W9-BPQ-410

NERD DO WELL

Simon Pegg

Simon Pegg is an actor, comedian, screenwriter, producer and author. Best known for his roles in *Spaced*, *Shaun of the Dad*, *Hot Fuzz* and *Paul*, he also plays Scotty in *Star Trek*.

Simon lives in London with his wife and daughter. This is his first book.

NERD DO WELL

Simon Pegg

arrow books

Published in the United Kingdom by Arrow Books in 2011

Copyright © Simon Pegg

First published in the United Kingdom in 2010 by Century
First published in paperback in 2011 by Arrow Books

Arrow Books
The Random House Group Limited
20 Vauxhall Bridge Road, London, SW1V 2SA

Addresses for companies within The Random House Group Limited can be
found at: www.randomhouse.co.uk/offices.htm

The Random House Group Limited Reg. No. 954009

A CIP catalogue record for this book
is available from the British Library

ISBN 978-1-78475-219-4

Typeset by Palimpsest Book Production Limited,
Falkirk, Stirlingshire
www.randomhouse.co.uk

Printed and bound in Canada

1 2 3 4 5   19 18 17 16 15

For Matilda Belle

Acknowledgements

Although these acknowledgements relate specifically to the process of writing the book, there are a few more general 'thank yous' I would like to express. Firstly, my mum, Gill, and my dad, John, for their endless encouragement and support over the years. It has been the foundation of everything I have achieved and a debt I can never repay. My wonderful wife, Maureen, for her understanding and willingness to be literally left holding the baby during the more intensive periods of writing this book. As always, I look forward to her thoughts the most. I should also give tribute to my sister, Katy, whose nerd credentials have often outstripped my own. Thanks for putting me on to all those great TV shows and being Robin to my Batman (I am of course talking about Carrie Kelly, the female Robin from *The Dark Knight Returns*). My brothers, Michael and Steven, for allowing me to make films with their toys and break them in the process. It was more than worth it for *Bogorof the Bad, Parts* 1 and 2 (my unseen first features). My agent, Dawn Sedgwick, for looking after me with such tireless devotion and having a confidence in me that even I didn't have. I'm not always the easiest person to motivate but her persistence in bringing out the best in me has never faltered and for that I am eternally grateful. Nods of thanks must also go to Alex Pudney and Nicola Mason Shakespeare who work by Dawn's side, chasing me down with pressing matters as the FBI chase down elusive terrorists. My editor, Ben Dunn, at Century who has demonstrated a seemingly indestructible patience in dealing with me. His enthusiasm, understanding and belief in my capacity to finish and indeed start this venture have been remarkable in light of my infuriating indecision and tendency to procrastinate. Elsewhere on the third floor of the Random House building on the banks of the River Thames, I'd like to thank Briony Nelder for looking after me so completely during the writing process and being someone with whom I could freely discuss the complexities of the final season of *Lost*. Katie Duce for assisting Ben in helping shape my somewhat shapeless train of thought into, of all things, an actual book. And Jack Fogg, not only for sounding like the alter ego of a Victorian superhero but for being part of the team that made me feel so welcome and, dare I say it, valued at Century. Thanks also go to Tony Kelly, the marvellously intuitive and gifted photographer, who I roped in for the cover shoot and who always makes things fun, and the great Simon Bisley for his spot-on rendition of me and Canterbury. And lastly, although their job has been to feature in this book rather than contribute to it, I would like to thank my dearest friends and closest collaborators for the material and, above all, the love. Michael Smiley, Edgar Wright, Jessica Hynes, Nira Park and of course, my inspiration and best friend, Nicholas John Frost.

1

The cave seemed to go on forever, a vast tectonic bubble receding to an infinity of shadow. Powerful spotlights lit various areas where trophies and keepsakes hinted at past adventure and an array of impressive vehicles gathered: an awesome assemblage of potential and kinetic energy. Elsewhere, the blackness folded in on itself, swirling into corners, endless, impenetrable, much like the mind of the man who sat at its flickering heart.

The hub was comprised of a central console, surrounded by various readouts and screens. Data from across the globe ticked into the mainframe to be displayed, analysed and evaluated by the figure sat in thoughtful repose amid the array. This was his lair, his base, the place he felt most relaxed, most centred, most at home; it was like the Bat Cave but with faster Wi-Fi.

Simon Pegg scanned the myriad infoscreens, searching, penetrating, squinting in a way that made him even more handsome. Across the feedbank, a dizzying strobe of information flickered before his, steel blue with a hint of rust, eyes. Stocks and shares rose and fell, disasters, wars, a cat attacking a baby on YouTube, an old woman ravaged by hunger holding out her hands in supplication to a faceless militia man, impassively pointing a rifle at her head.

'It's not fair,' Pegg's bitter mumble cracked across his lips. 'That cat should be put down!'

'There's a telephone call for you, sir,' a metallic voice chirped over the intercom.

'Jesus, Canterbury,' Pegg yelped, 'can't you make a ding-dong noise or something? It really makes me jump when you just speak like that.'

'I'm sorry, sir,' apologised the faithful robotic butler, 'I didn't mean to startle you.'

'Don't worry about it,' said Pegg, putting his feet up on the dashboard and pretending not to be freaked out. 'Who is it? Lord Black, I suppose, with another fiendish plot to bring about the end of the world.'

'No, sir,' replied Canterbury patiently.

'Good,' huffed Pegg. 'I hate that twat.'

'It's your editor, sir. Ben from Century,' replied the automaton gravely.

'Holy shit,' muttered Pegg darkly.

'Shall I bring the phone down, sir?' enquired Canterbury.

'Can't you just patch it through?' whined Pegg like a teenager who didn't want to go to the shops for his mum because he was about to have another wank.

'No, sir,' replied Canterbury. 'It's on your iPhone, which was down the side of the sofa in the drawing room.'

'I wondered where that was,' said Pegg, brightening slightly. 'Bring it down.'

'Very well, sir,' returned Canterbury, seemingly unaffected by Pegg's erratic mood shifts.

'Oh, and bring me a Coke Zero,' said Pegg, signing off.

He scratched his chin and narrowed his eyes, knowing full well what Ben from Century wanted and worrying slightly that his editor would think his telecommunications system was rubbish. On one of the infoscreens another YouTube baby emitted a classic guff, firing a cloud of talc into the air from its freshly powdered anus. Pegg laughed hysterically for two minutes before his guffaws subsided and he wiped the tears from his eyes, thus missing CCTV footage of an armed robbery approximately two miles down the road. He eased his demeanour back into seriousness with a loud sigh, and then shook his head with a chuckle, remembering the cloud-farting baby.

'DING-DONG,' said Canterbury over the intercom.

'FUCK!' said Pegg, clutching his heart dramatically. 'I didn't mean say "ding-dong", I meant get a thing that makes a ding-dong noise.'

'It seems to me, sir,' reasoned Canterbury, trying not to sound patronising, 'that any noise I employ to alert you to my presence will sound without warning and give you a fright.'

'What do you want, Canterbury?' growled Pegg.

'We've only got those Diet Cokes sir, the ones reserved for guests,' replied his faithful mechanised friend.

'Gak!' retched Pegg, 'Everyone knows Diet Coke marketing specifically targets women and effeminates and I am neither.'

'There is regular Coke sir,' offered Canterbury. 'The Ocado man delivered a six pack by mistake.'

'You allowed fatty Coke into this house?' Pegg whispered, secretly pleased.

Canterbury said nothing.

'I suppose it will have to do,' huffed Pegg quickly, 'but check the order next time. Remember that whole Volvic/Evian debacle?'

Pegg's response was met with an impassive acknowledgement from his chamberlain and silence fell across the cave once more. Pegg felt a tinge of guilt in his gut and fingered the intercom.

'Canterbury?'

Nothing.

'Come on, Canterbury, I know you can hear me,' insisted Pegg. 'It's not like you can hang up, the com-link's inside your head . . . Canterbury?'

An electronic bell sounded to Pegg's right, making him jump. The door to the elevator opened revealing Canterbury holding an iPhone and a Coke.

'Why didn't you answer me, Canterbury?' enquired Pegg, barely concealing a smile.

'I was in the elevator,' replied the stuffy robot who was absolutely nothing like C-3PO, 'the signal's not very good.'

Canterbury stood at roughly six foot tall; his torso was a barrel of sleek black metal, his arms and legs, an array of titanium bones and functional hydraulics. Despite being a super-advanced AI processor, driving a fully articulated, humanoid endoskeleton, there was something old-fashioned about his appearance, as if he'd been built in a bygone age or had stepped out of the film *Robots*, starring Ewan McGregor and Robin Williams. In an effort to make him appear more modern, Pegg had welded a small flashing stud to the automaton's left aural receptor. He had regretted it later but found it hard to remove. It was the eighties when he had installed the accessory, a time when men wearing earrings was cool and not in the least bit twatty.

Pegg smiled that famous smile that inspired instant sexual arousal in women and turned men into benders.

'I'm sorry I got annoyed about the fatty Coke, Canterbury,' Pegg said.

'Quite all right, sir,' replied Canterbury, and although not possessing a mouth in the human sense, his oral cavity being represented by a slot, behind which was positioned a vocal synthesiser, Pegg couldn't help feeling his old automated companion was smiling.

'Your phone, sir,' said Canterbury, passing over the handset. Pegg winked at the shiny butler as he put the iPhone to his nicely sculptured ear.

'This is Pegg,' said Pegg.

'Have you done it yet?' said an unpleasant voice at the other end of the line.

'Mmmmm?' said Pegg innocently.

'You were supposed to have written the ten thousand words by this morning', the voice continued like a sex pest.

'Yes, but —'

'That was the deal, Simon. If you don't meet your deadlines I'm going to have to ask you to return your advance. I don't care if you are a rugged, sexually devastating superhero.'

'Relax, Ben, I have it all under control,' countered Pegg, his voice suddenly resembling that of Roger Moore (in the seventies).

'I'm not so sure,' snarled the voice. Pegg detected an air of smugness in the voice of Ben from Century (a subsidiary of Random House Publishing).

'Are you a bummer tied to a tree?' enquired Pegg smoothly.

'What?' Ben replied.

'Answer the question,' insisted Pegg patiently. 'Are you a bummer tied to a tree?'

'No,' faltered Ben.

'BUMMER ON THE LOOSE!' trumpeted Pegg, terminating the call with a triumphant flourish.

Pegg chuckled, then looked across at Canterbury, a hint of sadness in his eyes.

'Looks like I'll be going up to the office for a while,' Pegg sighed. 'Will you be OK?

'Of course, sir,' replied Canterbury. There was an almost imperceptible catch in his voice, a flicker of static in his vo-com that others would have missed. Pegg heard it, though, and it warmed his heart.

'I guess I won't have to drink this after all,' Pegg winked at Canterbury, handing back the fatty Coke. His face stiffened as he punched up the recent calls menu on his phone and dialled the number for Century.

'You win for now but believe me, four-eyes,' whispered Pegg to his bespectacled literary contact, 'this isn't over.'

'I'm glad you've decided to see sense, Simon. I expect those ten thousand words in the morning.'

Pegg hung up without saying goodbye, which was impolite and he knew it. He also did the finger at the phone and said a rude word.

'Will you be gone long, sir?' Canterbury enquired.

'Not if I can help it,' replied Pegg, standing up to reveal his great body which was muscular but not too big (like Brad Pitt in *Fight Club*). 'I just need to find a little inspiration.'

Indecisions, Indecisions

It was never my intention to write an autobiography. The very notion made me uneasy. You see them congesting the bookshop shelves at Christmas. Rows of needy smiles, sad clowns and serious eyes, proclaiming faux-modest life stories, with titles such as *This Is Me*, or *Why, Me?*, or *Me, Me, Me*. I didn't want to do that, it's not really me. And who cares anyway? I don't and I'm the faux-modest sad clown with the needy smile and serious eyes who has to write the damn thing. There's something presumptuous in writing an autobiography, as if people's interest in your life is a given. Fair enough if your life is full of orgies; and murder and murder orgies, you can assume a little interest from outside; that stuff flies off the shelves. However, geeky boy comes good? I didn't see the appeal.

What I actually wanted to do was write fiction about a suave, handsome superhero and his robotic butler. The story of a tricked-out vigilante, with innumerable gadgets, a silver tongue and deadly fists; like Batman without the costume and a more pointed 'gay subtext'. Sure, it's not particularly original but it's far more interesting than my life. I don't even have a robotic butler. Not any more.

The literary public would be far better served with heroic tales of daring, midnight infiltrations and hip-smashing sexual prowess. The man I met from the publishing company, however, thought it would be better to write something a little more personal, more real.

'Oh boring,' I screamed at him, clearing my desk in one decisive swipe. How could my own mundane personal experience possibly outstrip the adventures of a man with a bullwhip and forty throwing knives concealed in the lining of his snug-fitting dinner jacket? 'Trust me,' said Ben, winning me over with a smile that reminded me of Indiana Jones and subsequently that I had subconsciously stolen the bullwhip thing from *Raiders of the Lost Ark*.

I liked Ben as soon as I met him. He was big, specky and friendly. Like a *Guardian* journalist who had turned into the Incredible Hulk while maintaining his smart, liberal sensibility, rather than succumbing to dumb monosyllabic grunts, like someone who writes for *Nuts* magazine. I knew we were going to get on after our first meeting, during which my dog Minnie honked up a disgusting heap of canine spew all over my office sofa. He laughed nervously and pretended not to be nauseated by the stink, for which I was immediately grateful. Minnie isn't a sickly dog, she chucks up with a corresponding frequency to myself (once every few months) and she doesn't even drink as much as I do. I appreciated Ben's tolerance of her gastric faux pas and thus trusted his judgement of my proposed book idea.

An autobiography then, I chin-scratched, weighing up mild naffness in the face of not writing anything at all. Ben offered an angle: an account of my journey from ordinary nerd to nerd participating in the world that made him nerdy in the first place. I liked this. The circularity appealed to me as a narrative device. I am often struck by the irony of my adult life in light of my childhood passions. Also, I secretly intended to ignore his suggestion and write about the superhero anyway. Resolving to humour him with the biographical stuff and sneak the real book in between the cracks. It might just work.

Much of what is written about me, usually during spurts of promotion, seems to dwell on the idea of an ordinary, guy-next-door, non-Hollywood, unattractive loser, somehow succeeding in this fabled land of facile opportunity, despite being handicapped by having red hair (I don't) and severe physical deformity (my wife thinks I'm handsome). So many articles begin with a passage about why I should not have succeeded, due to my lack of 'Hollywood' good looks, as if that has anything to do with being an actor.

And herein lies my initial reluctance to pen something biographical as opposed to fantastic. I'm not entirely comfortable with the 'fame tax'. There seems to be a consensus these days, a received wisdom, unquestioned even by those who are victim to it, that all actors do what they do because they want to be famous. Not because they enjoy the process but because they crave the product – not even the product, the consequence of the product, which is fame – and by this compulsion are considered to be 'show-offs', deserved of some kind of punitive comeback for their desire to be adored. It is as if some ancient rule setter folded his arms back when the concept of celebrity was emerging and said, 'OK, you can be famous, but by way of payment, you must surrender your private life and be willing to talk about it as if everyone is entitled to know.' I don't think that's particularly fair.

I hate it when I am asked about my family. I get all sweaty and agitated and subtly try to deflect the question towards my dog, whose private life I am willing to sacrifice because she doesn't read *heat* or watch E!. She doesn't consume any kind of media, be it entertainment or factual, although she did once watch the opening moments of John Carpenter's *The Thing*, mainly because it was on a really big TV and involves a husky dog running across a snowfield being chased by a helicopter.

She wasn't particularly concerned with the narrative context – a seemingly innocent and ordinary dog is pursued across the tundra by desperate Norwegian scientists who, we later learn, rightly believe the hapless pooch to be a shape-shifting alien life form intent on assimilating the entire human race. To Minnie it was just a dog running around in the snow. If she thought anything it would have been 'When did it snow? And where did that big window come from?' Of course she thought neither because dogs can't process abstract concepts, as much as we'd like to think they can. How could she think in such sophisticated terms? Her favourite pastime involves eating socks. See, there I go again. It's like a linguistic screen saver. Whenever my brain switches off I start talking about my dog. It happens all the time in interviews, as this extract from a recent interrogation demonstrates.

Journalist: So, you recently had a baby. What's it like being a father?

Me: My dog likes eating socks!

However, this book will require me to talk about my private life as well as my working life, since the two are inextricably linked. Events in my private life have greatly affected my creative decisions over the years, and in early life my decision to be creative. As such, this book is likely to be associative, in that it will hop around like a dog with a sock, as different events call to mind various forebears. For instance, when I was very small I used to fantasise about having a dog, to the extent that I used to confer with the phantom pooch while walking down the street. This eventually crept its way into *Spaced*, a sitcom I wrote with my friend Jessica Hynes (née Stevenson). Midway through the first series, Jess's character Daisy decides she wants a dog, having played out similar fantasies to my own as a small girl. The dog she eventually purchases is a miniature schnauzer, which she calls Colin (played convincingly by a two-year-old bitch called Ada).

Years later, I decided to similarly realise my childhood fantasy and add a dog to our family unit. Due to my wife Maureen suffering a mild dog allergy, we needed a breed that didn't shed. I immediately thought of Ada, who had not only been a delight to work with but also didn't leave hair everywhere. So, in May 2007, we drove out to a farm in Buckinghamshire and adopted a seven-week-old miniature schnauzer bitch. Her Kennel Club name was Wicked Willow but we called her Minnie. That's a double circle right there: life is imitated by art, which in turn is imitated by life, life then directly affects art due to my pushy stage-mother insistence that Minnie break into cinema. She was fired from *How to Lose Friends & Alienate People* (2007) for being too boisterous, cut out of *Paul* (which was shot in 2009), but finally made it into John Landis's period murder comedy *Burke and Hare* (2010), in which she expertly portrays a Regency period street mutt. Strange to think such consequences were born from the idle fantasies of a dogless child.[1] That was pretty personal, although it was still about Minnie.

---

[1] I should point out that the reason I was dogless as a child was simply because we had cats instead; two beautiful sealpoint Siamese called Bonnie and Clyde, who lived well into feline dotage and whom I loved immeasurably. The whole 'wanting a dog' fantasy was simply a consequence of wishing I could take the kitties everywhere with me, a notion they would quietly laugh at were they able to understand the suggestion. Despite Bonnie and Clyde being incredibly affectionate and devoted, they were still cats and as such were possessed of that wonderful aloofness their species often projects. If you call a dog's name, the response is 'What?' as in 'Yes, what do you need? Where are we going? Shall I bring this sock?' If you call a cat, if it even acknowledges you at all, the response is 'What?' as in 'Are you talking to me?' Clyde died in 1989 after losing a brief scrap with a tumour. I came home from university to say goodbye to him, knowing he was to be put to sleep the following week. It was the hardest door I ever closed. Bonnie followed not long after, such was their symbiosis – they were Siamese after all. I miss them even now.

There have been many of these moments of circularity in my life. I have so often found myself in situations whereupon I internally lament not owning a time machine that would enable me to travel back into the past and inform my younger self of future ironies. It's actually been a long-held fantasy of mine. We generally experience life in increments; we learn gradually as our reality evolves; there are rarely great leaps that shock us. Take the iPod for instance. If my older self had appeared in my bedroom, out of a glowing, electro-static ball in 1980, just as my ten-year-old self was lowering the needle of his red briefcase record player on to the tar-black surface of Adam and the Ants' *Kings of the Wild Frontier* and produced a sleek little super matchbox that could hold not just Messrs Ant and Pirroni's second, and arguably best, album, but the entire back and future catalogue of not just Mr Ant but twenty thousand other dandy highwaymen, I would have seen it as being some kind of joke (that's if the sudden appearance of an old me in an electro-static time ball hadn't already convinced me otherwise).

Remember when only a few people had mobile phones. Generally regarded as an object of derision, you would occasionally see business types clutching these ridiculous grey bricks to their faces and mutter to yourself, 'What a prick.' Nowadays, an eyebrow hardly flutters when we see a ten-year-old child happily texting away. You probably wouldn't notice anyway; you'd be too busy downloading an app that could definitively pinpoint who it was that had just farted in your Tube carriage.

Wouldn't it be great to grant someone the joy of truly appreciating the future, of surprising them with a turn of events that wasn't heralded and predicted through logical development? Getting to meet and work with Steven Spielberg was the culmination of many events, which had pretty much prepared me for it, and yet, if I could have travelled back in time and told the excitable young boy who had just watched *Raiders of the Lost*

Ark that one day in the future the man who created this brilliant piece of cinema would call you on your mobile phone (I probably wouldn't even notice the mobile phone part, I would have been so apoplectic with joy at getting to speak to the man who so spectacularly melted all those Nazis), I can only imagine the sheer joy and excitement that would have consumed me. It's not as if I didn't throw a complete nerdgasm when it actually happened, but to my younger, less mature self, with no idea where my career would take me or even a real idea of what a career might be? Surely, I would have burst into flames and melted like a Nazi right there and then. Thus, I will revisit those key times during childhood and retroactively try to inspire the wonder that would have been, had I been given access to an electro-static time ball, let's call it an ESTB (the idea and name for which I have copyrighted, by the way. In case I accidentally invent it in the future which, believe me, I do).

Despite all of this divulging of long-held secrets, what you won't be reading about in this book are salacious details of, say, for example . . . my first sexual experience.

Warning Signs

My first sexual experience involved a girl I shall not name, so as to preserve her dignity. Let's call her Meredith Catsanus, which, let's face it, couldn't possibly be her real name or that whole dignity-preservation thing would be a complete waste of time.

Meredith and I had been friends since the age of seven. Even at such a young age I felt the first tentative stirrings of physical attraction towards another human being, rather than towards a picture of Princess Leia or my Tonto action figure[2] when he wasn't wearing his little beaded suede two-piece outfit with the fringe. There was something about Meredith that really fascinated me. Possibly the fact that she looked a bit like Barbra Streisand, but perhaps more the way her hair fell down across one side of her face, covering her right eye, making her look

---

[2] Tonto was the faithful, monosyllabic Native American sidekick to the Lone Ranger. I had poseable, dressable action figures of them both. Tonto had pigtails and looked fairly feminine and stripping him naked gave me a strange thrill. I'm guessing this may have been an early indication of my sexual orientation, since I did not feel the same way about the Lone Ranger and he looked like a member of the Village People.

cute and demure, or perhaps to hide a hideous disfigurement (like Batman's popular adversary Two Face, he of the bisected personality/physiognomy). I was seven years old and would have found all possibilities equally appealing.

Aside from that tender romance with Carrie Fisher's profile page, which I tore out of *Look-in* magazine, I hadn't experienced romantic love before the age of seven. It's fair to say not many have. I had an odd crush on a boy called Ross but it wasn't motivated by any infant manifestations of sexual lust. He was just really lovely and I wanted to be near him. He was about three years older than me and I remember following him around the playground on one occasion, just aching to be his friend.

I also used to frequently snog my friend Kyle because it made all our other friends hoot with laughter. I hadn't been rendered homophobic by received notions of masculinity at the age of six and I had no problem doing 'film star kisses' with another boy if it meant getting a big laugh.

I had no intellectual understanding of sexuality other than the strictly hetero goings-on in films and shows I'd glimpsed on grown-up television while playing on the floor with my Steve Austin rocket and bionic operating theatre. There were the rumblings of future impulses implicit in the tiny waves of pelvic vertigo I felt with naked Tonto or read the section about the Romans in my pop-up book of history. At my sixth birthday party, my mother entered Nan's austere front room to find Kyle and myself going at it in the middle of a circle of screaming children and broke us up as though we were fighting, barely concealing a wide smirk of confusion on her face. I'm not sure if she was worried that I might be gay or just thought the behaviour was inappropriate for a children's party, no matter what the sexual orientation of the participants. I'm going to ring her and ask her now.

She says she doesn't remember, so it can't have been all that shocking to see two six-year-old boys locked in a passionate embrace on an armchair in the front room while other children clapped and laughed in some bizarre exercise in mini-pops dogging. It strikes me as something I'd remember if I caught my daughter putting on a display of sapphic passion for the amusement of her friends, but then Mum was always pretty liberal and progressive. As I am of course.

I did experience an icky sense of unease witnessing John Duttine from *Day of the Triffids* kiss a man in what must have been a *Play For Today* in the late seventies. It wasn't disgust though, more a primal fear of something to which you cannot relate, like gay men get around vaginas, or lesbians experience if they are unfortunate enough to stumble upon a cock. I'm not sure how my mother would have felt if she had interrupted one of the exploratory games I played in the shed with a number of the girls that lived in my nan's street, despite them being ultimately more socially conventional. Those very early forays into our sexuality that we all experience and which we seldom discuss unless under the umbrella euphemism that is 'doctors and nurses' have nothing to do with romantic love and are inspired by ancient curiosities buried deep within our DNA. I recall being no older than seven and getting naked with a girl my age on her bunk bed, just because it felt right. Grander concepts such as romance and love were beyond my understanding and separate from this strange little automatic event. It wasn't until a year later, when a young woman with Danish pastries on either side of her head knelt down in front of a walking dustbin to record an important message, that love truly came to town.

Anyway, before we explore that major obsession, let's get back to Meredith Catsanus. I have a clear memory of the first rumblings of sexual tension between us on a field trip to Gloucester Cathedral in 1978. I had attended a school attached to the cathedral as a very young child and found myself possessed of the confidence one feels in familiar surroundings, among those for whom the setting is new.

Meredith's mother, Mrs Catsanus, had accompanied us as a volunteer helper and her presence bolstered my old-boy boldness. I found it very easy to make her laugh by being mischievous and cheeky in a charming way. Wonderfully for me, Meredith found this skill endearing (we were at that age prior to parental validation being the kiss of death). My mother-charming antics took the form of various impressions and jokes, including my reciting of the tongue twister, 'The cat crept into the crypt and crapped', although I didn't say the last word because it was way too rude for an ecclesiastical field trip. Besides, Meredith's mum responded to the innuendo with a fit of giggles, whereas I suspect if I had actually said 'crapped' I would have been reprimanded on the spot.

This device was something that in later life I would employ in my stand-up routines and then in my film and TV work. Not the joke itself, although it's a stone-cold classic, but the idea that an audience were capable of putting the constituent pieces of a joke together themselves, arriving at the punchline before it is delivered, if indeed it is delivered at all. This perhaps was my first experience of collaborative comedy. Allowing Meredith's mother to know where I was going without actually going there and thus getting away with using a naughty word having inferred it rather than actually said it.

It's interesting that the memory of entertaining Meredith's mother remains so clear for me while countless other childhood events have evaporated. Perhaps its significance as one of my earliest comic devices is the reason it still twinkles in my reminiscences.

It certainly connected Meredith and myself in a pre-flirty flirty way and led to a relationship that would extend almost into adult life, depending on your definition of the word adult. Although I was thrilled and fascinated by girls, I was far more inclined to run across a building site, making the noise of a TIE fighter. All the juicy stuff wouldn't start happening until after *Return of the Jedi*.

And so, jump forward with me six years to 1984 (a year after the release of *Jedi*). I was fourteen years old, and living in a small village called Upton St Leonards in Gloucestershire. Actually, I'm lying, I didn't so much live in the village as in a newly constructed extension to it, which would eventually sprawl itself into the centre of Gloucester. Fortunately for Gloucester, much of the area is broken up by hills, on which it would be impossible, not to mention sacrilege, to build. At the time, the quaintly named Nut Hill and an area of farmland adjoining industrial grounds owned by the chemical company ICI separated Upton St Leonards from the neighbouring village of Brockworth. For the fit young boy in a hurry, the short cut was easy. A few fields, a number of fences and a seemingly disused airstrip, and I was in a whole new village, where a raft of new possibilities easily outstripped the meagre offerings available in my own leafy hamlet.

If one were feeling really daring, there was a treacherous bike ride down a winding two-lane road which was as exhilarating on the down as it was exhausting on the way back. I chose the second option that day and mounted my faithful Raleigh Grifter, knowing its heavily treaded wheels would be delivering me to something more than a kiss.

I had lived in Brockworth for four years as a youngster, so I knew it well. I was schooled there and continued to be schooled there into secondary education, after we had moved to a different area, delivered to the door of Brockworth Comprehensive by the Bennetts coach, which picked up the catchment kids on weekday mornings. To go there during leisure time felt adventurous and exciting. The village is bigger than Upton and the youth population was almost entirely comprised of school friends, acquaintances and bitter enemies. Meredith lived in Brockworth as she had always done and it was for Meredith's company that I cycled to Brockworth on that stifling summer's day.

By this time Meredith and I had experienced several on again/off again moments. In 1982, she'd had her hair cut like Lady Diana for which I teased her mercilessly. I realised during my persistent barrage of jibes, which included the stinging but covertly affectionate moniker Lady Doughnut, that I fancied her and subsequently I asked her 'out'.

Meredith turned me down, probably I realise now because of the whole Lady Doughnut thing; and a year later, probably out of pique, I did the same when she asked if I wanted to go 'out' with her. It was another year before we buried the hatchet and started 'going out' – that widely used euphemism for tentative teenage relationships. A relationship that generally involved 'hanging out' and occasionally 'getting off' with each other (what is it with these euphemistic prepositions?).

The degrees of what it was one actually got 'off' were in equal parts uncertain and legendary in the retelling from the more confident, sexually liberated boys. Tales of fingering and even blow jobs would filter back to the slightly naive kids (of which I was one) at the back of maths, and not always just from the boys. One particular girl used to regale me with stories of how she would 'gobble off' her boyfriend, leaving me slightly breathless and dry-mouthed as I tried in vain to understand quadratic equations.

Meredith and I finally succumbed to each other; indulging in a mammoth snog session on a sofa at some party, where guileless parents had abandoned their house to their teenage children, thinking it would never amount to anything more than pass the parcel and pop music, rather than the bacchanalian love-in it would inevitably become.[3]

---

[3] I remember being collected from one such event by a friend's father, who stepped into the living room to discover everybody just lying around in silence, snogging. I myself was on the floor with my hand up the back of Ann Tickner's T-shirt, having adapted very well over the course of the evening to the concept of 'open-mouth kissing'. My friend's dad coughed pointedly to break the spell (although I don't remember any of the other revellers stopping what they were doing), forcing me to get up and sheepishly follow him and my friend out to the car. He never commented on what he saw, or informed my mother what I had been doing, but I'm sure things would have been wildly different if he'd had a daughter rather than a son.

Eventually, Meredith and I agreed that we were going steady; although, once again, neither of us was entirely sure what 'steady' was. We had been friends for so long we often just fell back into each other's company when we weren't with other people.

On that fateful day in '84 she was wearing a sleeveless tigerskin-print T-shirt and was all of thirteen years old. We disappeared off to a remote part of a field which I'm pretty sure was part of the ICI empire, making it so much more daring. Not only could we have been caught, we could also have been prosecuted. Although most likely we would have been chased away by a grumpy security guard, imaginatively nicknamed Hitler by the local hoods. Canoodling plus trespassing certainly added that extra bit of exhilaration, and both of us knew, through an unspoken understanding, we would be progressing on from what usually constituted these little trysts.

We kissed for a while and nuzzled each other's necks, copying what we had seen people doing in films and TV shows. Almost as though the needle had stuck on the LP of grown-up sexual activity, limiting us to the first few bars, a never-ending prelude to a song we weren't quite ready to sing along with. That day, however, I decided to nudge the record player and touch her boobs. Not just honk them seductively but actually lift up her T-shirt, undo her bra and feel them, skin on skin. After the fortieth lips-to-neck cycle I changed rhythm. She didn't resist.

I remember her skin smelled like Boots. Not the footwear, that would be off-putting, rather the popular high street pharmacy. The Gloucester branch boasted a sizeable perfume and make-up department, where I had loitered many times waiting for my mother to finish buying toiletries. I appreciate that implies some odd collision between the Oedipal and the Pavlovic but now really isn't the time to get into that.

Meredith had sprayed herself with one of those aerosol perfumes for young girls that supposedly inspired men to go to enormous lengths to deliver flowers with breathless, dopey smiles. Flowers were possibly the last thing on my mind as she permitted me access to her bra strap, which I had no idea what to do with. I had never even seen one on a girl my age, let alone touched one. Meredith obligingly took over with an awkward smile and facilitated our blushing journey to whatever base boob contact qualifies as.

Afterwards, as I cycled home up over Nut Hill, I was suddenly racked with a sense of shame and regret. I don't know why I felt so bad about what I had done. Maybe I was worried about what my mother would think if she found out (there I go again, skipping through the psychoanalytical minefield), or I was just disappointed with the slightly embarrassed cessation of activity once we had travelled the distance we were prepared to travel at this point in our sexual growth. Whatever the reason, it was with a heavy heart that I pedalled up the difficult hill back towards Upton St Leonards.

About halfway up, the road becomes uneven, requiring a hazard sign at the roadside to warn motorists of the possible danger of tackling road humps. The sign is a red triangle with two symmetrical bumps in the centre. I had seen it many, many times on my travels to and from Brockworth, but today it proved a stinging reminder of my tentative step towards sexual maturity. As it loomed towards me over the hill and I spied those two suddenly significant mounds framed in that scarlet triangle, I closed my eyes and uttered the words: 'Oh God, what have I done?'

I'm not sure why I felt that way. It lasted only a few days and I never felt like it again as I progressed towards adulthood. It makes me laugh to recall it. My guilt and penitence in the face of this (hazard warning) sign from God seems hilarious to me now. God uses lightning and seas of blood to administer lessons, not the Department for Transport.

I actually waited for the feelings of guilt and remorse to return many months later, after the girl who lived in the house opposite mine came round one night and helped me fully understand what those conversations at the back of the maths room had been about. It was something of a shock. A year before, she had visited the house for a quick snog and protested angrily when my hand had found its way up her jumper (I must have been ready to get back on the proverbial tit bike). Now she was round again, and within a few minutes of necking on the bed, yanked my trousers down around my knees. Twenty-eight minutes later, I waved her off, shut the door and waited for the shame and regret to creep through me. It never did. I felt pretty good. Well, I would, wouldn't I? I'd just got gobbled off.

I know what you're thinking. What an absolute hypocrite! I open the book by railing against the notion of pimping my private life, then immediately don a felt fedora with a feather in it and whore out my secrets for cheap laughs. Intimate stuff too. Details of childhood sexual exploits, involving bras and fellatio. Truth is, I'm feeling my way along; it's a learning experience for me as much as it is for you and it's helped me understand something key. It's not talking about personal details that unsettles me, it's filtering personal details through someone else that makes me want to talk about Minnie. A stranger with a different agenda and priorities might distort, misinterpret or misuse the information, but if this information comes straight from the horse's mouth, that being the definitive subject – brain zero, me, me, me – it's not so bad.

2

'I'm supposed to be writing a book, you mongrel!' roared Pegg at the shrunken figure sat before him in the reclaimed dentist's chair.

'What's stopping you?' sneered Needles, a twitchy little informant who often featured in Pegg's adventures. 'Writer's block?'

'Gah!' inarticulated Pegg, betraying a frustration he had dearly hoped to conceal.

'Excuse me, sir.'

Pegg spun round, fire in his eyes. The black glove clutched in his manicured hand hung in the air like a floppy bat, ready to swoop down and give Needles another slap in the cake chute.

'What is it?' Pegg insisted through gritted teeth. 'I'm kind of in the middle of something here!'

'I'm sorry, sir,' trilled Canterbury, failing to subtract an air of haughtiness from his computerised vocal nodes. 'I know you don't like to be disturbed when you're interrogating a potential informant. Hello, Needles.'

Needles leaned out so he could see Canterbury beyond Pegg's hulking mass, which was muscular but nimble, like Oliver Hardy if he worked out.

'Hi, Canterbury,' said Needles with an apologetic smile.

'I was wondering if I might provide some refreshments?' Canterbury enquired with the kind of immaculate poise that could only issue from an ACH (automated cybernetic humanoid).

'Do you still have the SodaStream?' enquired Needles.

'I think so,' replied Canterbury. 'Although I fear it has been secreted in some high cupboard, along with various other novelty food-preparation devices.'

'That's a shame,' lamented Needles.

'We don't have time for this!' Pegg blustered, silencing them both. 'He can have a can of Fanta Orange and that will be the end of it.'

'Yes, sir,' conceded Canterbury, with a slight inclination of his thoracic servos. 'Coke Zero for you, sir?'

'What do you think?' Pegg growled with a throaty rumble that surprised even him (although he didn't show it for fear of losing credibility in front of Needles). Almost imperceptibly, Canterbury's neo-carbon-fibre shoulders sagged as he registered the disappointment in Pegg's velvety Patrick Stewart-style voice.

'Very well, sir,' he offered, with a hint of self-admonishment. He was almost back in the transit tube before Pegg stopped him.

'Canterbury?' Pegg blurted.

'Yes, sir,' he replied.

'That lasagne you made last night ...' Pegg's voice faltered slightly. His internal monologue cursed his weakness, then for some reason reminded him to get more bottled water for the cave and to tape *Mythbusters*.

'The lasagne, sir?' offered Canterbury with just a hint of concern, bringing Pegg out of his personal reverie.

'It was ... It was delicious,' Pegg admitted, eyes

fixed on the floor. 'I thought it was Marks & Spencer's, until later when I went to the kitchen for a Tunnock's Tea Cake and noticed you were steeping a dirty baking dish.'

'That was washed and stowed immediately after you retired, sir. I had to soak it,' assured the worried service-bot.

'It's OK,' Pegg reassured him with a smile. 'That doesn't matter. The point is, you made an amazing dinner last night, that, if I hadn't discovered to the contrary, I would have assumed was shop-bought. Impressive, most impressive.'

'You'll find I'm full of surprises,' said Canterbury, his mechanical body swelling with pride. They often quoted movies to each other as a means of expressing affection and *The Empire Strikes Back* was one of their favourites, closely followed by *The Shawshank Redemption*. Canterbury left, with a spring in his step, literally: his feet were cushioned by a system of helical metal coils.

'Good old Canterbury,' chuckled Needles, with a smile.

'SILENCE!' Pegg trumpeted, whacking the squealer in the mush with the black leather glove. 'Tell me the whereabouts of the Scarlet Panther.'

'Sorry,' apologised Needles. 'I was miles away.'

'Where is the Scarlet Panther?' Pegg reiterated.

'What about my Fanta Orange?' challenged Needles, defiance in his eyes.

'WHERE IS SHE?!'

The effect was instantaneous. Needles wilted under the force of Pegg's demand, his eyes widened and he seemed to shrink in size, and I can't say for deffo but I think he probably wet himself.

'The last I heard, she was in the Red City.' The

fight left Needles (like a shameful guff) as he gave up this vital infospurt.

'Liverpool?' questioned Pegg.

'No, Marrakesh, she was in Marrakesh.' Needles seemed all floppy like a smashed doll.

'Was? Was?' Pegg said twice for effect and to cover the fact that he thought the Red City was Liverpool.

'That's all I know,' sagged Needles, his puny shoulders shuddering in a way Pegg could never achieve due to his size and courage.

'"Was" is no good to me, Needles, I need to know where she is now.' Softer but no less insistent, Pegg closed in on the pathetic wanker.

'Can't you use your ESTB and go back to last week? She was walking across the Djemaa el Fna away from the Koutoubia Mosque and towards the souks at 10.15 a.m. last Wednesday.'

'Shitballs!' said Pegg breathily.

'What?' persisted Needles.

'It doesn't work,' Pegg admitted, cherrying up a bit. 'It never did. That's not to say it won't though,' he insisted, regaining some of that legendary composure.

'What about that piece in *Time Out*?'

Pegg didn't say anything. How could he admit to a lowly informant that he had fibbed to *Time Out* about inventing time travel?

'You'll never find her now,' cheeked Needles. 'Hell, you wouldn't have found her if you'd arrived there one minute later. She knows those alleys like the back of her hand.'

'So do I!' spat Pegg. 'I know them better than she does. I bought a riad off Sean Connery in 1998 and I go there twice a year.'

Needles was silent. Top Trumps.

Canterbury appeared at the passage pipe, pushing the drinks trolley.

'Your Fanta's here,' Pegg growled, putting an end to the conversation. Pegg snapped open his Coke Zero and took a long manly slug (unlike Needles, who sipped his fizzy orange like a Brownie). Pegg's thoughts turned to the Scarlet Panther.

'She's out there somewhere. The question is, where? Looks like I'll be taking a little trip to Morocco. I'd better pick up suntan lotion and some new Birkenstocks — my old ones are well knackered.'

'What?' said Needles.

'Nothing,' Pegg snapped, embarrassed that he'd said all that out loud. 'Drink your Fanta or I'll tip it down the sink in the downstairs toilet.'

'You wouldn't!' gasped Needles.

Pegg's expression said it all (he would).

A Little Racist

This is the first joke I ever wrote. When I say wrote, I mean thought up. I didn't purchase a small black book at the age of six with the intention of penning a library of classic material, which I would eventually leave in the back of a cab, forcing me to launch a heartfelt appeal to the thieves as part of an item towards the end of the second half of *London Tonight*. For many stand-ups the notion of writing material is actually a euphemism for just thinking stuff up and committing it to memory. Even when I was at my busiest, performing six or seven shows over a weekend, I never physically wrote material down. It existed intangibly in my mind, kept alive by constant performance, like a spinning plate or a campfire maintained by a lonely soul whose very existence depends upon its warmth. Looking back now, years after I hung up my microphone or legs or whatever it is retired stand-ups hang up, I can barely remember a single line of the routines I would perform nightly on the London circuit.

I never actually used my first joke in any of my stand-up routines. It was site-specific and traded somewhat on my status as a six-year-old child. I remember it very clearly though. I think the process of creating it secured it in my memory forever. It was, after all, a very significant moment for me. The creation of the joke and the subsequent reaction to it by my mum represented the first cycle of a process I would often play out through my childhood and into my professional life as an adult which, according to the number of years spent existing, is what I am now.

I was sat at the dining table at my nan's house in Gloucester, having lunch with my mum (shortcrust-pastry meat pie and veg). We were talking about school and the various friends I had made, in particular one friend whose father was a dentist.

'Nathaniel's dad is a dentist,' I declared.

'Where does he practise?' Mum enquired.

'He doesn't,' I replied. 'He's a real one.'

I clearly remember calculating the double meaning of the word 'practise' and seeing the opportunity to create a joke that would make my mother laugh. Not in a knowing sense, I wasn't a junior Groucho Marx; I saw the deliberate misunderstanding as a means of being amusing in a 'kids say the funniest things' sort of way. I had no intention of admitting that my comment was wilfully intended as funny. For some reason it seemed funnier to me if I played innocent and worked the humour from an accidental standpoint, so in that sense it was my first stab at character comedy too; the six-year-old me playing a slightly more guileless version of myself. A Simple Simon if you will.

It was around this time that I was suddenly lifted out of my exclusive Gloucestershire private school and supplanted to far more inclusive inner-city pre-school, with a far greater variety of class and ethnicity. Away from the rarefied rituals of Gloucester's King's School, the interior of which doubled as Hogwarts School of Witchcraft and Wizardry in the Harry Potter movies, I began to learn life lessons.

One of my clearest memories of Calton Road Junior School

involves a girl whose name I think was Karen, all hair and a tartan flannel dress, the faint smell of must surrounding her in an invisible cloud. Without any prompting, she leaned over to me in assembly one morning between hymns and asked if I wanted to hear the rudest word in the world. Intrigued, I nodded, at which point she shielded her mouth with her right hand, in case any morally indignant lip-readers were watching from the gym ropes, and whispered the word 'cunt' into my ear. I remember her solemn monosyllabic whisper, the way the 'c' formed a glottal rasp in the back of her throat, the way that the word itself sounded like a sort of nasal cough. This alien, magic word I had never heard before seemed dark and portentous to me, like I'd just been let in on a secret, the burden of which I did not wish to carry and nothing would ever be the same again. It made complete sense. I believed her. It sounded like the rudest word in the world.

I never told my mother about it, despite always feeling able to talk to her about anything, and always being keen to impart anything that might garner a reaction.

In fact, even by this tender age, I was already prone to showing off and was often accused of it by my peers, in that slightly bitter way that stifles creativity and shames children into shrinking into invisibility, although that didn't entirely work on me. Even as a baby, I would do impressions of my grandfather and send my parents into paroxysms of giggles. He was a conductor of brass bands and whenever my mum or dad would ask, 'What does Pop-Pop do, Simon?' I would wave my arms in the air, not because I understood the concept of coordinating the mood and tempo of a throng of musicians, but because such an action would elicit a peal of approving laughter, essentially what the comedic mind craves, *an immediate external validation by way of an involuntary, positive emotional response*. At least that's what my therapist said before I stabbed him in the cheek with a biro.

You could argue that the comic is the most impatient and

neurotic amid the ranks of the insecure. Not only do they require approval, they require it immediately, that evident and tangible assurance, asserted by an unquestionable reflex of confirmation: laughter. 'You love me! YOU LOVE ME!' internalises the mad clown, whilst looking confident and a tad smug.

Stand-up comics in particular are at the most severe end of this need to be liked. Such is their desire for affirmation, they stand before a group of strangers and risk hostility and disdain in the pursuit of their goal. This becomes easier the more experience you gain. Good stand-ups can go out in front of any crowd with an air of confidence and assertiveness that wins the crowd's attention before a word has been uttered. Even if, as sometimes happens, the gig isn't great, the comic is able to rationalise the factors behind this as being anomalous and move on to the next performance with the same self-assured swagger. This comes with time and experience and most budding stand-ups survive on nerves and adrenalin during their formative years; or, if you were me, the promise of boiled sweets.

I performed my first stand-up comedy set (I say set, really it was a single joke) as a seven-year-old, stood in front of a weekly gathering of old women at the local Salvation Army centre. Staying with my nan over the summer holidays, I would always accompany her to the Home League on Tuesdays, where she would sing hymns and socialise with similar cloud-haired, lavender-soap-smelling old dears who had nothing better to do. I can't remember if I was invited up on to the lectern to tell a joke or if I suggested to Nan that the service needed a little comedy to counterpoint all the hymn singing and tambourine battering, but step up to the mike I did. Unbeknown to me, it was a journey I would take many, many times and not just at the Salvation Army building on the Bristol Road.

Looking back now, I realise that the grinning faces of the elderly were as much a result of them seeing a cute little boy as they were a response to my joke telling. I doubt the ones at the back could even hear me amid the clatter of humbugs rebounding off their dentures. I felt an enormous sense of triumph every week as I stepped down from the podium to join my proud nan and receive a series of light to intense cheek squeezes from my leathery admirers.

In terms of material, I was essentially regurgitating jokes I had heard on *Tiswas* and *Des O'Connor Tonight*. The latter's material would invariably be the product of an unreconstructed seventies TV comedian, for whom casual racial stereotyping was a vocation. I clearly remember recounting a Jim Davidson gag centred round his West Indian character, Chalky White, which came complete with a bewildered, high-pitched comedy patois to seal the deal. It's incredible now to think of Davidson telling his Chalky stories to a hysterical Des O'Connor, who would roll across his couch, tears streaming down his orange face.

The purveyors of such material to this day cry political correctness gone mad, when criticised, complaining that it's all in good fun and shouldn't be ruined by the whinging liberality of those who would rather not offend and ghettoise minorities. Ultimately it boils down to motive. Satire can be regarded as such when meant as satire, but may become racist when intended as racist. We shouldn't be frightened of the differences between us. The old right-wing notion of 'political correctness gone mad' only really comes into play when we start to censure merely for referring to the idea that one group of people might be different from another, as though admitting variation is wrong.

A few years ago I was browsing the comedy section in HMV and saw a video for one of Jim Davidson's live performances, the cover of which showed him stood at a urinal between two big black men. The black men were looking down, presumably at Jim's derisory penis and laughing, while Jim looked at the camera with a sad expression as if to say 'Oh no, I've got a tiny cock'. This was Jim's misguided attempt to assert his non-racism, to compliment black males by conceding that they have all got giant cocks to make up for implying they are stupid. This was his concession, the promotion of another racial stereotype to compensate for the other. For me, it demonstrated the huge margin by which Davidson missed the point of his own transgressions and marked out the deeply ingrained, casually racist ideas that inhabited our collective consciousness at the time and how easily children accept this received wisdom as inoffensive.

Perhaps the term 'racist' is misleading, since its connotations somewhat exceed subtlety. Perhaps a new term has to emerge that isn't as extreme or inflammatory. 'Culturally irresponsible' maybe. Not very catchy though, is it? Knobhead works well.

It's not really fair to call a seven-year-old child a knobhead. I certainly didn't feel like a racist back then. I would have been horrified at the accusation. My best friend was black! I'm not just saying that in a 'some of my best friends are black' way. He really was. 'Is' I presume, he's not my best friend any more, not because he's black, but because I moved away. Quickly, move on to the next chapter, this one is going to explode in a shower of sweaty, white middle-class guilt.

Anyway, the amassed ranks of the Salvation Army Home League certainly didn't care, as they guffawed at my Chalky White impression. I was only little, but surely they were old enough to know better. It seems to me that, in the seventies, most old people were racists, which is ironic, considering they had all survived a desperate war against fascism, only decades before. Wait, I'm probably being ageist, how do I know what their political proclivities were? Now I'm the one being ignorant. They were probably laughing at the fact that I could barely see over the lectern. They were probably humouring me because I was a cute little boy. What else were they going to do? Throw rotten fruit at me and shout 'Piss off, you little Nazi'?

The realisation of my error came a few years later when I started my comprehensive education and my form teacher, Mr Calway, the first *Guardian* reader I ever met, quickly gathered that if he let me stand in front of the class and tell a joke every Monday morning, I would be easier to control, having vented my nervous energy through the catharsis of performance. He was a smart guy.

When I pulled out an old Chalky gag one Monday, Mr Calway (Gareth as I now call him, although still not entirely comfortably) explained exactly why the joke I had told was unacceptable. I listened very carefully, taking in everything he said. Five years later, for my English oral exam, I gave a five-minute oration on subliminal racial prejudice and got an A. So I guess some good can come of telling racist jokes, stolen from the telly. If I had relied on my dentist gag at the Salvation Army, I might never have learned such a valuable lesson or indeed got such a big laugh. Know your audience, I say – Jim Davidson certainly does.

Starting From Scratch

There is no danger of me forgetting the process of writing and performing my first comedy sketch because it is forever etched in my memory in blood and brick dust. It happened in 1978 at the age of eight as part of an assembly presentation at Castle Hill Primary School in Brockworth, Gloucester. Every so often one of the seven year-groups would host an assembly in front of the other six, mixing education and entertainment and giving the rest of the school a break from the classroom.

On one such memorable occasion, we put on a short play about the cathedral visit during which I had flirted with Meredith Catsanus and her mum. This involved me dressing like a punk (which was current at the time) and repeatedly kicking a papier-mâché model of St Peter's bell, which resides in the cathedral's belfry. It got such a big laugh the first time I did it, I did it again several times as part of an increasingly self-serving improvisation, which was eventually curtailed by our form tutor, Mr Godwin, an awkward bearded man whom we nicknamed Flash, on account of his moped. He leaned forward from his chair and hissed, 'Simon, stop it,' much to my disappointment and vague shame. This was two years after I had debuted my first written sketch and my comedy chops were already clacking. Two years before, I was altogether less experienced at performing my own material but no less enthusiastic.

Mr Miller, our avuncular and hugely likeable teacher, a man who walked with a significant limp and read stories with unparalleled skill, had been charged with organising an assembly project about journalism. My task was to write a short news piece that I would read to the class from behind a desk, as if I were Richard Baker or Angela Rippon or, my personal favourite at the time, *Midlands Today*'s Tom Coyne.

I immediately created the persona of Dicky Bird (I was unaware of the cricket commentator of the same name and thought I had invented the most hilarious comedy name ever) and wrote a story about a mysterious gas leak that was causing people across the country to spontaneously pass out. All spelling and (lack of) punctuation have been retained.

NEWSFLASH
With Dicky Bird

Here is the news hellow there has been Series of Spreading gas it has made its way up the west region and it is thought to be coming up to Belfast. A young lady by the age of seventy was walking up the road and she met her friend her friend said how are you and the lady said I feel abit and she fainted it was thouht to be the gas. The gas starded over in America when Lee magors alias Steve astin fainted during a bionic Jump he landed in a small allie nearby luckly he survied the producer said it was a narrow escape. A lady who own a purshen cat said her cat was chaseing a mouse its deadly claws were Just going to sink mousse inard body and then it fainted and that's all we have time for good night err.

The 'err' at the end was Dicky Bird succumbing to the mysterious toxin himself. I wasn't writing on Final Draft in those days and was unable to use parentheses or stage directions, nor was I aware of the signifying power of quotation marks, or commas for that matter; in fact, punctuation wasn't a concept I was familiar with at all at this point.

I was particularly pleased with the 'narrow escape' gag. I think it was my first encounter with a pun. I distinctly remember finding it funny but not being entirely sure why. I just knew it made me feel sort of clever and I wanted to discover if the rest of the school would feel the same. The assembly was set for the end of the day on Friday so I knew morale would be high. The show would effectively be starting the weekend; the kids would be running on the excitement of all their impending recreational time, so the chances of choking were pretty slim. I felt confident, determined and beyond excited.

That Friday morning I had a terrible accident.

The playground always seemed like a busier place on Fridays. Everyone was slightly more excitable than the mini zombies that wandered the concrete on Mondays. Another week had passed, an entire weekend was stretching out before us, and spirits were always high. Specific time frames feel longer when you are younger because they represent a greater portion of your life. At eight years old, a single year amounts to an eighth of your entire life; which is a heck of a long time. It follows that weekends felt like a huge, sprawling holiday and what's not to love about that?

I was particularly giddy, knowing that even before the weekend started, in five hours or so, I would be reading out my one hundred per cent guaranteed hilarious comedy news piece to a hundred or so other children. This was my big day.

A few months earlier, a new girl had arrived in class from another school. Her name was Denise Miller and she seemed slightly batty, or most likely, looking back, had a big personality and a great sense of humour – two things boys find threatening in girls and thus are more likely to dismiss as chronic mental illness. Denise had developed something of a crush on me, or so she said. Believe it or not, I was much prettier as a little boy with my mop of blond hair and big blue eyes. It was a face that made aesthetic sense as opposed to the frustrating Picasso that adulthood has seen fit to furnish me with.

Denise would often tease me with the threat of kisses, something I pretended to be disgusted by but actually encouraged because I was extremely flattered and relished the attention. That morning Denise was doing her 'isn't Simon dreamy' routine and declared that if she caught me, she was going to kiss me on the lips. I immediately took off at high speed, combining playing hard to get with a demonstration of my higher than average running speed. I think the accepted term is 'protesting too much'.

I sprinted down to the other end of the playground, through the melee of a football match towards a low wall that marked the beginning of the playing fields. I managed to dodge the midfield, sidestepped the defenders but fared less well with a striker from the opposing team who had made a similarly dazzling dash up the left wing. The boy, whose name was appropriately Simon Killen, ran in front of me, instinctively ducking down as he did so. My hips hit his flank at maximum velocity – catapulting me over his back, face first on to the wall.

I lay there for a second before hearing myself utter the words 'Oh God' in a way I had never uttered them before. I sounded serious, like a grown-up. I knew something very bad had happened. I have no memory of being picked up; the next thing I recall is seeing my reflection in the window of my classroom as I left the now silent playground. The bridge of my nose and my right cheek were covered in blood and my right eye was ballooning so fast I could see the swelling gathering beneath my eye.

It occurred to me, as I was led to the toilets by Mr Skinner, that I was not crying. Instead I was making an odd whimpering sound like a dog. Crying somehow felt inadequate at this moment, like I needed a new mode of expression to communicate the fear and surprise and, also, the odd sense of survivor excitement, although the last was probably just the confusion of shock.

In the toilets, I turned the sinks pink and red with my blood as I applied numerous paper towels to my face. Mr Skinner encouraged me to do impressions to prevent me from going into full shock. 'What would Margaret Thatcher say about this?' he enquired. 'This is very, very unfortunate,' I replied. It worked, I started laughing, I could see, nothing was broken. Miraculously, the angle of impact had been just right so as to avoid permanent damage or disfigurement. The brickwork had cut a line across the top of my nose to just beneath my right eye and gravity had dragged a deep graze down my right cheek. It looked absolutely horrendous but my skull and eyes remained intact and it left no scars when it healed.

Later, as I was being attended to by the school nurse, the most pressing issue remained: whether or not it would still be possible for me to read out my comedy news report at that afternoon's assembly; so much so that when I returned to class, a battered hero, receiving a worried look from Denise and a demure smile from Meredith Catsanus, and Mr Miller asked me if I wanted to go home, or at least sit out of the presentation, I declined emphatically. I sat down at my desk, my mind racing to come up with lines to comically explain away my injury.

That afternoon, with my right eye almost entirely closed and the graze on my cheek a suppurating badge of glistening gore, I sat down at my fake news desk, shuffled my papers and said,

'Good afternoon, I'm Dicky Bird and I have recently been in a fight with a cat.' The comic logic of it made sense to me: my name made me sound like a small bird and small birds get into fights with cats. I'd seen enough bird carcasses on our front lawn courtesy of Bonnie and Clyde, our two sealpoint Siamese, to know this was the case. Whether it was funny or the other children were just happy to see me making light of my hideous wound, it got a laugh and I carried on with my piece, which went down pretty well.

I went home in a great mood and when my mum returned from work, I covered my face with my hand and implored her not to be alarmed, like some sympathetic monstrosity, desperate for acceptance by the object of his affection, whipping my hand away and brandishing the damage with a face full of faux suffering. My flair for the dramatic had manifested itself quite clearly that day, not least in my dogged insistence to Mr Miller that the show simply must go on.

Who Do I Think I Am (Part 1)?

I wasn't born in a trunk at the side of a stage – that would be foolish and unhygienic. I was a full month old before I found myself backstage at a theatre and this fact is thanks pretty much entirely to my mother. She developed a love of amateur dramatics in her early twenties and imprinted a similar enthusiasm upon me as I grew up, never once giving me less than total support in my efforts to develop this hobby into a professional career, not just as an actor but as a writer, despite my tendency to indulge in long, rambling sentences that seemed as though they might go on forever (like this one).

Gillian Rosemary Smith was born in May 1947, to Albert and Emma Smith, the youngest of a gaggle of six sisters, kicked off by Doreen in 1927 and swelled at varying intervals by Margaret, Audrey, Marion, Jacqueline and finally Gill. The age gap between oldest and youngest sisters meant my mother became an auntie at the age of three, an achievement I always regarded as being extremely cool.

Growing up, Mum recalls developing a love of words and

poetry, instilled in her by her mother, who I knew as Nan and who possessed a similar passion for verse, not entirely usual for a working-class girl from Gloucester. Nan was able to recite Robert Browning's 'The Pied Piper of Hamelin' from memory, as well as Longfellow's *Hiawatha* and passages from Charles Dickens's *A Christmas Carol*. Her bookshelves were filled with poetry books and also included a *Complete Works of Shakespeare*, inscribed by my grandfather: *To My Beloved Pem – 1st May 1926.*

With six children and a household to run, Nan's love of poetry never extended beyond the bookshelves but she passed it on to her daughters, particularly Marion who demonstrated a talent for acting and joined a renowned local drama group in Quedgley, Gloucestershire, run by the RAF for whom she worked. Mum would go to see Marion perform in various plays as well as sit and listen to her read poetry at home. Marion may have even harboured a desire to attend drama school herself and probably would have done so had life not taken her elsewhere. Still, her influence on her youngest sister was powerful. To this day, Mum can remember the words to various Kipling poems favoured by the young Marion, and recalls being inspired to follow in her footsteps by participating in devised pantomimes at Sunday school and musical numbers at her school concert.

However, when Marion married, her dramatic activities ceased and twelve-year-old Gill's main influence disappeared. It was not until after she had met my father that she found herself being drawn back towards the theatre, or at least a large ice-cream and sausage manufacturing facility on Gloucester's Eastern Avenue. For reasons now forgotten, although presumably because of Dad's involvement in the local music scene (which I'll come to in a bit), my soon-to-be parents got involved with a production staged by a drama group at the local Wall's factory. Here, Mum discovered she had an aptitude for dance and was encouraged by a professional choreographer who had been hired to work on the show. She threw herself into things with a boundless enthusiasm that would one day result in her breaking both her elbows while executing a crazy dance move that nobody else in her drama group would try. That wouldn't happen for sixteen years though, and at this point, no amount of plaster of Paris would have held her back.

By 1968, John and Gill had married and moved into a bungalow in Churchdown, Gloucester, where they befriended Jim and Jackie Rendell, the couple who lived opposite. Jim and Jackie were members of a well-known local drama group called the Gloucester Operatic and Dramatic Society, or GODS (a far more austere abbreviation than their neighbour, Cheltenham's CODS, and infinitely preferable to the Stroud Operatic and Dramatic Society, who decided not to go with an acronym). As well as various smaller productions at their home theatre, aptly named Olympus, the GODS would mount an annual large-scale musical production, which would be performed at the ABC theatre on St Aldate Street in Gloucester, some five or so doors down from the music shop my parents would buy a few years later.

This particular production, to be performed in early 1969 (amateur drama requires a far lengthier rehearsal process than professional theatre since the participants all have proper jobs), was *My Fair Lady*. The GODS were an extremely respected organisation and their annual production would inevitably play to sell-out crowds and always make the front pages of local news-papers, The *Gloucester Journal* and the *Citizen*. (The latter would eventually receive a nod in our cop comedy *Hot Fuzz*, renamed the *Sandford Citizen* for the film's fictional Gloucestershire village setting.) There was, however, a slight deficit of male society members at the time, so Jim and Jackie cajoled my father into coming along and bolstering the ranks of men in the chorus. The ladies' chorus quotient was perfectly acceptable, and since my mother's participation would have effectively cancelled out my father's, she decided to assist backstage, dressing the actress playing Eliza Doolittle, with whom she became lifelong friends. Mum immediately fell in love with amateur theatre and decided she wanted to become an active member of the GODS. The following year, the annual musical production was to be Lionel Bart's classic, *Oliver!*. I'm sure Mum would have made a wonderful Nancy, had she not been heavily pregnant with me.

By the time the production went on, I was a month old and no doubt enjoyed the quiet excitement one always feels backstage at an active theatre on a matinee afternoon. I can't help thinking this would be a great ESTB moment, if not for me, then for my mother. It would be cool to step out of a crackle of fizzing electricity and point to the bundle in her arms, proclaiming that that baby was in fact me and would grow up to be a successful actor (and time traveller), although I fear with that proclamation, I might only serve to confirm the fears of Marty McFly: that in the future, we all turn into assholes.

Later that year and with me being a helpful baby and sleeping through the night, Mum was able to participate in her first play, Anthony Kimmins's *The Amorous Prawn*. It was a perfect hobby for her as a young mum, since she was able to put me to bed and then head out to the theatre, without me even realising she was gone. In this respect she was able to have her baby-cake and eat it: balancing her social and domestic lives. She appeared in many productions over the years. My first memory of seeing her onstage was in a 1976 production of *Brigadoon*, the musical about a magical Scottish village that appears every two hundred years. By the mid-seventies, the ABC theatre had been converted into a three-screen cinema and the annual GODS musical had been transferred to the Cambridge Theatre, a large auditorium at the Gloucester Leisure Centre. It was here that I stood on my seat as the actors took their bows and shouted 'That's my mum' at the crowd of pensioners surrounding me, including my grandfather's beloved Pem, who chuckled next to me, glowing with pride for her daughter and to a lesser extent her hysterical grandson.

Mum went on to become a leading light at the GODS, receiving rave reviews for her performances from the local papers, describing her 'marvellous timing and use of facial expression' and labelling her 'an undoubted show-stealer'. I have little doubt that had she been afforded the same opportunities, encouragement and dumb luck as me, she might have found herself working as a professional actress. In her more reflective moments, she will say as much. Never in such a way as to convey regret or resentment but more assurance to herself that though she did not choose to follow that path, it was a path she was more than capable of taking. Whether she followed her dream or not, I still have the same feelings of childish pride when I consider her achievements, not just theatrically but as a mother and a human being. 'Without you, I wouldn't be here' doesn't really cover it.

Who Do I Think I Am (Part 2)?

As well as Mum successfully infiltrating the local am-dram society, Dad was also a keen musician, having played the piano and guitar in bands since he was sixteen. (As an actress/musician pairing, they were in many ways a precursor to Pamela Anderson and Tommy Lee, but without the home-made nautical porn – as far as I know . . .)

John met Gillian at a concert at the Guildhall in Gloucester, at which his first band, the Beathovens, were performing. By the time I became sensible of the world at large (that is, when my own memories take over from details I know about myself from other people), we were living over the aforementioned music shop, a short walk from the Guildhall, and Dad was playing keyboards in a show band called Pendulum.

They were well known locally, and became even more so for a short while after they appeared on *Opportunity Knocks*, the 1970s precursor to *Britain's Got Talent*, presented by popular eyebrow wiggler, Hughie Green. We tend to regard the TV talent show as a modern phenomenon but it's been around a long time.

It's only recently, however, that we've begun to relish the failure of the contestants as much as the success.

Back in the day, the audition process was an unseen filter specifically designed to sort the talented from the not so talented, and was done and dusted before the show was aired. Either we didn't care about seeing people desperate for external validation, brutally humiliated in public, or we didn't know we wanted it, the urge lying dormant within the human genome, like herpes. I'd like to believe it was the former. I'm not suggesting we were somehow nobler, or better human beings back then (let's not forget, *The Black and White Minstrel Show* was enjoying huge audiences around the same time), I just think the culture of hate and humiliation associated with contemporary talent shows is a product of an age in which television has become a demythologised free-for-all.

The idea of actually being on television was entirely different in the 1970s. In those days, the 'box' was as enigmatic as its nickname suggested; a far more mysterious object, it was a conduit through which we were given passive access to a faraway world. It was magical and inaccessible, a means of happily observing a party to which we were not invited and that we didn't necessarily want to be at.

In the early eighties, everything began to change on a grand scale. The advent of home video gave us dominion over television, shaking us from its thrall. We could decide what to watch and when. We could record programmes and films and hold them captive, watching them multiple times then discarding them by erasing them from existence. We puffed out our collective chests at that once inscrutable piece of tech in the corner and said: 'Who's the daddy now?'

Video cameras became readily available in the high street, further eroding the mystique, not only of TV and TV production but of the very idea of actually being on TV. With a modicum of head-scratching and a few leads we could see ourselves on the small screen every night, so what was the big deal? This, coupled with the evolution of reality television, as we know it today, has arguably engendered a sense of entitlement among certain sections of the viewing public, who have morphed from happy observers into rabid participants in the scrum for media exposure.

Consequently, there seems to be a large amount of bitterness levelled at those who manage to get their faces among the pixels. For instance, the depth of bile levelled at contestants on Channel 4's *Big Brother* has markedly increased since the programme's first airing in 2000. The public interest began as fascination, even admiration, and transformed over successive series into a dedicated hatred for all but the final few and even then the admiration is somewhat short-lived and begrudging.

Similarly, the entertainment value of shows like *The X Factor* and *Britain's Got Talent* is, at least in the initial stages, about seeing hapless wannabes parade themselves before a panel of unforgiving 'judges' and cataclysmically fail for our pleasure, providing instant *Schadenfreude*. What else is the emotion behind the laughter? I always feel an enormous amount of sadness when I see people's self-belief shattered by these sneering 'determinators' with their corporate agendas defining what constitutes talent and art. Isn't self-delusion better than desolation?

Of course, it's eternally defendable by way of the argument that nobody is forcing these people to sacrifice their dignity to the masses, but that's not really the point, is it? *The X Factor* isn't a million miles from Channel 4's nineties car-crash magazine show *The Word*, presented by Terry Christian, in which people desperate to appear on television would eat bulls' testicles and lick pensioners' armpits as part of a segment poignantly entitled 'The Hopefuls'. The makers of contemporary talent shows know there will always be a supply of hopefuls, whose need for facile validation far outweighs their fear of public failure, or, worse, who are happy to settle for public failure as a means of attaining the moment of exposure they feel entitled to. In light of this conveyor belt of catastrophe, Warhol's famous prediction seems overly generous. Ironically, ten years after the show was axed, Terry Christian appeared as a contestant on *Celebrity Big Brother*. Talk about pap will eat itself.

Anyway, back in 1975, Pendulum's audition took place in Bristol and was presided over by the show's producer, Doris Barry, and Hughie Green himself. The band knocked out a version of Jimmy Webb's 'MacArthur Park' but were asked to perform something a little more poppy and so launched into an impromptu rendition of 'That's the Way (I Like It)' by KC & The Sunshine Band, impressing the judges enough to secure a place in the finals.

Sponsored by Iona Robbins, wife of the then Mayor of Gloucester, the band travelled to London to record the show. There they met the other contestants, the usual array of jugglers, magicians and ventriloquists, as well as a fellow West Country girl who wrote comic poetry, with whom the band struck up an immediate bond. They recorded their spot as live on the Saturday night and comfortably won the studio audience's vote on a sophisticated appreciation-measuring device called the 'Clap-o-meter'.

Dad returned from London on the Sunday, buzzing with success, and the whole family gathered the following night to watch the show air. It was all extremely exciting, staying up past my bedtime to see my dad on television (actually *on* the television!) was beyond amazing. At one point I fell over and got a cocktail stick stuck in my hand and yet even this momentarily worrying impalement failed to dampen my ardour at the wonder of it all.

I can still see him singing into the microphone, and if I really concentrate I can feel my grandparents' house unfold around me, filled with excitement and finger food. All the contestants are gathered together at the end of the show, waving and smiling at the camera as the credits roll. The only face I can recall is Dad's; he was, after all, the only one I was watching. Years later he told me that during the goodbye shot, Pendulum's drummer, Paul Holder, had placed his penis into my dad's hand, which was resting behind his back. I often lament the fact that there is no record of the show; it would be worth watching if only for the expression of surprise, which apparently exploded out of my father's cheesy goodbye grin as he realised that Paul's knob was lolling in his palm.

In the end, despite the 'Clap-o-meter' triumph, the definitive decision came from the viewing public. There was no phone voting in those days; public opinion was a strictly postal affair. Votes would be written on a blank postcard and mailed to Thames Television, then counted up to determine the victor. The result was announced on the subsequent show before the whole process kicked off again. Much to our collective disappointment, Pendulum didn't quite capture the public imagination as much as the talented young West Country poetess, who won the viewers' votes with a genuinely funny poem called 'I Wish I'd Looked After My Teeth'. Her name was Pam Ayres. The fact that Pam is still writing and performing to this day and often crops up on the television actually makes me very happy. It's a testament to her talent that she remains successful, and somehow makes her triumph over Dad's show band less disappointing.

Pendulum were approached by the Joe Loss talent agency and got a few high-profile gigs as a result, including the National Television Advertising Awards. However, Loss's desire for the band to work aboard cruise ships led to tensions, which eventually resulted in a split. Half the band had mortgages and children and couldn't really take off around the world at a moment's notice. I have a very vague recollection of Dad telling me about a possible trip but it never happened.

It's interesting that I have never heard Dad talk about his experience on *Opportunity Knocks* as an opportunity missed; the big break that could have propelled him to stardom. He is an extremely talented pianist and I have never known him not to be in some band or other. You can currently catch him performing in various venues in and around the South-West as part of a delightfully tight outfit called JB Jazz & Blues. The JB stands for John Beckingham, which are my father's first and second names respectively. Beckingham was my second name too until 1977 but we'll get to that later, maybe . . . Have I told you my dog likes eating socks?

An earlier incarnation of JB Jazz & Blues can actually be seen in *Spaced*. The band perform Louis Jordan's 'Is You Is Or Is You Ain't My Baby' behind Tim and Daisy as they dance themselves closer into one another's affections at the bitter-sweet conclusion to series one. It's a lovely moment and I was so proud and happy to have Dad be part of the show. The whole family didn't all gather in one place to watch that though. There was no sense of occasion or cocktail sticks. Everyone just watched in their own home or else taped it. Funny that.

Born Luvvy

Having been exposed to theatre at a very early age, I was keen to participate in drama as soon as the opportunity presented itself. The first major role I recall taking on was the young Francis of Assisi, in a play about his life staged in the Lady chapel at Gloucester Cathedral. I must have been extremely young, since the boy playing Francis in his dotage can only have been about ten, and the boy playing Francis's father was even younger at eight!

Appropriately, I played Francis as a tiny boy, in a scene where his father sits the future saint on his knee and imparts some nugget of wisdom, which motivates Francis in later life. The boy playing my dad walked on to the stage as if returning from work (not sure what Francis of Assisi's dad did for a living; maybe he worked at the Wall's factory on Eastern Avenue), at which point I leapt up and exhaled a booming 'Helloooooo, Father,' which reverberated around the walls of the Lady chapel and garnered an unexpected laugh from the audience.

Once seated on my eight-year-old father's lap, I was given a plastic tube full of fruit jellies, which I tucked into enthusiastically as Dad delivered his scripted words of wisdom. The cue for my next line came and went, but there were still three sweets left in the tube and I was determined to finish them before I spoke. The older kids in the front row were all leaning forward and hissing my line at me, which I knew full well. I nodded at them reassuringly and continued to chew.

The tittering started again and I realised it was because of me. I grinned broadly out into the auditorium with a face full of fruit jelly and calmly waited until I was able to advance the plot further, which eventually I did much to the relief of the assembled parents and clergy. I was never reprimanded for confusing my theatrical priorities with my sweet tooth, and my parents were clearly amused and even proud of my faux pas. I certainly didn't feel as though I'd done anything wrong, far from it, I felt it had all gone rather well.

The following Christmas, the inevitable nativity play rolled around, but much to my surprise, I was not cast as Joseph but instead some weary traveller, whose narrative purpose was to demonstrate that a lot of people had come to pay their taxes in Bethlehem and accommodation was in extreme demand. I was instructed to walk across the stage, looking for a room, which I did with ridiculous enthusiasm, getting down on my knees, looking under chairs and even under my own armpits, only to hear a frustrated voice sternly whispering 'Simon!,' similar in many ways to the voice I would hear five or six years later as I closed in for my fifth kick of the papier-mâché model of St Peter's bell, the real version of which had barely ceased to vibrate at the commencement of our nativity service and the debut of my man looking for accommodation character.

By the age of seven, I was performing alongside my mother and her friends in musicals such as *Carousel* and *The Music Man*. Even now, when I hear songs such as 'If I Loved You' and 'June Is Bustin' Out All Over' or even an orchestra tuning up, I experience a powerful sensation of excitement and anticipation.

It was a magical time for me; the shows were hugely popular and would play to audiences of five hundred every night for a full week with matinees at the weekend. Hanging out at the theatre, getting into costume, putting on ridiculously thick make-up, seeing my mum's friends in their bras was all a tremendous thrill.

As well as the physical and emotional rush of performing, I was developing a love of theatre as an extremely evocative mode of storytelling. I obviously didn't interpret that love as such, I just remember the shows having a huge emotional pull on me. *Carousel* had a particularly significant effect on my sense of the dramatic, probably because it dealt with themes such as love, death, loss and parental responsibility. It also includes a paranormal twist towards the end, when the main character, Billy, accidentally stabs himself, becomes a ghost and is transported fifteen years into the future to alleviate the stresses caused by his departure. To a nerdling it was appealing for obvious reasons – ghosts, time travel and moderate violence – but I think there were probably deeper emotions at work within me. My grandfather Albert had died a year or so before, my first intimation of death, and my parents had separated shortly afterwards. Those themes running through the play's narrative probably affected me more than I know, resulting in something of a subconscious catharsis, which engaged me with the moment and fastened it in my mind forever. It's strange how I don't remember *The Music Man* so well and that was a whole eighth of my life later, although if drunk enough, I can I still sing the first few verses of 'Seventy-Six Trombones'.

It was during *Carousel* that I experienced my first incidence of performing in the face of adversity (this being a full year before Denise Miller's threatened kiss inspired me to get intimate with a brick wall). There were a number of young people in the show, varying in age from my tender seven years to cool guys and sweet-smelling girls in their late teens. I loved being the little kid in the gang; there's always one: from the Double Deckers to the Red Hand Gang. I was the one who could fit through small windows, or sneak past the policeman, or pretend to be lost so that the security guard at the junkyard didn't notice the rest of the gang sneaking in behind him to rescue the mean old man's dog. In reality it wasn't like that – we just used to hang around at the bottom of a backstage stairwell before the show started and I would try to gain acceptance by acting like a monkey. I told jokes, did impressions, performed pratfalls, all in the pursuit of those status-affirming laughs that let me know I was 'in' with the big kids, although in reality I was never 'in', just tolerated.

I was a puppy for the girls and a chimp for the boys, which is quite versatile for a seven-year-old. Before one evening performance I was particularly eager to finish getting ready for the show and get down to the stairwell to commence hanging out, since my fellow gang members were already down there. I hurtled from the dressing room, down the corridor, through the fire door, then, just as I reached the top of the stairs, tripped. Much to the horror of my 'friends', I rolled head over heels, down the concrete steps, grinding my lower back against the hard corners, which were edged with an aluminium strip to limit wear and tear. I managed to right myself before I got to the bottom of the staircase and ran back up, barely containing the explosion of tears that issued, once I fully understood what had happened. I glanced back at them as I headed back to the fire doors and noticed their expressions of concern were morphing into smirks as they tried to contain their amusement. I clearly wasn't too badly injured or I wouldn't have got up at all, and their amusement was as much the product of relief as it was an enjoyment of my misfortune (probably about 30/70).

I was a little hurt by it though, because until that point the laughter I had elicited from them had seemed to me to be on my terms, whereas now I just felt like a clumsy little idiot. One of the older girls chased up the stairs after me and found my mum, who managed to calm me down and establish that nothing was broken. I had bruised my coccyx fairly badly, and as my first scene approached, the pain in my lower back grew more acute. I was playing one of the Snow children in the show, the prissy offspring of Enoch Snow, a stuck-up society type, if my memory serves me correctly. Our first scene consisted of a dance routine as the children follow their father somewhere, like obedient little ducklings. One of the moves required us to bend at the waist, something I was finding increasingly hard to do by the time it came to go on, I was stiff as a board, but to save face and, in my mind, the entire show, I persevered. I distinctly remember making a slightly pained face as we performed the move as if to show the audience that I was being a trouper, as if they would sit there in the darkness of the auditorium thinking, that kid sure has got a lot of moxie. It was an odd thing to do considering nobody in the audience had any idea that I had recently taken a spectacular tumble down a flight of stairs. Whatever my reasoning, there is no doubt that I relished the drama, which is somewhat appropriate for a budding actor, although I'm looking back now (as I often do while writing this book) and thinking, what a prick.

Look At Me! Actually, Don't Look At Me

As musicals go, *Carousel* could be said to be have affected me more deeply than any musical has ever affected any straight man, as it also provided me with my first brush against the complexities of celebrity. Specifically, how the desire to attain self-validation can ultimately have the opposite effect. It's something I remain conflicted about even today, and this small incident may have been implicit in shaping my feelings on the idea of personal visibility to this very day.

I was hanging about backstage in full costume shortly before the show began, my older crew having given me the slip, or perhaps found somewhere safer to hang out and 'forgotten' to tell me. In the show, the Snow children were dressed with Von Trapp uniformity in velvet jackets and little straw hats and knickerbockers. I needed the toilet before curtain up and I convinced myself the only way to do that was by leaving the backstage area, walking through front of house and out into the foyer where I knew there were male and female toilets. My memory tells me I knew this because of the Galaxian machine which stood against the wall between them; Gents on the left, Ladies on the right. However, having checked this out, I find it cannot be true because Galaxian didn't appear until 1979 and this was 1977.

Space Invaders didn't come out until 1978 so I have no idea what was between the doors of the male and female toilets on the first floor of the Gloucester Leisure Centre in 1977. Nothing? Was there really a time before video games? Strange to think of these invisible voids that exist around us, waiting to accommodate advances in technology that will soon become commonplace. So much so that it will be hard to imagine life without them. There were spaces on walls before light switches, let alone plasma TVs. Desks without computers, roads without cars, hands without mobile phones. Conversely, as microtechnology and digital storage maximise space and convenience, voids are opening up, subtly erasing any memory of the three-dimensional objects which filled them. The spaces occupied by photo albums, the box TV, filing cabinets, cassette decks, record players, books, ashtrays or more short-lived necessities like CD storage units, VHS players and tapes or hard-drive towers.

Computers have been shrinking since they first appeared. I wonder what the rooms that were filled with those huge, whirring, tape-spewing early computers are used for now. Are they empty? Or are they perhaps being utilised for an altogether more analogue form of storage? It makes you wonder what spaces will be filled or created by the next arrival or obsolescence. The mobile phone may well shrink out of our grip as the era of the cyborg approaches. Sounds like science fiction but we are inexorably approaching an era in which the phone will no longer be something we 'pick up'.

The threat to the key has long been a possibility since the magnetic strip began to give us access to hotel rooms and office buildings, but now contactless technology has equipped us with locks that recognise corresponding chips when brought into proximity. How long before the chips housed in those keyless entry fobs creep under our skin, making us technically part machine, recognisable to our houses, cars, workplaces, parking spaces? Who's to say these chips won't be able to communicate over longer distances and ringing a friend will only require you to think their name? Although this would potentially lead to a lot of unintentional calls answered with the question, 'Did you mean to call or were you just thinking about me?' Could be quite embarrassing.

The space around us has an intriguing potential to be cleared of things we need or filled by the things we don't yet know we need. That space between the male and female toilets at the Gloucester Leisure Centre was waiting for that Galaxian machine even before the leisure centre was built, when it was simply a volume of atmosphere, twenty-five feet above a field, or some woodland. The galaxy itself was waiting for the Galaxian machine in the same way it was waiting for Earth to settle into orbit around a sun that will eventually consume it. Oh balls, I've opened it right up now. I'm getting into the realms of chaos and consequence and our meaningless, flickering tenure, not only in space but also in time, when what I really wanted to do was tell the story of a seven-year-old show-off who needed a piss. I suppose what we learn from this digression is that you can't always trust your memory. It fills spaces with little inaccuracies, or else becomes a space in itself.

One thing I can be certain of is that there was a gentlemen's toilet on the first floor of the Gloucester Leisure Centre in 1977. I know because I distinctly remember entering it in my velvet jacket and straw hat and fishing my penis out of my knickerbockers to relieve myself next to a punter who regarded me with nothing more than a half-hearted double take. What I really wanted was for someone, not necessarily the pisser, but someone, to say, 'Wow, are you in the play? That's amazing! You're amazing! You are amazing for being in a play.' Nobody did. I don't even remember turning any heads, just experiencing a vague sense of embarrassment and regret and an awareness (even at my tender age) that my desire to be recognised was slightly pathetic.

When I returned backstage I was reprimanded by my mother, mainly for going missing for ten minutes but also for breaking the fourth wall, which apparently extended from the sides of the proscenium arch to the door that let the actors out into the auditorium. I remember her telling me it was unprofessional. I felt stupid and needy and suspected the people who had noticed me mingling, those that weren't in bizarre costumes, had thought me faintly ridiculous. This was the seventies though and, by contemporary standards, everybody was dressed in bizarre costumes.

I have never lost the perspective given to me by my journey to and from the real-world toilet, and although sometimes it's fun to relax and enjoy a degree of fame, I fully appreciate the transparency of the desire. The recognition that has resulted from the work I have done has fastened me into a pair of knicker-bockers, since at times getting noticed cannot be avoided. Being recognisable is like wearing a bizarre costume, particularly when you are with people that most keenly appreciate whatever it is you do.

The San Diego Comic-Con is an annual event, where almost half a million comic-book/sci-fi/movie fans gather together to buy cool stuff and see their favourite actors/writers/artists/directors talk about their work and sign autographs over a single weekend in late July. It is one of the most shamelessly enthusiastic celebrations of all things fantastic in the world and I love it. People dress as their favourite characters and walk the convention floor without fear of ridicule or cynicism. Indeed, they are admired, complimented, even regarded as celebrities by other attendees.

Since much of my work has dealt with the nerdier side of popular culture, either being about the kind of people who attend Comic-Con or being the kind of film people who attend Comic-Con are into, it's safe to say that the kind of people who attend Comic-Con are my demographic. I never feel more known than when I am there.

As an actor or writer or whatever, you hope deep down that those who witness your output enjoy and appreciate it, or better still connect with it on a personal level. You also hope to achieve some confirmation of that, not just through box-office receipts or viewing figures but by personal interaction. Receiving positive feedback is as eternally gratifying as enduring negativity is devastating. There is a pleasure in knowing you have made someone happy by sharing an idea or telling a story, and you can experience that pleasure only if the happiness is somehow relayed back to you.

I don't understand how any artist can reject positive feedback as if it is an annoyance or, worse, a burden. A friend of mine told me a story about seeing a popular British soap actor approached by a fan in a shopping centre car park and rejecting the admirer's request for an autograph with a resounding 'Fuck off!' We all have days when we want to be left alone, but even when you don't want your photo taken or have the time to stop and chat, you must surely decline with patience and good grace. Even if you have been approached a hundred times in an hour, whoever is approaching you is doing so for the first time and is probably nervous. The least you can do is acknowledge their good-natured bravery and respond with a smile, even if you don't have time to talk to their mate on the phone or allow them to lick your face.

It's not always the case that people's intentions are pleasant. I get shouted at a lot by people who simply want some facile interaction. Others will approach you specifically to tell you they don't know who the fuck you are, even though their coy mate, standing apologetically at the bar, does.

I hate being asked to list my celebrity credentials to rude, ignorant people who believe I owe them some sort of justification for my existence. Some people assume fame results in deafness and stupidity and, on recognising you, will point and stage-whisper, as if you're not there, 'Who? Where? It's not, is it?' as if they hope you will spare them the indignity of acknowledging their awareness of you, by holding your hands up in surrender and saying 'You got me'. In those situations, I tend to play deaf and stupid. This is why I generally try to make my figurative knickerbockers as inconspicuous as possible. Not because I don't appreciate affirmation from those who enjoy my stuff, or that I am even forfending against people who get a buzz from being nasty (fortunately the latter are rare), but more because persistent focused attention is actually exhausting whether it is positive or negative.

People who are super-famous have to live bizarre, rarefied lives, far removed from any accepted notions of normality, simply because a regular existence is prohibited by their enormous, unmistakable knickerbockers. I'm not complaining by any means; I don't suffer the weirdness that others do, people for whom the spotlight has become blindingly intense. I keep my head down and wear a hat. I try not to hang out in places where famous people hang out, although it's nice to take my mum to the Ivy once in a while, and every now and again a premiere invite will land on my doormat that is way too fun to ignore. I reject 99 per cent of the social invitations I receive and as such don't get photographed that much (I was once snapped picking up Minnie's morning bowel movement but didn't feel too invaded since technically I was setting an example to other dog owners).

At Comic-Con one year, determined to walk the convention floor freely, without having to make too many stops, I purchased a Joker mask from a *Dark Knight* promotional stand and moved across the floor unnoticed. The irony being that it was necessary for me to wear an actual costume in order to disguise the figurative knickerbockers my profession had inculcated me with. It was an act that represented a huge gulf of experience between me and my seven-year-old self, scurrying through the crowd in the Cambridge Theatre foyer, with the specific intention of drawing attention.

With the aid of the ESTB I might have nipped back and solemnly directed myself towards the backstage toilets. Although perhaps not. Perhaps I would be depriving myself of a valuable lesson about the consequences of fame. Besides, as a naive little seven-year-old, enjoying his first brush with show business, I would probably have looked into the eyes of the 38-year-old time traveller and asked, 'Why so serious?'

3

The jet lifted into the air like a big black aeroplane as the roof of Pegg Manor settled back into its mock-Tudor splendour, so that people passing on the A1 wouldn't know that billionaire philanthropist Simon Pegg had a heavily armed stealth bomber in his loft conversion. Canterbury, Pegg's faithful mechanical companion and butler, completed a number of pre-flight checks, flicking various switches and surveying an ellipse of readouts on the hi-tech dashboard.

'Shouldn't you have done that before take-off?' enquired Pegg.

'You seemed quite eager to leave, sir,' explained Canterbury. 'I thought I might do it on the hop.'

'I like your initiative,' mused Pegg with a small but devastating smile, which gave Canterbury a thrill even though he was a robot. 'And you're right, I was eager to leave. We have to get to Morocco and find the Scarlet Panther before it's too late.'

'That does sound awfully urgent, sir,' chirruped Canterbury, a note of concern in his synthetic voice. 'What will happen if we don't find her?'

'Well, you can kiss your metal ass goodbye,' Pegg returned with a gloomy heavy sigh. 'Not just your ass but all our asses, every ass on the face of this planet.'

'Go on, sir,' said Canterbury, encouraging Pegg to deliver much-needed exposition.

'Two nights ago, I received a mysterious tweet that I simply could not ignore,' confided Pegg.

'I thought you were switching Twitter off until you finish your book,' said Canterbury honestly.

'Yes, well, I was just having a look at it one last time before I started in earnest. I wasn't pontificating or anything.'

Canterbury said nothing.

'Look, the point is,' said Pegg heatedly, 'last week the Scarlet Panther broke into the Museum of Egyptian Antiquity in Cairo and stole the Star of Nefertiti.'

'Is that the thing that makes all the exhibits come to life?' enquired Canterbury.

'This is reality, Canterbury!' roared Pegg. 'The Star of Nefertiti is a magic diamond that when slotted into the lost tablet of Amenhotep IV fires a laser into the heart of the Sun, causing a solar flare that heats up the Earth's core and destabilises the tectonic plates that hold the very surface of the planet together, bringing about the end of days.'

'Like in that film *2012*?' offered Canterbury.

'Worse,' said Pegg with enormous seriousness. 'This makes *2012* look like *2001* in terms of action and excitement. We've got to stop her!'

'But what of the tablet of Amenhotep IV?' enquired Canterbury helpfully.

'Its whereabouts are unknown,' conceded Pegg grimly. 'It used to reside at the estate of Colonel Barnabus McCartney in Surrey but when the Colonel died mysteriously in 1994, his possessions were distributed privately according to his will. It could be anywhere.'

'Forgive me, sir,' said Canterbury, facilitating the divulgence of further information, 'but if the Scarlet Panther knew the whereabouts of the tablet, why would she want to bring about the end of days by combining it with the Star of Nefertiti? She's just a gorgeous cat burglar/nemesis, with whom you have a passionate and complex on-off relationship.'

Pegg's eyes became unfocused as his mind drifted elsewhere, followed by his penis.

'I see it!' Canterbury exclaimed.

'What?' said Pegg, adjusting his trousers.

'She doesn't want to destroy the world. She probably doesn't realise the true power of the Star of Nefertiti. She simply acquired it and someone paid her very handsomely to do so.'

'But whom?' mused Pegg.

'Who?' said Canterbury very quietly.

'That's what we have to find out, old friend, it could simply be a diamond collector or it could be someone who knows the whereabouts of the tablet of Amenhotep IV and wants to bring about the end of the world or else threaten to as a means of extorting money from the world's most powerful economies,' said Pegg without breathing. 'Set course for Marrakesh.'

'At once, sir,' replied Canterbury, snapping into important mode. 'You will need to return to your quarters before I fire the special stealth retros.'

'Can I just sit here for a bit?' enquired Pegg casually.

'No, sir,' returned the faithful automaton. 'The thrust in the cockpit would prove too much for the human body to endure without a flight suit.'

'All right,' said Pegg. 'Give me a minute.'

'Of course, sir,' said Canterbury, pretending not to notice the fact that his master was severely tenting.

Fear of a Blue Planet

When I wasn't adhering to a ludicrously heavy acting schedule as a nipper, I was often splashing around in the local municipal.

However, I wasn't a great swimmer when I was young. Nowadays, I can cut through the water like a buttered dolphin, but for a time I dreaded the weekly school swimming lessons.

It was a confidence issue more than a skill-in-the-water thing. You couldn't keep me out of the sea on family holidays, particularly after I discovered the many and varied joys of snorkelling. On one particular excursion, no bigger than an adult seal (unbuttered), I drifted out towards the open sea while exploring a beautiful cove on the Devon coast. I only realised I was straying into the English Channel when I felt a tap on my shoulder and emerged from my aquatic reverie to see my terrified mother treading water, with the shore some two hundred metres behind her.

My problem was more to do with the whole package, rather than simply the water itself. There was something nerve-racking for me about swimming pools. Great big, chemical-stinking rooms filled with wet strangers, emitting echoing screams of euphoric joy or genuine terror (it was never an easy distinction to make) as I failed to avoid gulping down mouthfuls of the old municipal blue. This somewhat specific aversion can be traced back to three childhood experiences relating to swimming that affected me deeply.

Two of them happened at Gloucester Leisure Centre, where I eventually and somewhat ironically worked as a lifeguard. I don't mean I worked in an ironic fashion – I didn't permit people to splash each other, run on wet surfaces and drown – I mean that, in hindsight, it seems ironic to me that I was paid to work in the very place that, for a couple of years, you couldn't have paid me to enter.

The first incident occurred when I was around six years old. As was our custom on a Sunday morning, I had gone to the public baths with my mum and my cousin Tim who was nine or ten years older than me. I had been confined to the learner pool, a smaller proposition to the huge, scary adult's pool annexing it. Bathtub-warm and full of tiny screaming kids and probably tiny screaming kids' urine (which explains the temperature of the water), I couldn't help feeling frustrated. I wanted to be in the main pool with Tim and hang out with the big kids.

I'd been in the shallow end a few times under supervision and played 'thumbs up underwater' with Tim. That's not some depraved game permitted in the seventies, a time when pool etiquette admittedly involved free rein to drown Rolf Harris (am I remembering that 'learn to swim' commercial correctly?), it was actually a game Tim and I had devised to road-test our goggles. We would stand opposite each other, count to three, then submerge ourselves into a corresponding position beneath the surface. We would then give each other the thumbs up until it was necessary to re-emerge into the light and noise to get air.

Whether it is the sea, the swimming pool or the bath, under-water is a fascinating place for kids. It is mysterious and other-worldly, rendering your surroundings in cool slow motion. We are guests of something awesome when we're underwater. It is a place where we do not belong and forces beyond our control govern our tenure; our body either propels us to the surface for air or the water keeps us for itself. It's alien and dangerous; it inspires our urge to explore, that primary force in evolution that conversely brought fishes from the sea to the land in the first place. Throw in an inevitable and arguably less subconscious uterine association and it's a wonder we don't spend our lives in scuba gear.

As a geeky teenager and finally rid of my phobia, I would dive to the bottom of the deep end of our school pool, during the precious ten minutes of free swim time permitted at the end of swimming lessons, and stand for a few seconds with my hands on my hips, pretending to be Superman. I would look around, as if in search of a Lois or Jimmy, then take off for the surface as if I was flying into the sky, and for twelve whole feet, I swear I could feel my cape flowing behind me. That was the other aspect of the aquatic world that appealed to me – the absence of verbal communication meant your internal monologue could fill the solitude with nerdy fantasy, unfettered. Even at the crowded Gloucester Leisure Centre in the mid-seventies, 'going underwater' was hugely exciting as it cut the pandemonium of the surface to a muffled silence in an instant. My frustration at languishing in the baby pool became too much to bear. I decided to escape through the verruca bath to the adjacent big pool, while my mother wasn't looking, and join Tim in the serious water, not just for 'thumbs up underwater' but for other legendary pool games, such as 'jumping off the cliff', 'caught by a shark' and 'can you tell that I'm relieving myself?'.

Emerging into the cavernous interior of the main pool, I spied cousin Tim some way towards the mid-shallows. What the heck? I thought to myself, I'm six, I'm wearing a rubber ring, I can handle the mid-centre with the teens, you just see if I can't! I had no idea about the level of panic involved in drowning. The hopeless desperation that floods your body, way before the water fully invades your lungs. I'm not sure what I expected my rubber ring to do as I rashly leapt in. Probably that it would do its job in preventing me from sinking beneath the water before I had a chance to hold my breath. It certainly fulfilled its primary purpose in remaining topside. In that respect, I let the rubber ring down by not remaining topside with it, as was admittedly my responsibility.

As I hit the water, the ring stayed where it was and I slipped through into the wash, kicking with sudden ineffectuality towards the surface, immediately aware that I was literally out of my depth. I can't remember who pulled me out. I don't think it was a lifeguard, I think it was a civilian man, with a beard; maybe it was Rolf Harris. Needless to say, the experience left me shaken and rendered me strictly baby-pool material for a while afterwards. A shadow of my former water-baby self, my confidence gone, I tried to rope a few toddlers into playing 'thumbs up underwater' but only got as far as asking a little girl's father before I was banned from the leisure centre for a year by a cabal of angry parents.

That's not true but it seemed like a good way to end the story, which, let's face it, petered out. I'm likely to do that from time to time. It comes from being a stand-up comedian. If a joke or story doesn't work, you keep adding to it until it gets the requisite response and then you move on. I promise to let you know when I do it, as I want this to be a truthful account as well as an entertaining read. The truth is always preferable in the context of a memoir because the enjoyment lives and dies by the reader's belief in the events being described. So, unless I tell you otherwise, I am conveying to you the absolute truth and not in a double-bluff, Whitley Strieber's *Communion*-type way. So now, with that short digression out of the way, let us plunge back into the suspiciously warm waters of my aquatic past and get to the bottom of this, as far as I know, nameless childhood phobia.

The second event (of the fabled three) occurred not in the voluminous blue of the Gloucester Leisure Centre main pool but in the changing rooms. The whole incident came about as the result of me accidentally kicking the person behind me in the eye as I exited the pool. Rather than apologise when I turned and saw him rubbing his face, I made a face as if to say 'Don't be such a baby'. He and his friend then acted out vengeance on me and my friend in an extremely cruel and scary way. They kept us in the changing rooms for at least ten minutes, holding Sean Jeffries and me hostage, and repeatedly calling us bummers before threatening to make us perform bum-based acts on each other, until I was a mess of terrified tears. I always remember being impressed by Sean, who remained stoic, even in the face of their chilling threats, while I whined and begged them to let us go.

In the end, I think they felt a bit sorry for me because I was such a baby and they did indeed let us go unmolested. I wouldn't go swimming for a few months after that. Years later, as a life-guard at the same pool, I caught a couple of kids terrorising a younger swimmer in the very same changing space and exacted cathartic revenge upon them, as if they were the very same bullies who had terrorised me ten years earlier. The two perps were probably in their mid-teens, both were already dressed as they circled in on a wet boy, no older than ten . . .

4

'What the hell's going on here?' asked Pegg, settling into a stance that projected strength and authority, a demeanour only augmented by his red, white and blue lifeguard uniform, which clung to his muscular form as though it could not bear to be separated from his sweet-smelling skin; a combination of natural musk and Brut 33.

'What's it to you, grandad?' said the more dominant of the two absolute shitheads.

'I'm not your grandad,' Pegg replied with a knowing smile. 'I'm not even old enough to be your father. Someone's clearly failing math,' Pegg quipped, firing a reassuring wink at the victim, whose face had become a glowing beacon of gratitude and admiration.

'What are you talking about?' spat the lowlife pool bully, his eyes disappearing into a hateful squint.

Pegg sighed. 'I'm saying, I'm not old enough to have fathered a child that could have given birth to you let alone fathered you myself, unless I impregnated your mother when I was five which would have been sick and impossible, not least because your mum is a right pig.'

The bullies looked at each other, simultaneously confused and enraged by Pegg's intellectual prowess.

The young future hero was already winning and hadn't even had to deploy any of his limbs.

'I could be your uncle,' he pursued, further confusing the rat-like attackers as they fought to keep pace with his brilliance.

'Look, just fuck off, all right?' said the alpha. 'This is none of your business.'

'Oh, I beg to differ,' Pegg intoned like an ancient wise man, despite being just nineteen years old. 'Anything that takes place in this changing room is my business. Not just this changing room but the general pool area, incorporating the boards and flumes, and roller-skating in the sports hall on Saturday.'

'Look —' the vocal bully spat.

Pegg cut him off with further affirmation of his inarguable status. 'I also oversee old people's water aerobics on the first Sunday of every month, so don't tell me it's none of my damn business.'

The bullies fell into a stunned silence. Pegg had them exactly where he wanted them.

'Now, if you don't mind, I'd like to get back to reading *The Dark Knight Returns* in the staff canteen,' crowed Pegg. 'So, let's bring this little encounter to a close, shall we?'

The bullies looked at each other, then, with a silent terrified agreement, produced a fine pair of lock knives, as if to say, back off or we will stab you to death with this pair of fine lock knives. Pegg shook his head slowly, a wry smile creeping across his taut young face.

'Oh, you've done it now,' he chuckled. 'I was going to let you off with a warning but I'm afraid that time has passed. If you want to play it this way, then this is the way it will be played and play it we will.'

Pegg knew full well his poetry would confuse them. It was all the time he needed. The bigger one fell first. He glanced at his friend for a split second as if Pegg's linguistic dexterity had short-circuited his brain.

By the time his beady eyes had flitted back to where the statuesque lifeguard had been standing, Pegg was upon him. Steel fingers clamped around the goon's bony wrist, twisting his warty little claws into open helplessness. The shiv hit the floor but not before a bright, sickening crack bounced off the tiled dividing walls of the recently refurbished changing area. A voice in Pegg's head suggested he stop with the wrist but he didn't listen to it. He ducked underneath the bully's willowy arm, pulling it straight, just as the first screech of agony left his thin lips.

Extending his own arms to their full impressive length, Pegg gave himself room to lift his muscular leg between them. With balletic poise, he curled the piston into his chest, pleasantly noting how his shorts revealed his bare thighs and the rolling muscle beneath the skin, which bunched into a terrifying coil of explosive power. Are you taking this too far? He didn't pause to answer the internal question. His foot sprang from his hip like a missile in a mid-price training shoe, the sole of which met the back of the scumbag's elbow with a formidable impact, snapping the arm in two, propelling the jagged ends of his ulna and radius through the soft flesh in the crook of his elbow, spattering blood across his cohort's horrified face. The defeated bully fell to the floor in a splutter of retching shock. Tears flooded his friend's eyes as thick blood glugged out around the snapped ends of his forearm, and a knife clattered across the changing-room floor as it fell from the terrified sidekick's fingers.

'I'm glad you see things my way,' Pegg whispered. 'You're both banned for a month.' The boys looked disappointed, even the one who would probably never do breaststroke again.

'Oh, and that's effective immediately,' Pegg asserted. 'Check in with Canterbury on the way out, he'll take your pictures for the wall of shame.'

'W-w-who's Canterbury?' stuttered the weaker of the two twats.

'You'll know when you see him.' Pegg smiled, thinking of his uptight robotic friend, whom he had only just finished constructing and who was in no way a derivative combination of various other famous robots.

The bullies left. The smaller herbert supporting his broken friend. The boy smiled at Pegg, his face a mixture of awe and admiration.

'Thank you,' he gushed. 'Thank you for helping me.'

'I wasn't just helping you, kid,' Pegg said in a way that was reminiscent of Harrison Ford talking affectionately to a small Chinese boy. 'I was helping every kid that has ever been intimidated in a swimming pool changing room and that includes me.'

'Y-you?!' the young boy stammered, as if he couldn't compute the notion of Pegg being a weedy little crybaby, terrified of being threatened and called a bummer.

Another lifeguard entered, a beautiful French girl whose name was Murielle. She seemed worried, approaching Pegg at speed.

'Simone, Simone,' she cooed lovingly, despite the note of concern in her sing-song voice. 'Someone did a bellyflop off the top board and his tummy has exploded!'

'Excuse me,' Pegg apologised to the grateful young boy. 'I'm needed elsewhere.'

He was gone before either of them realised (because he was so quick like the Flash or Mr Muscle), leaving an air of confused wonder between the Gallic goddess and the small boy, a boy whose long-term sanity Pegg had just rescued from a future of regret and obsessive, cathartic reimagining.

Pegg opened his eyes.

'Remember Murielle back then, Canterbury?' asked Pegg, drifting out of his reminiscences back to the reality of his luxurious quarters aboard the hi-tech private stealth jet.

'Indeed I do, sir,' Canterbury's voice sounded over the intercom, startling Pegg slightly, despite the fact he had asked the question. 'A true beauty then as she is now.'

'It still amazes me,' Pegg mused. 'What she became.'

'Perhaps it was fate, sir,' offered the droid thoughtfully.

'Perhaps it was,' agreed Pegg with a rueful smile. 'How long until Marrakesh?'

'Thirty minutes, sir,' returned Canterbury.

'Good. That gives me enough time to watch the escape montage from *The Shawshank Redemption*,' fizzed Pegg excitedly.

'How many times do you think we've watched that film?' added Pegg.

'I've lost count,'confessed Canterbury.

'Really?!' worried Pegg.

'No,' admitted Canterbury. 'It's 137.'

Return of the King

The whole experience of lifeguarding the big pool at Gloucester Leisure Centre had a pleasing sense of completion for me. As if I had finally conquered an old fear by returning to hold partial dominion over it, or at least uphold its ancient laws. I would sit in the high chair at the edge of the deep end (roughly where I had almost drowned fifteen years prior), swinging my whistle, a languid prince meting out justice to those who transgressed the list of very clear rules. Rules that are well known to any of us who have frequented the local baths; rules which, in the main, make complete sense. With a few variations between principalities, they are as follows:

1. No running.
2. No pushing.
3. No acrobatics.
4. No bombing.
5. No swimming in the diving area.
6. No diving in the shallow end.
7. No unaccompanied minors.
8. No heavy petting.

These commandments were usually emblazoned upon a poolside billboard, each diktat accompanied by a cartoon illustration, in case swimmers were too busy bombing, running and petting to address the written word. They were all very clear in their depiction of the prohibited act: a naughty-looking person running; a suave-looking, hairy-chested brute balancing a bikini-clad young woman on his shoulders; a hapless swimmer oblivious to an imminent collision from above. The only cartoon that failed to convey its intent or reasoning was the coy representation of heavy petting: a man and a woman in a tentative embrace, looking amorously at each other as tiny love hearts popped in the air between them.

As a child, this was particularly confusing to me. I had no idea what light petting was, let alone the heavier variety. I still recall the sense of bewilderment as I regarded the poster, not understanding why this particular pastime was banned in the water and where one might indulge in it legally. Even now, I'm not entirely sure what they meant by heavy petting. Was it simply a case of saving the embarrassment of others, or were these strictures put in place to prevent more sinister hazards? A watery collision with a freshly released skein of bodily fluid for instance could really spoil a Sunday-morning swim and, as a lifeguard, you never truly know what goes on beneath the ever-moving surface.

The other poolside warning sign that sticks in my memory is the one that whimsically reminded bathers that the baths were not a toilet. 'Welcome to our "OOL". Notice there's no "P" in it? Let's keep it that way.' I always felt the designers of this poster missed a trick by not going one step further and proclaiming 'Welcome to our "L" . . .'

I actually used that gag in my very early stand-up routines, which I would perform wearing my lifeguard's uniform. It was a fun joke to tell because it required the audience to apply the final piece of the comedic jigsaw themselves. In the same way that Meredith Catsanus's mother had got the giggles in the Lady chapel of Gloucester Cathedral having mentally contributed the word 'crapped' to the end of 'the cat crept into the crypt' tongue twister, the audience for my lifeguard character comedy would do a little linguistic arithmetic and come up with the word 'poo', no doubt followed by a visual representation all of their own. Terribly juvenile, I know, but there is often comic value in juvenility and the process by which this gloriously childish punchline is reached is gratifying by its collaboration, which, in contrast to giggling at a floater, is quite grown-up.

The rest of the act consisted of me demonstrating how I administered discipline with a whistle while wearing ill-fitting shorts. I also performed comedy poems, having witnessed the brilliant comic and poet John Hegley on BBC2's festival highlights show, *Edinburgh Nights*. The poems mainly dealt with my hopeless infatuation with a girl whose heart I eventually won but who five years later spectacularly broke mine, filling me with enough impotent rage to smash a window with my fist and wind up in the casualty department of the Hendon Garden Hospital. However, it all seems formative and necessary in hindsight, since it gave me the emotional reference to create the wounded comic-book artist Tim Bisley and the opportunity to escape a lifestyle that through domestic routine had rendered me somewhat inert. She'll crop up a few times here and there since she was something of a muse at one point and instrumental in my making the move to London where things really started to happen for me. Out of respect for her, and in the spirit of the Meredith Catsanus approach to dignity-preserving pseudonyms, she will henceforth be known as Eggy Helen. I'm sure she won't mind. She's been referred to indirectly before in *Spaced*, although in that instance she was called Sarah.

The second most frequent subject of my comedic ditties were the inner, often political thoughts of my goldfish, which would always accompany me onstage. I'll talk about that in more detail later. For now, while we're poolside, here's an old poem about some of the more power-hungry guardians of the gurgle I used to share the staffroom with at the Gloucester Leisure Centre.

Get out of my swimming pool, Jack!
Wild and whistle-happy, cries a megalomaniac,
With his Hi-Tecs on the tiles and his hands behind his back,
He's making up for problems that he's having in the sack.
Because every angry spasm,
Is a failed orgasm,
That is waiting in the chasm of his deep end,
Round the bend,
Will these problems never end?
His poolish pride he can defend
But in bed . . .
He's only running round the side.

My own authoritarian poolside persona, ready to admonish bad behaviour or dive in at a second's notice to save a stricken bather (in two years of lifeguarding I never had to resuscitate anybody, or indeed even get my uniform wet), wasn't quite the little Hitler of the poem, although I learned quickly that a little power was a dangerous thing. I often caught myself looking a bit serious, while chewing my whistle like a cigar, or shaking my head with grim prohibitive insistence at a young splasher, as if he were about to steal a priceless magic diamond.

When I joined the lifeguarding core, the pool had just been refurbished with two large water slides, which snaked their way around the outside of the building back inside to a splash pool in a newly constructed annexe. What made these brightly coloured flumes even more fun was the addition of the 'flash flood' feature. The sliders would sit themselves in position at the top of the slide, while a huge twenty-gallon tank would fill with water. When it reached the required level, the lifeguard on duty would operate a pedal, which released the built-up water in an explosive torrent, catapulting the screaming rider into the tube and down the slide.

As a lifeguard it was the best of the stations on the rota (shallow end, deep end, flash flood, splash pool), because it was the most fun. The kids absolutely loved it, which was infectious. The adults were almost as easy to wind up; either by withholding the flood blast for an inordinate amount of time, or by unleashing it suddenly at the start without any warning at all.

However, one of the most gratifying tricks one could play at the flash-flood station was one we always reserved for the most obnoxious and annoying children. They would appear at the top of the slide, often resembling the vicious little thugs that held Sean Jeffries and myself hostage, and I would instruct them to lie on their fronts with their heads facing the top of the slide and, on the count of three, scream as loudly as they could. As they opened their mouths, I would kick the release pedal and blast them in the face with twenty gallons of water.

Even as I type this, I'm thinking what an absolute arsehole I was. Sure those kids were annoying but they were only kids. Perhaps the poem was a subconscious admonishment of the man I feared I was becoming. A power-hungry maniac, frustrated by the impotence of the tiny authority he was permitted to wield. I wasn't referring to myself with the literal impotence stuff – I was nineteen and doing very well in that department, thank you very much. Never in the pool though, that was illegal.

Whatever I was, it was a long way from the nervous young boy whose Saturday-morning swimming practice was often marred by nervous headaches and nausea. Particularly on one occasion, where I vomited boiling orange sick into the toilet bowl in the boys' changing room and had my tummy rubbed by my swimming instructor. I dimly recall feeling vaguely uncomfortable as this man in his forties vigorously massaged my abdomen. Nothing untoward transpired – this isn't some heartfelt confession about being taken advantage of – I'm certain he was trying to help me, but I do remember being embarrassed by his touch. Despite his doubtless honourable intent, the idea of administering this kind of tactile therapy to a seven-year-old nowadays would doubtless set great hooting sirens off across the country and rightly so; although perhaps it's a slight shame for the majority who act with solely good intentions. I remember breaking down in front of my form tutor, Mr Calway, once. I was having a few emotional problems, teenage stuff but nevertheless real and raw. He was being extra hard on me as a means of keeping me focused but it backfired. I asked to speak to him privately and attempted to explain how I was feeling, only to unleash a torrent of tears. He leaned over and patted me on the shoulder when what I really wanted was a hug, which procedural etiquette prevented him from administering.

Not sure where I was going with that, but you'll be delighted to know all this has been leading up to an account of the third and final swimming-related incident which I regard as a formative moment in my journey towards becoming an actor and a comic.

The Mars Bar Incident

You might remember Mr Skinner as the teacher who had helped to soothe my bloodstained face following my run-in with the brick wall in Class 5, but he was also our PE and swimming teacher. And a pretty cool one at that. He wasn't particularly old – junior to the beardless Mr Miller by ten or fifteen years – nevertheless Mr Skinner sported a great full-face beard, which not only projected strength but also suggested the ability to grow hair out of your face. He was tall as well which made him physically imposing for us little people, although that was never his intention.

He had a no-nonsense air about him and his default demeanour was usually one of intense seriousness. What stopped him from being terrifying and served to make him that much cooler was the fact that he was funny, really funny. His approval or his amusement were achievements to be savoured because he always made you feel as though you had earned them. Such was the edifying power of his laughter, I all but forgot I had just scraped half my face off as we filled the sinks with blood in the boys' toilets on the day Denise Miller drove me to destruction. And the final piece in the jigsaw of cool that made Mr Skinner so hip in our young eyes: he looked great in a tracksuit. It's perhaps more superficial than some of his other winning attributes but it cemented the physical aspect of his authority. He was clever and sporty, what is often referred to as an all-rounder, and this Clark Kent/Superman duality really upped his stock.

Although not a fan of either playing or watching league football (I half-heartedly supported Liverpool as a kid), I clearly recall the first football lesson I ever attended as a child and a piece of sage advice given to us by Mr Skinner that has stayed with me to this day, which was 'remember the rope'. This spatial awareness aid served to remind us to consider the proximity of opposing players when passing the ball to fellow team members. We were asked to imagine a fictional rope, stretching between the player we intended to pass the ball to and ourselves. If a player from the opposing team is able reach the rope, then the ball is vulnerable to interception. It makes complete sense and I keep meaning to include it in a letter, which begins, 'Dear England . . .'

I don't play football myself but I do use the strategy when kicking balled-up socks across the kitchen to my wife while Minnie tries to intercept. I have also used the expression when watching national games, yelling at a player whose lazy pass has been foiled by a defender. 'Remember the rope, you fucking prick!' I will scream with a mouthful of lager and dry-roasted peanuts. This is just one of a number of Mr Skinner-based incidents that have inspired me throughout my life, the biggest of which was the day we both performed an elaborate comedy sketch in front of the entire school.

I wasn't enjoying swimming lessons at school, and although I had displayed a certain amount of aptitude for a nine-year-old, my aforementioned wariness of swimming pools had rather slowed my progress. Nevertheless I had moved from the beginners group taught by Mrs Hortop, through to the intermediate group taught by Mr Miller, and eventually, and reluctantly, to the advanced group, which was of course taught by Mr Skinner.

My first lesson as an aquatic A-lister didn't go so well. The group was populated by the kind of sporty kids who had been swimming since they were babies and possessed cool goggles, nose clips, bathing caps and unusually broad shoulders. The lesson required us to swim an alarming number of widths, wearing a pair of nylon pyjamas, which was exhausting and tiring and in my mind pointless, since I usually made an effort not to sleep-walk near large bodies of water.

Psychologically speaking, I couldn't shake flashbacks to that all-consuming sense of panic I had felt struggling, rubber-ringless, beneath the surface of Gloucester Leisure Centre's 'big pool'. After a few lessons of feeling exhausted and literally out of my depth, I approached Mr Skinner and asked him if I could return to the intermediate level. I felt a little pathetic; it was hard to ask for voluntary demotion from a teacher whose respect I craved, but I didn't really have a choice. Mr Skinner considered my earnest expression for a moment, and obviously detecting something other than laziness in my entreaty, granted my wish. He did, however, make one proviso, this being to buy him a Mars bar as compensation. He smiled at me and sent me off to change, unaware that I had taken his condition very seriously.

But I didn't want to just hand him the Mars bar like a normal person; I wanted to use the opportunity to play a practical joke on him. The previous Christmas, the object of my desire had been a digital watch. Not the kind with a calculator or the super-slim model that played 'Scotland the Brave' or 'The Yellow Rose of Texas', but the kind with a seemingly blank ruby face which would display the time in glowing red if you pressed a button on the side. It wasn't entirely practical and its supersession by the grey-faced, silver, ditty-playing next wave of digital timepieces is understandable, since surely the convenience of the wristwatch is that it requires only a glance and does not require any assistance from other digits or limbs. Despite its super-modern feel, in practical terms it was a return to fob-watch fiddliness. At the time, however, the novelty was sufficient to make it highly desirable, and the idea seemed awfully futuristic to this pint-sized sci-fi fan. Also, nobody else in my class had one, making me at the vanguard of new-wave timepiecery.

Christmas drew nearer and presents began to stack up beneath the tree. Every day I would survey the packages, attempting to identify the one that must surely contain my brand-new digital watch. However, the elusive little box failed to materialise and on Christmas morning, having scored an impressive haul of toys and games (that I now wish I'd kept boxed and never played with), I came to my main gift. This last remaining package represented the grand finale to the day's gifting; the crescendo to which all the other presents had been building. But, the box was big and, although still exciting, couldn't possibly contain a digital watch. I hastily tore off the wrapping to find a nondescript box, inside which was another wrapped box. This happened several times until I eventually got down to a small square box.

I was buzzing with excitement, and inside, just as I had hoped, was the watch, all the sweeter for coming as a complete surprise. I remember thinking what a clever way to deliver a shock and still give me exactly what I had asked for. It was this cunning practical joke that I borrowed from my parents the following year when delivering Mr Skinner's Mars bar. I wrapped it in a box and placed the box within a box, then wrapped up that box. I repeated the process several times until the chocolate bar was housed at the heart of six boxes and appeared to be something far bigger. I inscribed the gift card: *To Mr Skinner, Just like I promised.*

I took the gift into school, snuck into Mr Skinner's classroom when he was off somewhere else being cool in a tracksuit, and left it on his desk. That lunchtime he found the gift and began to open it. I watched through the glass in the door as he negotiated his way through box after box. Mr Miller was in the classroom with him and I remember seeing him hooting with laughter, slapping his good knee as each new box presented itself. I ran back to my classroom before they emerged and sat in my seat the very picture of well-behaved innocence.

Mr Miller entered the room shaking his head and laughing and asked if any of us had given Mr Skinner the present. I remained silent. A few moments later, Mr Skinner entered the room and playfully demanded to know who had left him the cryptic offering. Still, I didn't say a word. I realise now, looking back, that I slightly overestimated Mr Skinner's recollection of his own jokey stipulation, which had meant so much to me. To him it was more of an offhand comment intended to make a young boy feel better about not being a confident swimmer.

It became obvious that he hadn't got the joke at all, assuming one of us was just having a bit of fun. He singled out a boy in the class who looked the guiltiest and asked him to step to the front. I could see I was going to have to do a little of the work myself, so I raised my hand and confessed, at which point Mr Skinner feigned outrage. I can't remember exactly how things transpired at this point but I seem to remember him threatening me with some sort of corporal or even capital punishment before asking me if I had any last requests. I asked if he would permit me to sing 'One Million Green Bottles'; he accepted and sent me down to the hall, where I stood in the corner singing for about an hour.

Eventually he came to see me and I explained the specificities of the joke and what had inspired me to perpetrate the prank, which he found amusing if perplexingly detailed. Term was coming to an end at this point and the relaxed atmosphere inspired him to push the joke a little further, suggesting I make an impassioned public confession in front of the whole school. He played the stern teacher, while I played the penitent villain as he wheeled me from class to class to make my plea.

I'm not entirely sure why I was being painted as the bad guy; I had after all bought him a Mars bar with my own money and gone to the trouble of elaborately wrapping it up; but I played along because it was fun and because it was Mr Skinner. After the confession in front of my class, we had a little confab in the corridor and came up with the next part of our charade. He told me to wait a few minutes, then burst into his classroom and beg for forgiveness, like a prisoner begging a hanging judge for clemency. This was more nerve-racking than messing around in front of the younger children. Class 7 was the top class and was full of really ancient kids, some as old as eleven. They were aloof and wise and slightly taller and barely ever paid any attention to the juniors, unless it was to belittle them or else send them hurtling into a corridor wall.

Everyone in Class 7 was infinitely cooler than me, just by being in Class 7. Standing outside Mr Skinner's classroom, waiting nervously to perform my little improvisation in front of the high council of cool kids at Castle Hill Primary School, I was suddenly infused with an unexpected and enormous sense of excitement and pride.

I burst in with a thespian wail and threw myself on Mr Skinner's mercy, in a performance which included fake tears and dramatic supplication, much to the one part bemusement, two parts amusement of the assembled class. Even Mr Skinner was at a slight loss in the face of my histrionics. When I had finished my act, I flung the door open with a dramatic flourish, unaware that my own classmates were outside pressing their ears against the door. A huge heap of them fell into the room, much to the further amusement of the class, although I seem to remember Mr Skinner shouting at them angrily, signalling an end to the frivolities.

This picture was used in a newspaper advertisement for my grandfather's music publishing company, so technically it is my first professional engagement.

Looking like a human corkscrew with Mum in our garden in 1970. My hips were held in place by a splint due to them being not quite formed when I emerged. I was two weeks late as well. How long does it take to make hips? My elbows were perfect. I chose the outfit.

Dad and Mum with me just after my christening at St John's Church in Churchdown, Gloucester. It was a big day for me, I was fucking knackered.

My mum, then Gillian Rosemary Smith, as a bridesmaid in the early fifties. She really hasn't aged that much since.

My Dad, John Beckingham, as a King's School chorister in what must have been the mid-fifties. I've only just noticed that he's holding a pair of leather gloves, clearly a vital accessory for the choir boy on the go.

My first photoshoot. Apparently, a photographer came to our bungalow in Churchdown in 1971. I pretty much ran the gamut in this session as you can see, expertly playing out complex emotions such as shouting and burping.

Me (in the anorak) with my grandparents Ma-Ma and Pop-Pop on the Isle of Wight in 1973. The sleeping baby is my cousin Vicky. She was such a lightweight!

Me in a spaceship with a gun in the flat above the music shop in St. Aldate Street, Gloucester in 1973. Sometimes destinies are set at a very early age.

'Dad, I am not going to say it again, get the hell out of bed and make me some Weetabix.' Bursting into the parental sleeping quarters on my trike in 1973.

Holidaying in Devon, 1974. There's something about this picture which entirely encapsulates the British seaside in the seventies. Barely undressed people braving temperatures of up to nineteen degrees Celsius, eating candy floss and planting a flag in the ground as if to say, this is England and the rest of you can go fuck yourselves.

Slightly awkward photographs of me in my new school uniform on my first day of attending Hogwarts School of Witchcraft and Wizardry ... sorry, King's School, Gloucester in 1974.

This was my original 10x8. I didn't get much work.

Me thoroughly enjoying time with a donkey at the Cotswold Wildlife Park in 1973. My Dad had a terrible reaction to a wet horse and came out in giant red hives. It was a day of mixed emotions.

Christmas morning at Castle Hill Drive, Brockworth, Gloucester, 1977. I supported Liverpool for many years before I realised I didn't really like football due to it being a horrendous corporate money making machine. I still support *Star Wars* though. Not the new ones, I dropped them for much the same reasons as football.

Me and Mum somewhere, but I'm not entirely sure where, in 1977. I think it was Devon. The important thing is we are swinging from a tyre and that's not easy.

In the garden at Castle Hill Drive in 1978. Admiring Bonnie and Clyde, our two Seal Point Siamese cats. They aren't ignoring me, cats are just like that.

(L to R) Me, Libby Cox, Peter Rolf and James Stewart at Brockworth Comprehensive's 1982 production of *Tom Sawyer*. I don't know what happened to Libby and Peter but James Stewart was simply mesmerising in *Rear Window*.

Dressed for German TV, filmed at Gloucester docks in 1982. I have nothing more to say about this picture.

A cutting from the *Gloucester Citizen* from 1983 accompanying a story about our school revue show showing Glen, Darius and me in full robotic mode. It really is almost as if we really were soulless automatons clunking and whirring our way through various mechanical sub-routines, despite the photographer not letting us wear our robot glasses.

Another picture choreographed by a local newspaper photographer, this time *The Stratford Herald* in 1988, covering our college production of Chicago. (L to R) Caroline Higgins, Dale Crutchlow, Me, Steve Diggory, Gabrielle Starkey and Jason Baughan. I know those names probably don't mean anything to you but I wanted to give them a shout out and it means a lot to me that my memory still works.

For a time afterwards I was adopted by some of the older kids, like an amusing puppy; I was famous for being the funny kid and I relished it enormously. My enjoyment of the attention wasn't motivated by insecurity or a deficit of affection at home. I'm sure psychoanalysis would probably identify some sort of desire for approval in the light, or rather darkness, of my father's departure, but I think I was always like that, even before I could possibly comprehend the abstractions of my own ego. In wordy psychoanalytical terms, my parents' divorce and my attempts to rationalise a degree of abandonment may have exacerbated an existing compulsion to perform but does it really matter? And what the hell does exacerbate mean anyway?

The point is, this incident remains firm in my memory as a key moment in the evolution of my interest in performance and comedy. Having won over a tough crowd – a potentially very tough crowd – the success of the impromptu show left me with a sense of accomplishment and confidence that compelled me to do more. I felt confident and assured. Swimming pools? I shit 'em.

Not in them obviously, that's against the rules.

Nerd Rising

Now that you know all about me and my once toxic relationship with chlorinated H_2O, let's return to Gloucester and the business of my mother and father – literally. Shortly after Pendulum broke up, Mum and Dad let the music shop on St Aldate Street go. We moved in with Dad's parents (lovingly referred to as Mama and Pop-Pop) and lived with them for a year.

At some point towards the end of that year, Mum and I moved to Nan's house (Mum's mum) on Clegram Road in south Gloucester. My grandfather Albert (Grampy) had died a few months earlier and Nan was alone in the house for the first time in forty years. I don't remember the process of uprooting from Mama and Pop-Pop's to Nan's; I didn't even notice that my dad didn't come with us. I remember waking up one morning, going into the middle bedroom where Mum slept and asking her where Dad was, to which she replied, 'He's gone away for a bit.' The truth was, for various reasons, they had decided to separate. I took it pretty well, considering.

A few weeks later, Dad walked up the side passage to Nan's back door wearing a check shirt and I ran into his open arms.

We saw each other regularly from then on, thanks to my mum's typically selfless goodwill, and developed a relationship closer to friends than father and son. In that respect, I look back on my parents' divorce as a good thing, at least for me. It galvanised my relationship with both of them, forming a powerful bond with my mother and facilitating the removal of the kind of male tension that causes rival stags to lock antlers.

Shortly after that, Mum embarked upon a relationship with a man called Richard Pegg, whom she knew from the GODS. His father, John Pegg, another regular at the Olympus Theatre, worked in the Lloyds Bank on Westgate Street, central Gloucester. Whenever my mum and I went into this austere establishment, which was deathly quiet but for the echoing thump of rubber stamps, I would shout at the top of my voice. 'Where's John Pegg?', completely unaware that a few years later, I would call him Grandpa.

Pegg Junior worked in Terry Warner Sports, some five doors down from what used to be John's Music on St Aldate Street. While living at Mama and Pop-Pop's, I had become obsessed with *The Six Million Dollar Man*[4] and, subsequently, *The Bionic Woman* (although my love of the latter was mainly because Lindsay Wagner's Jaime Sommers gave me a funny feeling in my tummy). In a pre-*Star Wars* world, Steve Austin was my ultimate hero; a cool, handsome, cyborg astronaut, everything I was looking for in a friend at the time. I was actually slightly jealous when Barney Miller, the Seven Million Dollar Man, appeared in one of the show's story arcs and distinctly recall feeling a certain amount of *Schadenfreude* when Barney found himself emotionally incapable of accepting his new super-strong prosthetic limbs

---

[4] According to CNNMoney.com, adjusted for inflation, the Six Million Dollar Man would cost closer to $100 million today. I'm sure the price of a mint-condition Steve Austin action figure, Bionic Repair Station and Maskatron have increased just as prodigiously from the retail price in 1976.

and went rogue, only to be apprehended by Steve in a thrilling bionic showdown. Eat that, Barney, I thought to myself as his bionic arms and legs were conveniently dialled down to a 'normal' setting, Steve's my friend, not yours.

The Christmas of 1976 was a clear material reflection of my love for Colonel Austin. It was the first Christmas we had spent at Nan's without Dad, and perhaps out of some unnecessary sense of guilt, Mum really pushed the sleigh out. Presumably through a combination of credit cards and self-deprivation, she made sure I didn't want for anything that Christmas morning and woke to a plethora of *Six Million Dollar* goodies. A Steve Austin rocket ship, for the Steve Austin action figure I already owned, which transformed into a bionic repair station, complete with magnifying window and multiple pipes and switches. I also received a Maskatron action figure, the multiple-faced, bionic nemesis and mad scientist I had never heard of but really wanted.

It's fair to say I was Austined up to the bionic eyeball(s). It's interesting to note that two years later, my main Christmas present was a *Doctor Who* action figure, complete with Tardis and talking Dalek. I was a huge fan of the show, and in 1978 I was lucky enough to meet the fourth Doctor, Tom Baker, at a book signing at Merrits newsagent in Gloucester city centre. He gave me a jelly baby and inscribed my copy of the *The Talons of Weng Chiang*, a novelisation of one of the television stories. His inscription read: *To Simon 8, from Tom Baker, 888.*

I still remember drifting away from the signing table, staring at the ink drying on the page and attempting to process the experience of seeing my hero in the flesh. Before the next person could step up to the table, I cut back in line and proudly informed Tom that I been given an effigy of his likeness for Christmas. I recall our conversation clearly.

Me: I've got an action man of you.

Tom: That's marvellous. Have another jelly baby.

I accepted the extra helping of character-based confectionery and walked away a very happy little boy. Twenty-five years later, in the guise of the Editor, evil human nuncio to a bizarre creature called the Mighty Jagrafess of the Holy Hadrojassic Maxarodenfoe, I faced off against the ninth Doctor, Christopher Eccleston, in a moment of circularity that would have floored my eight-year-old self, had I appeared with the news from the electro-static time ball (ESTB), or perhaps more appropriately a Time And Relative Dimension In Space (Tardis).

Getting back to *The Six Million Dollar Man*, it was my love for this earlier sci-fi hero that in some respects led to my mother and Richard Pegg getting together. Having already been bought a Steve Austin-style red tracksuit, I asked Mum if I could have a pair of red-and-white Adidas trainers to complete the look. She knew there was a sports shop near where we used to live, and that John Pegg's son Richard worked there, so we'd have a friendly face to help us locate the correct pair of bionic shoes. In the summer of 1976, we dropped in to make the purchase. The style was in stock but the size was not. Richard promised to order them in and bring them round to my nan's house, which, a few weeks later, he did. He also asked Mum out on a date. They got married six months later. We moved out of Nan's house and into 10 Castle Hill Drive, a small semi-detached house in Abbotswood, Brockworth, directly opposite Castle Hill Primary School. Wait, divorce, marriage, emotional turmoil . . . Minnie, come back with my sock!

Castle Hill Primary School in Brockworth, Gloucester, was (and probably still is) separated into seven classes, handily referred to as Class 1, Class 2, etc. Back when I was there, each class had a teacher with whom you would spend a year of your school life. I joined Class 4, halfway through the spring term of 1977. I liked the school immediately. It was bright, clean and exciting. In my recollection, the colours seem more vivid, the light brighter, the air somehow sweeter. It may have been the contrast between my new environment and the grim urbanity of Calton Road Juniors that I had left behind, but I attribute the sensation of freshness associated with those memories to the emotional experience of starting a new life in a slightly more rural setting.

My Class 4 teacher, Mrs Hortop, was a wonderfully maternal and skilled teacher who possessed a killer stare if you were naughty but offered endless encouragement and praise if you applied yourself. Her style of teaching was a far cry from the grim, mean-spirited instruction of my previous teacher; a stern woman with a cloud of dry grey hair who had once blankly informed my mum that I had no academic potential and was somehow at fault arriving at the school with an existing knowledge of cursive handwriting, thanks to my previous place of education. I think she childishly resented me for being something of a smarty-pants, just because I had transplanted from the slightly posher King's School. Her bitter resentment towards me had actually reduced my mother to tears after one parents' evening. Mum already felt guilty for removing me from a school I enjoyed attending and suffered deeper insecurities that her divorce may have affected me more than had first been thought. I disliked this teacher almost instantly and consequently had little motivation to meet her twisted standards, sinking into a cycle of insubordination. Fortunately I had an impeccable taste in 'old school' trainers (although at the time, they were just 'school') and my bionic red-and-white shoes initiated a chain of events that would facilitate the much-needed change of lifestyle.

I made friends quickly in my new environment. I wasn't particularly shy as a child and had always done well when it came to integrating with other youngsters in parks or on holiday.

As the new boy, I was briefly a point of interest and palled up with two of the more naughty boys, one of whom I later discovered was my second cousin. That happened twice during my time at Castle Hill; both occasions I was already friendly with the person before I found out. Small towns are like that. Occasionally you will discover a person you have known socially for years is your uncle or your cousin. Sometimes they're both.

Eventually I forged the lasting friendships I would sustain throughout my school career and indeed into my adult life. A boy called Lee Beard caught my interest on my very first day. When I arrived that morning, I was late into the class, having spent time with Mum and the headmaster, getting welcomed and orientated. I walked into Mrs Hortop's classroom and was introduced to my classmates, who greeted me with that slow, mechanical voice children collectively employ when saying 'good morning' or 'hello' or 'join us'. I sat down at my new desk, noticing Meredith Catsanus's attractive fringe, and got on with whatever fun task we had been set that morning.

Presently, Mrs Hortop asked for a volunteer to go down to the headmaster's office. Before I could raise an overeager hand, Lee Beard leapt up, causing my stomach to perform a small involuntary somersault. Lee's right leg was encased in a complex caliper splint made of metal and thick leather, which forced the limb into permanent, enforced extension at an obtuse angle to his body. The shoe at the end of the apparatus had an oddly angled sole, enabling Lee's foot to make even contact with the ground when he walked, which he did awkwardly but at great speed. I later learned that Lee had a condition called Perthes' disease, which softens the femoral head of the thigh-bone due to an interruption in the flow of blood to the hip joint. I was extremely shocked that first time I saw Lee's bionic leg. Half thrilled, half appalled, he seemed to me the living embodiment of those little boy charity recepticles often seen outside supermarkets.

Despite this initial shock, I felt an immediate affinity with

Lee. For the first six weeks of my life I had worn a splint to restrict movement in my legs due to my hip joints not being properly formed. This, combined with Lee's infectious exuberance and obvious sense of humour, inspired me to make a friend of him. I regularly volunteered to carry a chair down to the assembly hall for Lee to sit on (essential, since Lee could not sit on the floor with his mad robot leg) and we developed a closeness that has kept us in contact to this day.

Why is this relevant to my journey towards becoming an actor? Well, Lee and I took two key roles in the first school production I participated in that didn't involve shepherds. Two years before I performed my Dicky Bird news report with a grazed face, Mrs Hortop cast me as the eponymous and indeed ambiguous hero of Robert Browning's version of 'The Pied Piper of Hamelin' (the same version my nan had committed to memory so many years before), which we performed in front of the school as part of an assembly in 1977. Lee played the little 'lame' boy, who cannot keep up with the rest of the village children, as they are led away by the disgruntled Pied Piper, and fails to enter the wondrous portal in the mountain. I remember watching Lee playing out his disappointment at being left alone, eliciting a huge wave of sympathy from the assembled children, and being aware that he had somewhat stolen the show.

By this time Lee's condition had improved and he no longer wore the rigid brace. Instead his heel was attached to a leather strap around his waist that kept his leg bent up behind him at all times, necessitating the use of crutches. It was the last phase of his treatment before he dispensed with the corrective contraptions completely and embarked upon a mad spurt of energy that lasted about a year before he finally settled down to being a normal little boy.

At the time of the 'Pied Piper', he was perfectly cast and cut an affectively poignant figure as he limped away from the closed cave entrance/sports utility cupboard. I remember feeling a little jealous as the audience hung on his every step, but I also felt admiration for his skilful portrayal of rejection and isolation and couldn't help feeling it was coming from the heart, even then at the tender age of seven, and I never once thought him to be a jammy little fucker.

Performing the show and seeing how it affected the audience made me want to act more, to do something that would make an audience vocalise their emotions the way they did at Lee Beard's lost little boy – jammy little fucker.

Old School

Moving up to Class 5 in my second year at Castle Hill Primary, we graduated into the combined tutelage of Mr Miller and Mrs Harvey, the latter having only recently joined. She was younger than Mrs Hortop and for this reason alone she seemed very cool. Whereas Mrs Hortop was the very embodiment of the wise, authoritative schoolteacher, Mrs Harvey possessed a distinct, summery laid-backness, which hinted at the possibility that a teacher could be as much a friend as an educator. She wasn't the only such teacher at Castle Hill.

Another young, female teacher called Miss Eglise, who taught us music, possessed a similar casual amiability. I had the unsettling experience of seeing Miss Eglise out of school once, playing Tuptim, in a production of *The King and I* staged by the CODS in their native Cheltenham. In the show, Tuptim is given to the King of Siam as a gift and potential wife, but Tuptim is in love with Lun Tha, the young man who delivers her to the palace, and (SPOILER ALERT) eventually tragedy ensues. It was strange seeing Miss Eglise in a non-school setting, let alone portraying a beautiful young woman with frailties and desires. Towards the end of the show, Tuptim is severely reprimanded for staging a play, which plainly reflects her dismay at being forced to marry someone she doesn't love. She escapes with her lover but is captured and faces corporal punishment administered by the King himself.

Seeing Miss Eglise play out these emotions, in silky oriental garb, was fairly intoxicating for me. I was fascinated to see her after the show socialising in the bar. She came over to say hello to my mum (and me) and I told her how much I had enjoyed the show, at which point she gave me a playful hug (an act that was still legal back then). She was glowing with post-performance exhilaration and I remember she smelled lovely. The emotion of the play and the unusual interaction with this suddenly exotic and attractive teacher left me with something of a crush on her and I spent the following Sunday sighing heavily and dreaming of Siam.

When I walked into the assembly hall on the Monday, my heart was racing, I felt as though I knew her better than any of the other children in the school; it was as if we had had some kind of an affair, not that I knew what an affair was. I hadn't enjoyed any masturbatory fantasies about showering together in a bed and breakfast just off the A40, Shurdington Road. I was pre-masturbatory at the time, although I did regularly pore over the pages of a *Lovebirds* magazine that I kept under a caravan in an alley near my house (pore over was perhaps the wrong choice of words there).

I saw her across the room standing by her piano in a cream cardigan and blue dress and walked towards her, hoping she would notice me. Sure enough, she glanced across and spotted me, smiling broadly back at her. I placed my hands together as if in prayer and bowed to her like a Siamese prince, at which point all my dreams came true as she reciprocated with a bow that turned into a curtsey. This little in-joke meant the world to me in that moment, it was an acknowledgement of a connection we had forged outside school and as such made us more than teacher and student: we were sort of friends. She married that year, which vaguely disappointed me, I think. She changed her name to something I don't remember, my lack of recall in this matter being significant perhaps since my strongest memories are as a single woman with an exotic French-sounding name.

I didn't have quite the same feelings towards Mrs Harvey, although I liked her enormously and looked forward to seeing her every day. She was the first teacher I ever accidentally called 'Mum', much to my enormous embarrassment, but I think this was due to the relaxed, informal atmosphere she engendered in the classroom. She was also a slightly softer touch than Mrs Hortop, and the rowdier boys, the ones that befriended me on the first day, pushed their luck a little more forcefully with her, trying to look up her skirt and asking asinine questions like 'What's love juice, Miss?'.

One of the key factors in my appreciation of Mrs Harvey was that she was something of a nerd. She didn't look like one particularly. She was pretty with a fuzz of curly black hair and dressed in loose blouses and flowing skirts that you had to lie on the floor to look up. Not that I did, nor in fact needed to. I have a vague memory of being able to see her legs through the material when the sun shone through the classroom window and giggling breathlessly about it to whoever was next to me, probably Sean or Lee or Matthew Bunting, a boy I eventually drifted apart from due to conflicting feelings about sport (he liked it, I didn't).

Mrs Harvey's nerdiness extended mainly from her fascination with the paranormal. She had a grandmother who was reputedly psychic and Mrs Harvey would regale us with stories of how her granny participated in regular conversations with dead relatives. These stories would simultaneously thrill and terrify us and inspired us to sit at her feet (trying not to look up her skirt) or gather round her desk at any given opportunity.

It wasn't just the spirit world that fascinated Mrs Harvey; we had long discussions about Big Foot and the Loch Ness Monster as well as other aspects of parapsychology. She particularly nurtured in me a fascination with UFOs and even gave me a book on the subject called *Mysterious Visitors* by Brinsley Le Poer Trench, which featured a pictorial supplement, illustrating how certain biblical conceits, such as the luminous cloud/pillar of fire that accompanied the Israelites, or the 'wheel' witnessed by the prophet Ezekiel, may have actually been visiting spacecraft. I still believed in God at the time, as children tend to do, and this made stuffy old religion ten times more interesting.

We discussed how the immense geoglyphs carved into the Nazca Desert floor, which can be seen only from a great height, could be messages intended for extraterrestrial visitors. I loved talking about this kind of thing. I had been fascinated by unexplained phenomena from a very early age. I avidly watched television shows such as Arthur C. Clarke's *Mysterious World* and *In Search of . . .* presented by Leonard Nimoy (a man I would eventually meet on an ice planet called Vega 4). I subscribed to *The Unexplained*,[5] a monthly magazine about the paranormal, which could be collected into volumes and housed

---

[5] *The Unexplained* was published in the early eighties and covered every aspect of the paranormal. The pages were filled with grainy images of flying saucers, alleged ghosts, Big Foot and partially burnt pensioners, the latter being the supposed victims of SHC (spontaneous human combustion). Even as a child, I remember noting that in all the pictures, the charred body (usually complete with one intact, slipper-clad lower leg) would be lying next to a fireplace or a three-bar electric fire. Some years later, I saw a bizarre public service announcement, warning old people to practise care with their heating appliances as every year (and this is a hell of a statistic) an average of sixty old-age pensioners burnt to death as a result of negligence. I leapt up triumphantly and shouted, 'Yes! I knew it!' Then I felt bad that I had celebrated the annual incineration of sixty old people so enthusiastically.

in an attractive binder, available gratis if you purchased all twelve issues.

Looking back, this fascination was formative in my journey towards geekdom, further inspiring an existing love of all things alien and unknown that compelled me to close the curtains whenever I watched *The Clangers*,[6] or enjoy spending time under-water. Thirty-five years after Mrs Harvey handed me *Mysterious Visitors*, I found myself in the deserts of New Mexico with my best friend Nick, making a film about an alien called Paul, who enlists two British nerds to help get him back to his spaceship, idly wishing I could fizz off back to 1978 and let me know.

Around this time of fantastic, inspiring teachers, we were lucky enough to also be taught by the limping, storytelling genius that was Mr Miller. Stern yet avuncular, he inspired a similar desire for approval as his predecessors but somehow made that approval even more of a mission to attain. Maybe male approval was more important to me because of latent abandonment issues brought on by the creeping realisation that my father had walked out on

---

[6] *The Clangers* was a peculiarly atmospheric stop-motion animated TV series, which ran as part of BBC Television's afternoon children's programming from 1969 to 1972. It centred around a community of pink knitted alien mouse/elephants living on a moon-like planet in the furthest reaches of space. The Clangers were accompanied by a mechanical chicken, a horde of frog-like creatures appropriately called 'froglets', and a single-parent family of dragons consisting of a mother and son whose life revolved around the mining of soup from the depths of the planet's core. The show had a unique ambi-ence, which thrilled me as a child. The echoing whistle of the Clangers in the vastness of this magical model space, combined with Vernon Elliot's oddly affecting score, would drive my infant self into paroxysms of glee, whenever it flickered from the television. Conditions had to be just right for viewing. The room darkened, my feet tucked up beneath me away from the floor. This is probably my earliest memory, since I cannot have been any older than three. Perhaps it was something to do with the endless potential of the cosmos that so inspired my euphoric enjoyment of the show; the boundless possibilities concealed in the blackness of the unknown; a metaphor for the future, played out jerkily with pink wool and tinfoil. I can still locate that sensation in the recesses of my memory and feel it still under particularly starry skies.

me as well as my mother, although I never really thought of their divorce in those terms, at least not until I was older and even then I didn't regard it in such a self-pitying, egocentric way.

Still, these experiences do manifest themselves in our behaviours and it's fair to say I looked for fathers for a while, despite having a brand-new step model at home. But perhaps the desire to please Mr Miller was keener, simply because he was enormous fun when he was pleased and quite scary when he was cross. He was the first teacher to make me stand in the corner and it made me cry with shame and disappointment. For some reason the whole class had collectively decided to make the popping sound achieved by putting your index finger in your mouth and firing it out against the inside of your cheek. We've all done it to demonstrate how the weasel goes at the end of that bizarre nursery rhyme. The Class 5 popspasm inevitably got out of hand and Mr Miller sternly proclaimed that the next person to emit a finger-assisted explosive would be in big trouble. Without thinking, I called his bluff. He wasn't bluffing.

I realised I had been quite literally cheeky, the moment I felt the air on my wet finger. Mr Miller ignored the wave of suppressed tittering that skidded across the room, and zeroed in on the transgressor, me. The order to stand in the corner was given with what I can only describe as disappointed indifference, as if in that one second he had given up on me completely. I sobbed remorsefully in the corner until he took pity on me and relieved me from my position of shame. I can't remember exactly what he said to me (something like 'try not to be such a silly billy'), but he said it comically from the corner of his mouth and accompanied every other syllable with a painless kick up the backside, which was harmless and affectionate but today he would be fired for.

I remember Mr Miller with great fondness; his natural air of authority was gently undermined by the pronounced limp, which gave him an appealing vulnerability. He had a wonderful way with words, regularly using antiquated phrases such as 'by jove' and 'by jingo', and referred to our schoolbooks as 'goods and chattels'.

He was undoubtedly the best storyteller I had ever encountered (perhaps second to my dad who I still recall reading me *The Hobbit* when I was just four). At the end of each day, we would all put our heads down on our folded arms and listen to Mr Miller read from a variety of books which continue to exist in my memory because they were all read to us with such passion and vigour. *Tom's Midnight Garden*, *The Little Captain and the Seven Towers* were delivered in daily, nail-biting instalments, and I attribute any understanding I have of the importance of drama in narrative storytelling to Mr Miller and what was clearly his and our favourite part of the school day.

The other significant recollection I have of him is far less salubrious but remains fixed in my memory as one of those occasions where laughter segues into great heaving sobs, indistinguishable from hysterical crying and emotionally not that dissimilar.

There are two more occasions on which I recall this happening during early childhood. The first occurred while watching *Morecambe and Wise* perform a sketch in which Eric, dressed as a Cossack, was repeatedly pulled off the front of the carriage he was driving by a disobedient horse, while Ernie sang a love song to a female guest. With each successive 'giddy up', Eric would leap out of shot and the level of my hysteria would increase, until I was helpless on the living room floor.

The other transpired as a result of a game I was playing with Sean Jeffries, which involved running towards one another in the dark at high speed, wearing vampire fangs, illuminated only by torchlight, presumably to try to elicit some sort of visceral scare. On the fourth or fifth iteration of the 'my turn/your turn' cycle, Sean came haring round the corner of his house and fell over on his arse. It doesn't sound particularly funny in the recounting but it crippled me with laughter at the time. I folded up into a breathless heap on the floor for about five minutes and howled uncontrollably at the night sky. I wrote about the event in my schoolbook the following week, as part of an essay about my weekend activity, complete with a drawing of Sean, bearing his fangs, mid-skid.

However, neither occasion quite matched the levels of hilarity that ensued on the day Mr Miller sat on the corner of his desk and farted it to pieces. Bear in mind, I was a typical eight-year-old, for whom bodily functions, slapstick and the humiliation of authority were among the most amusing things on the planet. Now imagine, if you will, this triple threat of child-spazzing rib-tickling comic factors being unleashed on a class of thirty-five eight-year-olds, all of whom were likely to be buzzing on sugar and tartrazine from all the Space Dust they had ingested at break time. It was comparable to a bomb going off, a blast wave of gut-busting hilarity that spread through the room in a microsecond from Mr Miller's red-faced ground zero at the front of the class.

It happened in tiny increments as I remember. Mr Miller sat on the edge of the desk, which shifted slightly; the sudden exertion of the correction he had to make to regain his balance resulted in a double blow-off; two little rasping braps, accompanied by an expression of amused shame on his face, before the table suddenly lurched, cracked and then collapsed on to the floor with Mr Miller on top of it. There must have been a nanosecond of disbelief and amazement at the confluence of this combination of farcical ingredients before the class exploded into frenzied, screeching giggles, which Mr Miller simply had to allow, since his embarrassment and indignation would have only made it worse.

The ramifications continued long after the event, with random class members suddenly bursting out laughing, the result of post-comedic stress disorder. Mr Miller himself grew used to the odd light-hearted raspberry, which would erupt behind his back, accepting the reminder with a reluctant nod of the head. He actually moved up with us from Class 5 to 6, so that we enjoyed his company for nearly two years. I'm sure he privately lamented not getting to teach a new group of kids, one who hadn't witnessed the calamity.

However, the incident in no way undermined his status among the children; such was his reputation, it could withstand any ignominy, even a furniture-destroying guff. The first thing I think about when he comes to mind is resting my head on my arms, closing my eyes and listening to him read us those classic stories. It's only after further reminiscence that a smile twists itself across my face and my shoulders start to shake at the thought of his marvellous, impromptu and entirely unintentional comic *coup de grâce*.

5

Like most riads, Pegg's consisted of a living space built around a central garden or courtyard, with the majority of the building's windows focusing inwards on the central outdoor space so as to give the residents protection and privacy.

The transition from the featureless mud-brick exterior to the often ornate atria proved an inevitable surprise to those unfamiliar with this introspective architectural style, but how much greater would that surprise be if the unwary visitor witnessed a sleek black stealth aircraft lower itself gracefully into the centre of the building, as the zellige-tiled fountain folded in on itself and the citrus trees, heavy with fruit, parted to allow the silent aircraft to further lower itself into its subterranean hangar? They would probably shit themselves.

The hangar had been built by previous resident Sean Connery back in the seventies in order to house the personal helicopter he assumed would be commercially available to the general public by 1981, but alas it did not materialise until 2006, by which time Connery had sold the riad to Pegg and moved to a delightful property in Spain with two tennis courts and a weather-changing laser cannon which he sold to the comedian Jimmy Tarbuck who gifted it to his daughter Liza.

The hangar remained intact until Connery vacated it in

1995, used mainly for storing wine bottles and mountain bikes. On his purchase of the property, Pegg had the hangar tastefully restored to house his experimental aircraft. He had to smile to himself when he went to see the first *X-Men* film at the Canon, Frogmore Street, in Bristol, and noticed that the students of Professor Xavier's school for gifted youngsters had a similar hangar in their basement but there was no way he had stolen the idea because his was built when Bryan Singer was just a gay baby (gaby).

'Power down,' said Pegg, easing the hefty bird to a perfect landing. 'Secure the tethers.'

Canterbury's metallic digits flickered over a bank of instruments and the sound of clamps, closing around the landing gear, resonated through the plane as it released a final, breath-like whine.

'Welcome to Morocco,' said Pegg like he always did when they landed in the riad, usually around Easter and the last half-term break before Christmas.

'Should we start looking for her?' enquired Canterbury.

'Let's get some rest,' said Pegg. 'You need to recharge and I didn't really get any sleep on the plane because *The Shawshank Redemption* came on the TV and I was only going to watch the first ten minutes but I ended up watching it all.'

'Get busy living or get busy dying,' mused Canterbury.

'Look, I'll be a mess if I don't get at least six hours,' snapped Pegg. 'It's all right for you, you're a robot.'

'It's a quote from *The Shawshank Redemption*, sir,' said Canterbury apologetically.

'Oh, yeah.' Pegg inwardly cursed his failure to pick up on the reference. 'I'm tired, I told you,' insisted Pegg. 'Otherwise I would have definitely got the quote and prob-ably quoted the next line back to you. Give me another one.'

'You know what the Mexicans say about the Pacific?' asked Canterbury in a perfect imitation of the actor Tim Robbins.

'Not a general knowledge question,' said Pegg testily. 'Give me a quote from *The Shawshank Redemption*.'

Canterbury's neural servos whirred quietly as he considered his options. His vocal capacitor crackled very slightly before he spoke.

'Brooks was . . .'

'Here!' screamed Pegg triumphantly. 'Brooks was here. I love that bit when the old man hangs himself because he can't hack it in the real world. It's so funny!'

Pegg's hysterical laughter echoed around the hangar as he performed a short self-congratulatory dance.

'Y'see, Canterbury?' trilled Pegg, 'You have to be firing on all cylinders to catch me out when it comes to quoting *The Shawshank Redemption*.'

'Indeed you do, sir,' conceded Pegg's lovable robotic counterpart, 'indeed you do.'

Pegg stretched the ache of confinement from his toned body, snapping a crackle of pops from his crispy joints. He was in the best shape of his life, but as he had wittily attested when his *Raiders of the Lost Ark* VHS had become unwatchable due to overuse, 'It's not the age, honey, it's the mileage.' To say Pegg had seen action would be a gross underestimation of his exploits and adventures over the years and his body was worn from too much brawling and having it off. Despite the wear and tear, he was still well fit in both senses and looked genuinely good in skinny jeans, which is rare for someone in their thirties.

Pegg stabbed at a button on the dash and a ramp extended silently to the ground beneath the jet. Pegg disembarked with his faithful robotic assistant, butler and acupuncturist in tow and took a lungful of the warm night air.

'Let's hit the medina first thing,' Pegg suggested. 'If the Scarlet Panther is here, we'll find her, and when we do, she'll wish she'd never set foot in the Museum of Egyptian Antiquity.'

'Do you think she'll be easy to find, sir?' enquired Canterbury.

'That depends on whether or not she wants to be found,' said Pegg knowingly. 'If she's in the mood to remain inconspicuous, we could be eating couscous for days. If she's feeling playful, she'll come straight to us. In which case, there's a Wimpy out near the airport; I'll probably grab myself an eggy bender.'

'She will come to us?' said Canterbury, confusion in his synthetic voice.

'If I know the Panther like I think I know the Panther, then yes, we just need to make our presence known. Should have brought the personal helicopter rather than the stealth jet,' Pegg mused. The pair were silent for several moments. About eight.

'Will that be all, sir?' enquired Canterbury, aware he was due to recharge his power cells.

'If you've got enough juice, can you nip over to that vending machine by the bus station and get me a Coke Zero?' said Pegg with childlike hope.

'Of course, sir,' Canterbury replied immediately and without complaint. 'I'll use the usual disguise.'

As Canterbury pottered off to prepare for his errand he stopped and turned back to his master. 'You think we'll definitely find her then?' He faltered slightly. 'The Scarlet Panther that is.'

'I hope so,' replied his handsome creator, pausing dramatically before saying it again. 'I hope so.'

Canterbury nodded. 'Remember, Red,' he said, once again quoting Frank Darabont's much-vaunted prison saga, 'hope is a good thing, maybe the best of things, and no good thing ever dies.'

'Who the fuck's Red?' enquired Pegg.

Fabulousity

I n 1979, the news that there was to be a *Star Trek* movie proved immensely exciting to me. Thanks to the renewed interest in science fiction generated by George Lucas, BBC2 had started showing the original series again at 6 p.m. so that I would invariably find myself wolfing down my evening meal so I could leave the table and rush to the living room in order to boldly go.

Prior to this (and of course *Star Wars*), my budding inner nerd had been serviced by a variety of sources. Like most young boys, I became obsessed with dinosaurs at a very early age and can recall roughly sticking together a model Allosaurus long before I should have ever been permitted to wield powerful glue.

My love of big creatures and dinosaurs and films like *The Valley of Gwangi* and *The Land That Time Forgot* was further sated when I discovered David Attenborough presenting a TV show called *Fabulous Animals*. The show aired as part of the BBC's afternoon children's programming schedule, and covered such famous myths as the Loch Ness Monster and the Abominable Snowman, as well as examining the more classical creatures from Greek and Roman mythology. I watched it avidly;

not entirely certain that it wasn't a documentary about creatures that might exist or in fact did exist at some point. I remember desperately wanting to believe in the Sphinx and Phoenix and being certain that these histories must have some foundation in truth. It was the beginning of my love for unexplained phenomena at a time when I was far more Mulder than Scully.

I remember being annoyed at my mum for interrupting my viewing of *Fabulous Animals* one winter evening, then promptly forgetting about griffons and centaurs, as she informed me that my grandfather had died. I was six years old at the time and that memory will always be inextricably linked to David Attenborough's soft, breathy voice. It's interesting that I should recall so precisely what I was watching on TV at the time. I'm not sure whether it was the shock of my first bereavement that imprinted the moment so vividly in my memory or the sharp contrast between the fantasy of the show and the reality of my mother's tears. I certainly didn't understand the concept of death, and as such, I didn't truly experience a great sense of loss, I just remember feeling guilty that I had complained about missing my show, as I witnessed Mum struggling to give me the news, a sight far scarier than the Abominable Snowman or the Fiji Mermaid.

A much happier monster memory involved going to see *Sinbad and the Eye of the Tiger* at the ABC on St Aldate Street with my dad. We walked the five or six doors down from our shop to the cinema, where two years later I would see *Star Wars* and where five years before I had entered my first ever theatre. Witnessing Ray Harryhausen's marvellous animations on the big screen was amazing and I watched open-mouthed, even more than I had done at my grandmother's house a year or so before, when Dad had introduced me to *Jason and the Argonauts*. I look back at both films as seminal moments in my development towards geekdom. *Jason and the Argonauts* had a particularly significant effect on me, becoming the focus of much of my art and stories for some time afterwards. Dad and I would re-enact scenes from the film with me as Jason and Dad as the bronze giant Talos. He would kneel very still then crane his neck round making a loud creaking noise, at which point I would erupt into giggling screams and attack him with a plastic sword. Earlier this year, director John Landis invited Ray Harryhausen to cameo in *Burke and Hare*. Ray signed a copy of his book for me and gave it to John to pass on. To be honest, I'm quite relieved he didn't give it to me in person: I probably would have erupted into giggling screams and attacked him with a plastic sword.

My other nerdy pre-*Star Wars* interests included the television series of *Planet of the Apes*, *Lost in Space* (for which John Williams provided the score), *The Invaders*, Gerry Anderson's marionation classics, *Thunderbirds*, *Captain Scarlet* and *Joe 90*, Jon Pertwee as Doctor Who and the animated series of *Star Trek*. The cartoon version of the classic live-action TV series ran from 1973 to 1974 and featured original cast members providing their voices. As a pre-schooler, I found the live-action show a little scary and I much preferred the animated adventures. It wasn't until after *Star Wars*, as my interest in the genre became more sophisticated, that I started to lap up the live-action adventures of Kirk, Spock and that Scottish guy. Even then some of the episodes would give me a serious case of the creeps.

An episode called 'The Corbomite Maneuver', in which Clint Howard, star of *Gentle Ben* and brother of the more famous Ron, plays an alien child, who uses a terrifying alter ego to put the shits up the *Enterprise* crew, gave me an equal if not more intense case of the space willies. The scary proxy's name was Balok and his appearance was deeply troubling to me as a child. A dome-headed, blue-tinged humanoid with piercing slanted eyes, his glare was so intense it forced me to hide behind my hands and make squeaking noises. It was a triumph of model-making at the time and the programme-makers made good use of it by featuring his image in the closing-credits stills montage of the show, so that even if I hadn't been frightened by the episode, I'd get a dose of Balok all the same. The montage wasn't always the same though, so watching it would amount to a game of visual Russian roulette. Would it be the green Orion slave girl caught in the middle of her sexy dance, or would it be Balok with his terrifying death stare? Interestingly my daughter makes the same face now, when she's filling her nappy. Maybe that's what Balok was doing.

By the time *Star Trek: The Motion Picture* rolled round, I considered myself a proper fan and felt abuzz with excitement when my Uncle Greg picked me up and took me to the ABC. The movie was criticised for its solemnity and for being a little wordy and grown-up, but I don't remember being disappointed at all. With the absence of a weekly budget big enough to afford spell-binding effects, the series had compensated by concentrating on character rather than setting. The stories, though fantastic, often boiled down to basic conflicts of emotion and morality. *The Motion Picture* did the same, only with the aesthetics the series never had. By the second and arguably best *Star Trek* movie instalment, the film-makers had got the mix right for commercial success, but the first movie remains an enjoyable cinematic outing for the characters.

Star Trek: The Motion Picture came with a lot of pre-existing mythological weight, having already established itself culturally. Although not a massive success on its first airing, the series had proved a cult favourite in syndication and found fans around the world. The film-makers exploited this familiarity, reintroducing us to the characters and settings as if they were old friends. Seeing the *Enterprise* for the first time on the big screen felt special because we knew it so well from the television. The sight of Spock with long hair gave me a thrill as a kid because he had always been so immaculately groomed in the TV show, so seeing him all unkempt was very cool.

In some respects, this was my first experience of intertextuality, something that would become very important to my own creative output in later life. Although basic scene-setting to the untrained eye, these dramatic touches in *Star Trek: The Motion Picture* were gifts to the faithful and could be truly appreciated only by them. That frisson of enjoyment at seeing scruffy Spock could not possibly be experienced without a pre-existing knowledge of his spirit-level fringe. One might have simply thought, 'Who is that scruffy guy with the pointy ears?', not 'Wow, Spock's really let himself go' or 'Hey, Leonard Nimoy looks good with a shoulder-length bob'.

As I sat there in the darkness of the ABC, I was of course totally oblivious to the personal significance the event had for me. I was witnessing the commencement of a series of cinematic adventures that would one day include me. As I witnessed Spock step from his shuttle on to the *Enterprise*, I was unaware that one day that character, not just the actor but that character, would look me in the eyes and say, 'You are Montgomery Scott.' It's a little indulgent, I know – though a memoir is after all the height of indulgence – but it blows my mind to consider the circularity of these events. It is hard to describe being in your late thirties and acting with a character you have known almost all your life. It's exciting enough to meet actors you have long admired, but to be transported into a fictional universe that you have witnessed countless times from afar is really something else.

The first time I set foot on the bridge of the Starship *Enterprise*,[7] I tapped director JJ Abrams on the shoulder and smiled, knowing as a fellow fan he would appreciate the

[7] Technically, that wasn't the first time I had set foot on the bridge of the Starship *Enterprise*. In 2002, I attended the premiere of the last *Star Trek* movie before the one I was in, *Star Trek: Nemesis*. The party for the event took place at a *Star Trek* exhibition at Hyde Park in London, which featured a full set of the *Enterprise* from *The Next Generation*, which my sister and I ran around, pretending to be in *Star Trek*.

significance as I took my one small step on to the impressive set housed in one of the sound stages at the Paramount Studios lot in Los Angeles. This was the culmination of a lifetime's fandom. A journey which had started with a cartoon, continued through the gaps in my fingers as I waited for Balok's terrifying face to appear, and had drawn ever closer the day JJ sat down to watch *Shaun of the Dead*. Eventually, as I touched down in London, having spent a month in New York shooting the exteriors for *How to Lose Friends & Alienate People*, I switched on my phone and noticed I had received an email from JJ. We had become friends a couple of years earlier after he had telephoned me at my London office and asked outright if I wanted to be in *Mission: Impossible III*. Of course I said yes;[8] I knew JJ from his hit show *Alias* and was extremely flattered that he had contacted me so forthrightly. Eighteen months later I opened the email from JJ and found it to be similarly forthright. 'Do you want to play Scotty?'

[8] The decision to join IMF was an act of atrocious hypocrisy on my part. While doing press for the release of the *Shaun of the Dead* DVD, I had said in an interview that I wasn't going to desert the UK to go off and do, oh, I don't know . . . *Mission. Impossible III*. What's odd is that at this point I didn't even know there was going to be a *Mission Impossible III*. It was an imaginary blockbuster that I plucked out of the air to demonstrate my disdain for Hollywood ephemera and my loyalty to the British film industry. It turned out to be a naive comment on a number of levels. Firstly, the movie turned out to be a cracking adventure flick, wound taut by JJ's flair for action directing and a characteristic all-or-nothing action performance from Tom Cruise, not to mention the rest of the cast, including me as a nerdy IT guy called Benjamin Dunne, which also happens to be the name of the man who commissioned me to write this book (this really is a labyrinth of coincidence, isn't it?). Secondly, because you don't have to defect to America to participate in the hugely prolific Hollywood movie machine, you can just as easily commute. We have an odd attitude towards our actors here in the UK, which condemns them to a sort of 'damned if you do, damned if you don't' limbo. Working in Hollywood is sometimes seen as simultaneously the pinnacle of achievement and the height of self-serving treachery. The truth of the matter is that Hollywood is simply a place where a lot of films get made, where there is a lot of money to make films and where there are a lot of people who want to make them. Any actor looking to work

regularly in film and diversify beyond the limitations of their own creative environment is bound to want to go there at some point. Of course, I wasn't of this considered opinion as I sat on my high horse and proclaimed my reluctance to cross the checkpoint into Tinseltown, never to return. A year or so later I boarded a flight to LA destined to work for two days on the movie and eternally render myself an enormous hypocrite.

This is too much of a digression to have put into brackets while I was in mid-flow above, but I wanted to share a memory of Debenhams that encompasses both Debenhams and the Wombles and is thematically linked to the events I have described. One afternoon, presumably to promote something or other, the Wombles visited Debenhams. They weren't the real Wombles, they were tiny and fictional, although the success of Mike Batt's *Womble* music did lead to the formation of a Wombles band for the purposes of appearing on *Top of the Pops* and the like. Just put 'The Wombles' into YouTube and you'll be able to witness the bizarre spectacle of grown humans in furry suits miming to catchy pop standards in front of gambolling seventies teenagers. It isn't all that weird, considering the Teletubbies had an unforgettable number-one single in 1997, but then Tinky Winky, Dipsy, Laa-Laa and Po (see?) weren't presenting themselves as a jobbing band. Anyway, the Wombles band, which to some degree were the real Wombles (it was a complicated mythology), visited Debenhams, presumably for an album launch, and arrived in a van at the back of the store, visible to myself and my dad in the shop. At the time, soon-to-be briefly popular TV show band and Clap-o-meter victors, Pendulum had a number of Wombles songs in their Saturday-night repertoire and kept a Wombles costume in their dressing-up box, which also included a Telly Savalas bald cap for 'If' and a monkey outfit for 'King of the Swingers'. On the day the Wombles came to Debenhams, Pendulum's mischievous drummer, Paul Holder (he of the cock-in-the-hand incident) decided to don the costume, and crash the Wombles party, presumably to try and get into the *Gloucester Citizen* and drum up some publicity for the band (Pendulum, not the Wombles). I watched excitedly from my bedroom window as Paul, dressed as the timid, studious Wellington, crossed the road and intercepted Orinoco as he left the building. I remember Paul's costume looked decidedly shabby and threadbare next to the real thing, which was plush and expensive-looking. There was an odd poignancy to the scene, as if Paul's Wellington was an old friend, down on his luck, trying to derive some reflected glory from his more successful friend. 'Orinoco, it's me, Wellington. Do you remember? We used to hang out in south-west London and pick up litter? No? Come on. Orinoco? Fuck you!' That isn't what Paul said. Actually, it might have been, I was watching from some way off.

A Long Time Ago . . .

S tar Wars was released in the UK in December 1977 and it's fair to say, like the peaceful planet of Alderaan, I was totally blown away.

It wasn't just the effects either, far from it in fact. The chemistry between the actors was genuine and irresistible, the comic touches were subtle and well pitched, and John Williams's brilliantly emotive score was a hair-raising stroke of genius in an age when orchestration was unfashionable. The caption that preceded the first orchestral blast of score was hugely intriguing and immediately hinted at the story's mythic weight: 'A long time ago in a galaxy far, far away . . .' A frown flickered across my face in the darkness of the ABC cinema in Gloucester, that same building that until a few years earlier had been the venue for the annual GODS musical production. *So this is science fiction but it isn't the future?* Also, whether it was intended to do so or not, the fact that this first outing for the franchise was billed as *Episode IV* gave it instant historical presence, as though the story was already a classic tale, we just hadn't been aware of it.

I left the cinema in a daze of excitement, deliriously enthused by what I had just witnessed. I wanted to go back and see it again immediately and I envied the long line of people waiting to go in as we left.

I bought a poster at a merchandise stand in the foyer and brandished it like a light sabre, all the way back to the car, which became a landspeeder and X-wing fighter as we drove home. I can distinctly recall the sensation I experienced directly after seeing the film. I had entered the cinema in daylight buzzing with excitement and re-emerged into the night charged with joyous satisfaction. Everything had changed, not just the fact that the sky was now a deep blue but that it seemed bigger and more full of potential than ever before.

My first intimation of *Star Wars* in any shape or form was at a friend's birthday party in 1977. He had received a *Star Wars* Letraset[9] action transfer kit, which consisted of a cardboard diorama depicting what I later learned to be the Death Star hangar bay and two sheets of dry transfers to be rubbed on at your discretion. I had no idea who these characters were but they fascinated me.

There was an old man in a cloak carrying a glowing blue sword, a man dressed entirely in black with a helmet like a dog's face and a glowing red sword, a young blond boy in pyjamas, a cool-looking guy in a waistcoat firing a big pistol, a similarly armed girl in a white dress, a gorilla, a dustbin with legs and a gold homosexual. There were also loads of guys in white suits, all carrying guns and in varying action poses. I had no idea who was who, although apparently the blond boy was called Han. Already, even before I had seen the film, I found myself seduced by a marketing campaign based heavily on merchandising. I was playing with these characters and growing ever more desperate to actually meet them.

[9] Letraset was a brand of dry rub-on transfers, which primarily provided lettering for posters and artworks, etc., before computer printing made it obsolete. Letraset also produced a number of action transfer sets in conjunction with various film and TV merchandising campaigns.

The film was not released in the UK for a full seven months after its release in the US, so that by the time it reached our shores, it was already being heralded by an awesome juggernaut of extraordinarily positive pre-publicity. Seven months earlier, in the States, it had been a completely different matter. The inside word on *Star Wars* was extremely negative and a nervy Twentieth Century Fox even moved the release to avoid a trouncing from other summer movies. When it was released, it opened on only about forty screens. To give you an idea of how few that is for such a significant film, in 2004 *Shaun of the Dead*, a small, low-budget comedy horror film from the UK, opened on eight hundred screens across the USA. Lucas had, however, been extremely smart in his personal efforts to promote the film, having retained the merchandising rights (an act of stupendous short-sightedness on the part of the studio) and taking on genre whizz Charles Lippincott as marketing director. Lippincott was able to establish a core buzz about the movie with the science-fiction fan base at events such as the San Diego Comic-Con.

At that time, the event was nothing like the industry behemoth it is today, but it was still a nexus for the film's key audience and Lucas and Lippincott cannily identified that these enthusiasts could be the touch paper required to set *Star Wars* alight. A novelisation of Lucas's original story was released in 1976 and by the time the movie was released on 25 May 1977, half a million copies had been sold. Despite uncertainty about the film's potential, even from those within Lucasfilm itself, *Star Wars* smashed the house box-office record in every theatre it played at and started a chain reaction which would propel it into the history books and make it one of the most successful films of all time.

The enthusiasm was contagious. The American cinema-going public, desperate for some positive, life-affirming entertainment, embraced it with hysterical enthusiasm. Not only did it entertain and amaze, it promised something the nation had been reluctant to address: a future. A future that was bright and exciting and full of good-looking young Americans.

Ground zero was the famous Grauman's Chinese Theatre at 6925 Hollywood Boulevard, Los Angeles, where the premiere for the movie took place. As news stories filtered across to the UK about the success of the movie, TV reports often featured shots of the ornate building, with crowds of fans wearing *Star Wars* T-shirts and 'May the Force be with you' badges lined up outside waiting to see the film. It seemed so magical and exciting to me, sat in front of the television. It may have been happening there before my eyes but it seemed like a galaxy far, far away to me then, like something other-worldly and untouchable. If there was a bright centre to the universe, Gloucester was the town it was farthest from, particularly for a young enthusiastic country boy, dreaming of escape to a place of excitement and adventure.

You see what I'm doing here, right? I'm comparing myself to Luke Skywalker. Interestingly, I did always assume the role of of Luke when playing *Star Wars* on the fields and building sites of my youth, and not the infinitely cooler Han Solo. Maybe I identified with him a little more, maybe his predicament as a dreamer in a quiet uneventful place did strike a chord with me, even at that tender age. Maybe it was just because I had the same haircut. Whatever the reason, it was a powerfully poetic and ESTB-craving event, when, thirty-two years later, I pulled up outside Grauman's Chinese Theatre in a big black limousine to attend the premiere of a different science-fiction blockbuster. Sure the T-shirts and badges read 'Trek' and not 'Wars', but I have my own affectionate history with that other most famous of space sagas, so the poetry of the moment was layered with several boyhood dreams.

What's interesting about *Star Wars* is that although now we regard it as the ultimate expression of dumb moneymaking cinema, at the time space-based science fiction was regarded as esoteric, with such films as Kubrick's *2001: A Space Odyssey*, Douglas Trumbull's *Silent Running* and John Carpenter's *Dark Star* leading the field. The most successful science-fiction story thus far had been the *Planet of the Apes* series which was very pointedly Earthbound, even if at first it appeared to be somewhere out of this world. (You didn't know it was Earth? I am so sorry.) Despite the crowd-pleasing theatrics and the classic story implicit within the film, from the outside *Star Wars* probably looked to most like another highbrow, space-based nerd fest. The trailer was certainly very po-faced and portentous without any of John Williams's rousing score and only partially finished special effects. Nevertheless, the word of mouth generated by those early showings, and the infectious sense of well-being with which it filled its audiences, sent a positively virulent wave of elation through the populace, so that by the time the film reached other shores, it was supported by awesome box-office statistics and tales of audience hysteria. It was the marketing momentum every film-maker dreams about and it hit Britain like a tsunami.

The explosive impact of *Star Wars* was thus a combination of a number of factors, the coalescence of which created a blast wave that engulfed much of the globe. The holy grail for every film-maker is an effective marketing campaign. Rubbish films regularly do well with the force of aggressive exposure, and though they evaporate in the memory and contribute nothing to the medium of cinema or anyone's life, they make the requisite amount of cash to justify their being made in the first place and possibly again, at least for the people that put up the investment.

Studios are reluctant to get behind films that don't have obvious mainstream appeal because the risk of losing money is too great. But audiences are generally more sophisticated than they are given credit for and respond to smarter fare if they are exposed to it. Generally, though, we are given fireworks rather than theatre because ultimately the mainstream audience will avoid challenge if they can help it. Life's too short. Occasionally, a *Little Miss Sunshine* or *Napoleon Dynamite* will slip through the net and gather a head of steam through word of mouth. Strange to think that *Star Wars* once had more in common with these hopeful little indies than with the monuments to profitability it now stands beside.

For me, as a seven-year-old boy, the hype and the hysteria were only a small part of it. It was fun to be swept up in and be part of the thing that everyone was talking about, but its true effect on me went beyond the social and economic forces that brought it so keenly into my consciousness. I have no doubt my interest was nourished and maintained by all the toys and books and paraphernalia that accompanied the release and defined the very concept of merchandising thereafter, but my love of *Star Wars* was also incredibly personal. It inspired my imagination, increased my vocabulary, encouraged an interest in film production and music, it was in many ways my childhood muse. This wasn't to do with it providing any sort of psychosocial release for me. I was unaware of America's bleak mood in the early seventies or how it affected the rest of the world, and was oblivious to any of the anxieties to which *Star Wars* was an antidote. I loved it for what it was, a great story, told well with relatable, lovable characters and the added attraction of awe-inspiring visuals, even if George Lucas insisted Carrie Fisher suppress her boobs with gaffer tape.

That's No Moon, It's an Understatement

As you can probably by tell now, *Star Wars* had quite a big effect on my life; not just as a child, but by extending its influence beyond that first encounter to so many facets of my adult life.

It has affected my relationships, my education, my intellect, my decisions and made a significant contribution to making me the person I am today. I'm not suggesting this is due to it being some indispensable work of art or the single greatest film ever committed to celluloid. It was, however, for all its superficial inconsequentiality, of seismic importance as a social and cultural event at that particular point in history, as well as being a piece of blisteringly entertaining fun.

People will often cry gross over-intellectualisation when popular culture is critically addressed, as if it is somehow exempt from serious consideration because it is itself 'non-serious', just a bit of fun that doesn't require or deserve dissection. I disagree; every expression of art is a product of its environment and as such will reflect the concerns, preoccupations and neuroses of the time. Mainstream entertainment particularly, by its very nature, has to reflect the dominant modes of thinking in order to qualify as mainstream, and in that respect, mass entertainment is even more fun to pick apart.

The first *Star Wars* movie is an extraordinary example of this, and its impact was so extensive, it resonates to this day, helped along by a superior sequel and despite the spiralling decline in the quality of subsequent instalments. Now, you're probably thinking, what the hell? I thought this chapter was going to be a continuation of the previous chapter's whimsy about a sci-fi blockbuster shaping a little boy's dreams. Well, that's absolutely what this chapter is; it's just slightly more complex than that. Stick with it though, there are far more personal recollections on their way and I promise you the preceding theoretical musings are interesting and fun in equal measure. It's *Star Wars* – how can it not be?

First things first, I want to identify why this film had the effect it did, not just on me but also on millions of people over the course of a third of a century. It isn't the story, which is wilfully classical and familiar; it isn't the script, which is joyously clunky at times; it isn't the characters, which are archetypes lifted from stories told many times before; it isn't the acting, which I think is great particularly from the central players, but it's only a space opera; it isn't even the effects, which were groundbreaking and dizzying to behold at the time. It is somehow all of these things combined (crucially) with the timing of its release, the collective American psyche at the time and, in global terms, the tremendous hype that ensued as a result of the US population's *Star Wars* hysteria.

If you didn't already know, or haven't guessed from my rambling, I studied film for a while. I relished being able to pick apart my favourite films as a student; it was amusing and fascinating all at the same time. Easily dismissed but powerfully persuasive when argued well, film theory seems from the outside like an awful lot of brainpower for something so inconsequential. During my studies, I wrote a thesis entitled 'Base and Supersucker: A Marxist Overview of Consent in *Star Wars* and Related Works'. In the most basic terms it was about how when we experience art without critical awareness we consent to the ideas being promoted, either intentionally or unintentionally, by the film-maker. For instance, if you watch a racist comedian and laugh at his jokes, you are consenting to the prejudices inherent within them. Similarly, if you watch a movie which perpetuates conventional ideas about race, gender, etc., you are consenting to them and not affecting change in any way.

A film or TV show might not set out to be political, but its refusal to challenge or upset received modes of thinking makes it so. Here's a fun example. Towards the end of the Cold War, our obsession with weapons of mass destruction was endemic. The possibility of total annihilation filled us with the vibrations of constant low-level panic. Who among us remembering this period can't recall waking from a dream similar to the one Sarah Connor has in *Terminator 2: Judgment Day*? Fire sweeping through our neighbourhoods, houses disintegrating in the wake of a devastating blast wave, 'people flying apart like leaves'.

We lived in a constant state of concern that our deepest fears might be realised at any moment, signalled by the siren from the beginning of Frankie Goes to Hollywood's 'Two Tribes' or the television caption in the video to Ultravox's 'Dancing With Tears In Our Eyes'. This preoccupation frequently manifested itself culturally; not just in eighties gritpop or bleak, overtly realist dramas like BBC's *Threads* or Nicholas Meyer's *The Day After*, but also in populist, mainstream entertainment, in which the WMDs were presented figuratively and metaphorically.

The Force, the Death Star, the Ark of the Covenant, Project Genesis are all atomic avatars that not only enable us to address our fears in fantastic terms, but also help us formulate a social morality which helps justify the existence of our own nuclear arsenal. These formidable weapons are totally justifiable in the hands of the righteous and the good. The Death Star is a monstrous orb of evil controlled by the largely faceless, militaristic galactic Empire, but it is perfectly acceptable to use that awesome power against the Empire and wipe out its entire population. After all, it blew up Princess Leia's home planet of Alderaan, just as the Russians could potentially destroy Alaska.

We (the rebels) even employed a little WMD action of our own, using the Force to nail the thermal exhaust port, although in our hands this power is a means of achieving good.

The Project Genesis in the *Star Trek* movie series is similarly confused. In the hands of the Klingon Empire, another autonomous group of demonstrative military aggressors (China, North Korea, Russia, take your pick), it is a force of death, a destroyer, a means of extinction. In the hands of the righteous federation, however, it is the very opposite: a bringer of life and renewal, a force for good and the creation of a new order. Genesis even looks like a missile, similar in appearance to Cruise or Trident.

It would be easy to dismiss this kind of theorising as a bit tenuous, but these moral dilemmas were tightly wound into our collective subconscious at the time.

I'm not suggesting Steven Spielberg and George Lucas were somehow in the government's employ and were charged with encouraging the masses to consent to the ongoing stockpiling of nuclear weaponry. I'm simply saying that our deepest thoughts, desires and preoccupations manifest themselves in art, whether we intend them to or not. That's what art is for; it's not cerebral, it's emotional.

So, if you're still with me, here's why *Star Wars* is so popular. Firstly, we have to look at the film in the context of its time. In the mid-seventies America felt like shit. Having participated in a sixteen-year-long war against an indomitable and tenacious guerrilla force (remember that phrase, I'm going to use it again later) and receiving one of the most significant psychological ass-kickings in the history of military engagement, the nation found itself in a deep depression. No longer buoyed by the cocksure self-confidence engendered by the victories in Europe and the Pacific during World War II, it faltered in a malaise of self-doubt and moral confusion.

A growing surge of angry internal dissent inspired an equal and opposite display of entrenched, right-wing, nationalistic rage and the country was gripped by a schism of insecurity and confusion. Notions of good and evil became muddied and unclear as faith in leadership dwindled to an all-time low, in the wake of the Watergate scandal and both Lyndon Johnson and Richard Nixon being accused of abuse of authority under the War Powers Act of 1973.

Away from the war, the progress of the civil rights movement had sharply divided public opinion on matters of race and equal opportunity, and polarised the nation into violent clashes between old and new thinking. The country's cinematic output was appropriately bleak, reflecting the moroseness and self-hatred that riddled the national psyche. Anti-heroes such as Bonnie and Clyde, Travis Bickle, Popeye Doyle and the Corleones dominated the box office and the public wallowed in a morass of guilty introspection. There was never a country in more desperate need of a blow job than the United States of America: enter George Lucas.

Born in Modesto, California, on 14 May 1944 (if only it had been May the fourth), George Walton Lucas Jr initially had aspirations to be a racing driver until a near-fatal accident in 1962 led to a change of direction. He became interested in cinema and, significantly, in-camera special effects while studying liberal arts at community college, a passion which steered him towards the avant-garde in his formative film-making years. More interested in non-narrative, associative film-making, Lucas focused on creating abstract works that evoked emotion using sound and vision, cinematic poems that foreshadowed not only his obsession with aesthetics but also, perhaps, his reluctance to work with actual actors. Lucas's transfer to USC eventually led to his remaking one of his own short films into a feature for cinematic release. *THX* 1138, a science-fiction story of oppression in a dystopian future and most likely a civil rights metaphor, was a not a success in commercial terms, although it is regarded as a cult classic by some, and Lucas's next feature could not have been more different.

Inspired by his youth spent racing cars in Modesto and, as his later career might suggest, driven by a desire for commercial recognition and remuneration, Lucas wrote and directed *American Graffiti*, a massive box-office success, eventually grossing $115 million, and subsequently proving a significant calling card for the young director.

With the success of *American Graffiti* under his still modest belt, Lucas grasped the opportunity to adapt the manageable mid-section of a space opera he had been developing. *Star Wars* was a grand reworking of the old RKO serialisations of *Flash Gordon* and *Buck Rogers* and initially consisted of four trilogies, which fortunately, although sadly not forever, he whittled down to one. After initially finding it hard to get the project off the ground, Lucas eventually got the support he needed from Twentieth Century Fox, and what was to be a bumpy production began at Elstree Studios, England, in late 1975.

The film represented many of Lucas's preoccupations, combining sophisticated visuals, use of music and sound design, as well as objects travelling at great speed, robots and midgets. It was everything America was crying out for, and on its release could not have been more warmly welcomed by the cinema-going public. *Star Wars* was and is a simple tale of good vs evil, which shamelessly celebrates the thrusting positivity and optimism of young, white America, clearly defining the boundaries between good and evil so there can be no mistake who are the good guys and who are the bad.

The bad guys are faceless and aggressive or else wear uniforms reminiscent of the Third Reich during World War II (a time when notions of good and evil were seemingly as clear-cut) and represent an enormous technologically advanced superpower, intent on extending its influence across the galaxy. The good guys (and here's where it starts to get really interesting) are represented by an *indomitable and tenacious guerrilla force*, who refuse to give way to the superior aggressor, even in the face of insurmountable odds. Sound familiar? This is a theme that continues to leap out from behind Lucas's creative bush throughout his diminishing returns. Six years later, in *Return of the Jedi*, one of the three climactic battles takes place in a huge forest between the Empire's formidable army of laser guns and mechanical chickens and a makeshift army of ill-equipped, relatively primitive jungle fighters, who eventually prevail, despite the bookies heavily favouring the guys with the robo-cocks. The word Ewok even sounds faintly Far Eastern.

Was the mass psychotherapy of *Star Wars* a cathartic transference into the mind of the enemy? A sort of hypothetical revisionism allowing the audience a little subconscious self-flagellation from the safety of the imaginary moral high ground? Not just for Vietnam but for other dishonourable histories yet to be reconciled, not least the subjugation of the country's indigenous population, a regret played out again and again in American cinema, most recently in James Cameron's *Avatar*.

Was *Star Wars* the history that America craved? Young, good-looking, enthusiastic and plucky teenagers overthrowing a staid older order, represented largely by British actors (we wrote the book on guilty histories after all) and even subtitled *A New Hope, Star Wars: Episode IV* (as it eventually and somewhat irritatingly became known) represented a distancing from the ways of the past and a renewal of the positivity and determination that infuses America at its best. This opportunity for self-reassessment and fantastical distraction is a key element in the success of the movie, although it would be unfair to say it is the most important factor – that's due to the fact that *Star Wars* is just really fucking great!

The clearly defined role and function of each character (the hero, the princess, the rogue, the wise man, etc.) and the classical development of the story made it easily accessible to a mainstream audience of all ages. Lucas succeeded in infusing familiar themes and situations with a freshness and originality, by way of his epic fantasy recontextualisation. The *Star Wars* universe was postmodern in a conceptual sense if not a literal one.

A strong feeling of antiquity persists throughout the movie, particularly in the production design, which appears weathered and used. With the exception of the sleek angular Imperial environments, the settings feel lived-in and old, and even in the newer structures, there is a classical simplicity. Science fiction generally dealt either with Earthbound encounters against technologically superior aliens, who usually wanted to eat us, or enslave us, or else with projections of our own future (technologically advanced and expanded beyond Earth into the reaches of space). The *Star Wars* universe was entirely removed from our own reality, it had nothing to do with us, or our planet, and as such, perhaps, proved a more effective metaphor. Even as a child I thought this was clever as it enabled total escapism to a place unsullied by familiarity.

Unfortunately, Lucas seemed to forget this when creating his prequels, gleefully including sly winks to decidedly Earthly concepts, such as the evils of smoking cigarettes and smart-mouthed sports commentators. The computer-generated, dramatically weightless robot armies of the trade federation constantly use the phrase 'roger, roger' as an affirmation, which is old-fashioned US Air Force speak, taken from the Able Baker phonetic alphabet. Couldn't he think of something more other-worldly? All that money was spent trying to create a galaxy far, far away and the risible dialogue keeps bringing us down to Earth with a bump. Even Captain Scarlet and Thunderbirds had their own call signs in S.I.G. and F.A.B. and I never cared a jot that I could see their strings.

This was just one of the multitude of niggles that hampered my determination to enjoy *The Phantom Menace* in 1999, having flown to New York especially to see it. I dimly recall the British playwright Howard Barker speaking of the supreme discomfort we experience when embarrassed by the people we respect. This was most certainly the case at the AMC Lowes cinema on 34th Street as the demolition of my childhood obsession unfolded before my eyes. I should have noticed the signs as I pretended to like the needless augmentations of the original films when they were re-released as 'special editions' in 1997.

If I'm totally honest, I should have accepted that things were going awry when I pretended not to hear Chewbacca yelling like Tarzan as he and a couple of space bears swung from a vine on a mission to hijack an electric chicken in *Return of the Jedi*. Hindsight, as they say, is 20/20 and back in 1977, way before I required glasses, my jaw slackened in anticipation of the film everyone was talking about and the curious legend proclaiming a distant time and location faded on to the screen. I was hooked even before the three neat paragraphs of expositional text receded into infinity, setting up the first dizzying scene.

The opening sequence of *Star Wars* must surely be one of the most effective in the history of modern cinema. John Williams's iconic march settles into a dreamy reflection of the spacescape. A single moon hangs in the starry, silent depths of space over a sandy-coloured planet. The score sweeps and gathers into urgency as a large ship passes overhead, establishing a brief standard for the size of interplanetary cruisers, but as the music swells to percussive insistence another ship rumbles into view, profoundly dwarfing the first. Its mammoth hulk widens into a seemingly never-ending triangle of awesome military might as it fires red energy bolts at the hapless, now tiny, blockade runner, which in response sends back an ineffectual volley of soft green laser blasts.

There is a wonderful economy of storytelling, which grips the audience from the outset, even before we meet any of the characters. It is entirely a bonus that the visuals are so extraordinary and this is key to the success of this first film. If the context were removed, an appealing and easy-to-follow story would still exist. Lucas then superimposes a rich and complex fantasy environment over this story, enabling us to experience classic tropes in a new context. We have seen the relationships and even the situations before in other films (Lucas himself once referred to *Star Wars* as his '*Searchers* in space'). But the roles usually divided up among ethnic supporting actors in war films and westerns are allocated to genuinely alien characters and robots. He adopts a narrative device used by Akira Kurosawa in his 1958 film *The Hidden Fortress* to present the story from the point of view of the lowliest of characters. This is a clever means of easing us into the environment at the first social level, allowing us to look up to the protagonist Luke Skywalker, even at his lowliest phase as a whiny farmhand and before the classic narrative device of 'the call to action' which elevates him to hero status.

In Kurosawa's film, these characters are two peasants called Tahei and Matakishi who befriend the protagonist, General

Rokurota Makabe. In *Star Wars*, the job goes to C-3PO and R2-D2, a couple of affected robots whose actions facilitate the entire plot. We certainly hadn't seen this before. Hal 9000 was a bit camp but he was most likely bi, particularly when compared to C-3PO, a bot who wouldn't look twice at an artificial girl, even Daryl Hannah in *Blade Runner* or that chick out of *Metropolis* with the metal tits.

Interestingly, there was a photo spread in my secret copy of *Lovebirds* that featured an erotic model displaying her wares in a science-fiction setting while wearing silver boots and futuristic make-up. In the little blurb that accompanied the series of pictures (a sort of humanising personal message from the model no doubt written by the magazine's male editor), she spoke of not being able to sit down due to 'the rogering [she] got from C-3PO last week'. Even as a child I felt this was profoundly wrong. Not just because C-3PO was clearly incapable of 'rogering' anybody, but because he wouldn't, even if he could. He wasn't interested in such things, he was too busy being fluent in over six million forms of communication and being posh like Jeremy Thorpe.

Extra-Curricular Activity

'For the love of God, let me act!' I felt like screaming, amid the shocking dearth of extra-curricular drama in Gloucester and the surfeit of opportunity to chase cheese wheels down a hill.

Luckily, my drama teacher at school noticed my frustration and suggested that I join the Gloucester Youth Theatre as an outlet for my dramatic urges. The teachers' strike was ongoing at the time and our educators had ceased supervising extra-curricular activities as part of their industrial action.

This meant that the usual plays and inter-house drama competitions were cancelled in the name of financial justice, and all my performance energy was expended being disruptive in class. Dora Brooking, a wonderful drama teacher beloved by the students for possessing a maternal energy that soothed even the thugs, decided I needed something more than school plays to satisfy my passions. She had cast me as the lead in a school production of *Tom Sawyer*, one year before the harsh reality of staff underpayment brought an end to all the fun, having noted my enthusiasm for the performing arts. In what can sometimes be a sea of apathy, teachers are drawn moth-like to kids with light bulbs hovering over their heads. It gives them something to work with. I will be forever grateful to Dora Brooking, for not only spotting my light bulb but also helping me turn up the wattage.

Tom Sawyer was an amazing experience for me. I had been cast at the end of my first year at Brockworth Comprehensive and taken a big thick script home with me for the holidays. I underlined all my dialogue with a red biro and was thrilled to see that barely a page turned without multiple scarlet slashes reminding me just how much I had bitten off. The show went on in November of the following school year and proved to be an extraordinary adventure.

I developed a huge crush on the girl playing Aunt Polly. She was sixteen, a full four years older than me, and was widely regarded as the prettiest girl in school. The smell of her perfume, coupled with the adrenalin rush of performing in front of five hundred people over two nights, created in me a powerful memory, which I can recall in full detail even now, twenty-eight years later. I didn't necessarily decide to become an actor that year, but my love of performing was utterly secured and Dora knew she had found an ally who wouldn't simply see her subject as a doss.

So it was that Dora called Mum and Mum called her friend Barbara Luck who ran the Gloucester Youth Theatre and arranged for me to start attending the weekly get-together, held on a large barge moored down at Gloucester Docks. I was extremely nervous about going, despite my love of performing. I didn't know anybody other than Barbara who I had also developed a slight crush on after seeing her in *Sweet Charity* at the Cambridge Theatre in Gloucester Leisure Centre (I fell in love all the time as a kid).

As we pulled into the car park at the docks in our red Ford Escort, I could see the assembled theatre youths waiting for Barbara

Me at my 18th birthday party in 1988. Notice the ripped blacked jeans, the red and white stripey top and heavily crimped hair. Also, the birthday cake in the shape of the Aristotelian faces of dramatic art. I was still a bit of a dick at this point.

Me and my sister Katy at Mum's house in Gloucester in zombie mode for Halloween 1989. Katy has a cameo in *Shaun of the Dead* as one of the zombies that break through the back door of the Winchester.

God's Third Leg and the Black Candles, keeping it real in London's seedy Soho in 1987. We didn't go in.

Steve Diggory, Andy Harrison and me, really looking the part at Glastonbury 1987. It was my first festival and I made sure I saw as many bands as possible. Crazyhead were amazing!!

Me and Mum at my graduation from Bristol University in 1991. Check out the earrings and quiff. What a knobhead. A knobhead with a degree though.

Faking a fall in the Australian Outback in 1996. The design on my t-shirt is an alien face very similar to that of Paul, the main character in a film I would shoot in Santa Fey, New Mexico, eleven years later.

Michael Smiley, King of the World, Adelaide, Australia 1996.

Me and Smiley in the flat we moved into together in 1996, after returning from Australia. These were the rave years, we wore a lot of hats and shorts.

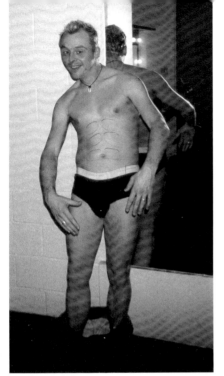

On tour with Steve Coogan in his live show *The Man Who Thinks He's It* in 1998. Those are my real abs, although I may have embellished my knackers with a sock or a boner.

NOT YET COMPLETE

EXT TIM & DAISY'S HOUSE
EP2 SC20 (Mike)

A continuity polaroid from the second series of *Spaced* at the Spaced house in Tufnell Park, London in 2001.

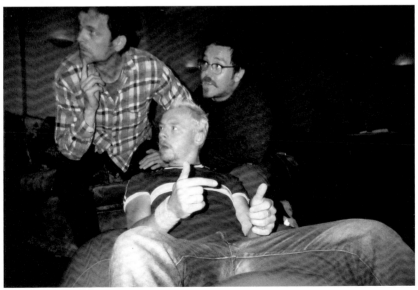

(L to R) Mark Heap, me and Nick Frost in rehearsals for *Spaced* series two at The American Church Tottenham Court Road, London in 2000. Note my expert demonstration of video game hands.

Jessica Hynes and I reading a fanzine containing an article about *Spaced* whilst writing the second series at our Queens Park office in 2000.

Nick and I rehearsing a scene for episode four, series two of *Spaced* in 2001. Nick is in his *Matrix* gear whereas I am still dressed as Tim. I am not sure why this is. I'm sorry.

One of Tim and Daisy's fake holiday photos from the first series of *Spaced* in 1999. The shot was taken against the window of a travel agency in Palmers Green, London.

Promoting *Shaun of the Dead* in Sydney, Australia in 2004. It's quite exciting when you happen upon a poster of yourself in the street.

Looking pleased with myself on the set of *Shaun of the Dead* in 2003. We spent weeks in that garden in Crouch End, having to suffer persistent delays due to the weather. Good times though.

Me and my stunt double relaxing on set.

Looking worried in Crouch End. The weather was so erratic we came up with an idea for a film set in the deserts of America about two guys who befriend an alien called Paul.

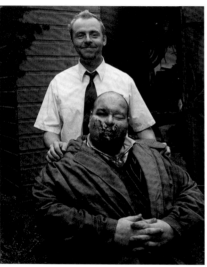

I look so proud of my necrotic, mouthless friend. A zombie known as 'the hulk', played by Mark Donovan.

Me, and behind me is our chief sound man Simon Hayes, riding a BMX.

to arrive to let them on to the show boat. The group were rehearsing for their Christmas production, *Follow the Star*, on which I would serve as a technical assistant, having arrived too late in the season to audition for a part. I squinted into the darkness to get the measure of my fellow drama types and noticed very quickly that they were all female. This group of confident, outgoing women, who all knew each other, were about to take delivery of a goofy fourteen-year-old boy with a tendency to fall in love and a sense of moral confusion with regard to his carnal desires. This was only a matter of months after Meredith Catsanus's titmageddon and a full two years before the girl over the road would so confidently unbuckle my belt. Suddenly, I was alone in the car. It was just me and this shadowy crowd of mysterious and exotic women. I couldn't help myself. It just slipped out of my mouth, like an opportunistic prisoner noticing a hole in the fence. It was out before my brain could sound the alarm.

FUCK!

My mother's shrill admonishment barely concealed her amusement and my own gasping apology was lost amid a fit of giggling. The Freudian significance of the comment was lost into the ether; so much more was the shock of hearing my barely broken voice utter this profanity in the back of a Ford Escort in 1984. There was no punishment though, only a warning about putting my brain into gear before I spoke. The incident progressed my relationship with my mum into a more adult phase, as if a certain spell had been broken between us, like discovering the truth about Santa, the Easter Bunny or God, and now I would occasionally hear her swear for comic effect or at least refer to swearing by making an 'eff' sound. It was a while before I dared utter the C-word in front of her, and when I did, it was met with far less amiable acceptance. I was a college boy by this time with some grasp of etymology and linguistics and my casual use of the word had been wilfully inflammatory.

'Oh, come on, Mum,' I sighed at her protest. 'It's just an old Anglo-Saxon word for the female organ which has been adopted by an inherently misogynist language as a negative epithet. It's the same as "fuck", it basically means the same as copulate, but the latter is perfectly acceptable. Why? Because copulate has its roots in Latin and Latin reminds us that we are a sophisticated, learned species, not the rutting animals that these prehistoric grunts would have us appear to be, and isn't that really the issue here? We don't want to admit that we are essentially animals? We want to distinguish ourselves from the fauna with grand conceits and elaborate language; become angels worthy of salvation, not dumb creatures consigned to an earthly, terminal end. It's just a word, Mum; a sound meaning a thing; and your disgust is just denial of a greater horror: that our consciousness is not an indication of our specialness but the terrifying key to knowing how truly insignificant we are.'

She told me to go fuck myself.

6

The smell of the medina crept seductively into the courtyard of the riad and punched Simon Pegg full in the face as he wound the traditional Berber keffiyeh around his head.

'Oooh, I'd love a tagine!' Pegg enthused.

'Sir?' enquired Canterbury, who was dressed in a full burka so as not to anger the locals. This had nothing to do with the edicts of sharia law; robots were permitted to wander freely in Islamic territories. King Mohammed IV's own robotic chamberlain, Abd Al-Ala, was often seen clanking through the souks purchasing spices or bartering over leather goods (the King had a thing for satchels). The problem was that Canterbury was something of a celebrity, famous for being aide to the world's most famous international playboy and adventurer, and his presence in Marrakesh would doubtless cause alarm. This in turn would render Pegg's disguise as a handsome, swarthy Berber trader absolutely pointless.

Also, Pegg had spray-painted a pair of tits on Canterbury's breastplate after he got drunk on sherry at a Soup Dragons concert in 1991 and couldn't get it off. He regretted the act enormously and had thought many times about spraying over the lewd graffiti but had refrained from doing so in case it invalidated his warranty. It was the same reason Pegg had refrained from removing Canterbury's flashing earring, resulting in the asexual android being called 'gaybot' by some of the other automatons at the 1998 science expo at Earls Court.

'A tagine . . .' hissed Pegg through a day of stubble, which added to his disguise and also made him look even more handsome, which was impossible but if it wasn't, it would have done, even though it couldn't have but it did, '. . . is a sort of slow-cooked, North African stew, named after the ceramic pot in which it is cooked.'

'Forgive my impertinence, sir,' beeped Canterbury, 'but I know what a tagine is. My own recipe for quail tagine with prunes and almonds received first prize in the 2005 Great Robotic North African Cook-Off, held at the Birmingham NEC and sponsored by ASDA. You were there.'

'I know I was there,' retorted Pegg hotly, 'I was just slightly distracted by the little matter of Lord Black trying to turn the Oasis Centre into a hydrogen bomb. Do you have any idea how many goths would have died?'

'That was the following year,' replied Canterbury calmly, 'you were actually one of the judges at the Great Robotic North African Cook-Off.'

'Cock off!' dismissed Pegg.

'Cook-off,' corrected Canterbury.

'No, I mean cock off, I wasn't there,' clarified the charming adventurer.

'Yes you were,' Canterbury insisted.

'You're absolutely right,' conceded Pegg. 'I remember

now, I voted for the Prime Minister's Sexbot. He made these amazing Moroccan harost balls with dates, raisins and nuts that were absolutely to die for!'

'What?!' buzzed Canterbury, his computerised voice riddled with consternation.

'Nothing,' backtracked Pegg. 'Forget I said anything.'

'He stole that recipe off the Internet!' seethed Canterbury. 'And those balls were undercooked.'

'Canterbury —' Pegg tried to calm the indignant robochef down, even though he knew in his heart he had royally fucked up.

'I had to go to south London for those prunes. Do you know how difficult that is? It's all spread out and confusing.' Canterbury's agitation seemed to be getting out of hand and Pegg couldn't afford a rogue robot at his side, if they were soon to leave the riad and penetrate the market in search of the Scarlet Panther.

'Reset code delta one zero,' Pegg said casually. Canterbury snapped to attention, his eyes became fixed and glowed a deep red colour, like a Cylon from *Battlestar Galactica* but not going from side to side and making a noise like Knight Rider.

'Please state reset perameters and confirm.' Canterbury's voice was monotone and businesslike, reminiscent of Pegg's fourth wife Sienna, who worked in a call centre although she talked like that normally too. Pegg looked at his watch. He squinted and went over their recent conversation in his head.

'One minute should do it. Confirmation alpha seven.'

There was silence but for the barely audible clicking of Canterbury's processors crunching the override procedures. Pegg checked his emails on his iPhone 4 as he waited but found nothing but a spam email from a Scottish souvenir website. He cursed himself internally for buying those cashmere socks for his mother's birthday.

'It was a one-off, damn it! I don't want a fucking newsletter!'

'What would you like to do first, sir?' chirruped a suddenly animated Canterbury, making Pegg jump.

Pegg took a deep breath. 'I'd love a tagine,' he said breezily, massaging his chest and trying to emulate his earlier tone.

'Sir?' enquired Canterbury.

'A tagine,' replied Pegg helpfully, 'like the one you made at the Great Robotic North African Cook-Off at the NEC in 2005. It was so delicious. I shouldn't tell you this but I voted for you, you know.'

'Thank you, sir,' stumbled the flattered droid. 'I'm extremely grateful for your support. To be honest, I thought perhaps you had voted for the horast balls made by the BJ5000 after I saw you emerging from the utility cupboard together.'

'Don't be absurd,' replied Pegg, a bead of sweat forming on his brow. 'Your tagine was by far the best dish. For me to vote for those tasteless, undercooked doughy balls would have required some serious buttering-up.'

'Thank you, sir.' Canterbury seemed happy and did not press the subject, much to Pegg's relief. 'I only question your judgement, sir, because we have more pressing matters at hand. We must locate the Scarlet Panda as soon as possible, and discover the where-abouts of the Star of Nefertiti, or face the destruction of the Earth on a scale that would give Roland Emmerich a fatty.'

'You're right, I . . . Wait a minute.' Pegg suddenly tensed, looking at his robotic friend through partially closed eyes. 'What did you just say?'

Canterbury made a rewind noise.

'Give Roland Emmerich a fatty,' replied Canterbury.

'Before that,' pressed Pegg.

Another high-pitched squiggle signified Canterbury's reviewing of his vocal tapes.

'Discover the whereabouts of the Star of Nefertiti?' offered Canterbury.

'Before that.' Pegg wound his hand in the air, a note of impatience in his voice.

Canterbury wound back further, before pressing his internal play mechanism.

'We must locate the Scarlet Panda,' Canterbury repeated.

'Scarlet Panda? Don't you mean Scarlet Panther?' Pegg's confusion was evident.

'That's what I said, wasn't it?' insisted Canterbury with insistent insistence.

'No,' corrected Pegg with measured confidence, his muscles tensing one by one as his body became aware of its surroundings. The earthenware plate on the wall to his left would make an excellent improvised Frisbee-style weapon, as would the ornate Berber sword mounted on the wall which wouldn't require as much impro, being as it was already technically a weapon. Pegg also had two Israeli-made Desert Eagles under his djellaba, so he was fairly prepared.

'The Scarlet P-P-Panda,' stammered Canterbury. Something was definitely wrong. Canterbury shook slightly; a trickle of white liquid issued from the side of his audio slot. 'I seem to have acquired a virus, sir, it's affecting my cognitive centres. It's ... it's wiping my memory.'

'When was the last time you interfaced with a potentially infectious node?' enquired Pegg, knowledgeably.

'I can't remember!' panicked the ailing bot. 'Wait, the vending machine at the bus station. Someone must have ...'

'Oh God, Canterbury,' whispered Pegg, his voice riddled with concern. 'What about all those recipes?'

'I backed them up on one of those little stick things ...' said Canterbury, trying to be helpful, despite the ongoing destruction of his memory centres. 'You know? A ... a ...'

'Flash-drive?' shouted Pegg.

'That's it,' returned Canterbury.

Pegg gave the air a victory punch, delighted that he'd got the right answer.

'The memory loss is a side effect though, sir,' said Canterbury ominously. 'The virus was not intended to destroy my info-storage platters, it has done something far worse.'

'What?' said Pegg, the smile falling from his classically good-looking face.

'It knocked out my early-warning sensors.'

Pegg's body filled with the hot sensation of readiness, which usually precedes a proper tear-up, and had to admit internally that he was shitting himself.

'The Scarlet Panther, sir,' said Canterbury.

'There you go.' Pegg's body relaxed into a slump of relief. 'See? Your memory's coming back. Now quickly, get your sensors back online. For a minute I thought we were in trouble.'

'We are,' said Canterbury flatly. 'My memory centres

have been all but wiped clean. The only things still working are my primary recognition functions.'

'But if the only things working are your primary recognition functions,' said Pegg, catching on, 'then that must mean you are actually looking at the Scarlet Panther and if you are actually looking at the Scarlet Panther she must be ...'

'Behind you.' A voice like velvet covered in chocolate slid through the warm air, spinning Pegg round to face his old enemy/love interest. ''Ello, Simone.' Pegg felt her voice in his underwear, even as it issued from her full, red, round lips. 'Don't worry about Canterbury, eet's not permanent.'

Pegg and the Scarlet Panther stared at each other, a smile playing across both their mouths, their bodies tensed with anticipation. Things were about to get extremely physical and they both knew it. The question was, would it be violence or would it be sex? Pegg hoped it would be both.

'Why is my watch a minute fast?' asked Canterbury.

'I'll tell you later,' said Pegg as he lunged towards his quarry.

A Fine (B)romance

I was never allowed to watch *The Sweeney* due to excessive violence, swearing and use of Dennis Waterman, so I can't really tell you much about it. (*Starsky & Hutch*, however, was a firm favourite of mine, to the extent that the first poster I ever bought and Blu-tacked to my bedroom wall was a huge diptych of the actors, Paul Michael Glaser and David Soul. It was probably the last obsession I had before that giant star destroyer rumbled over my head and made everything else seem trite.)

There was something beguiling and different about *Starsky & Hutch* that sucked me in and hooked me completely. It wasn't an elusive ingredient or a special *je ne sais quoi*; it wasn't the set-up or the storylines; it was entirely the chemistry between Glaser and Soul and the close friendship between their two alter egos. There was an affection and sweetness in their interaction that went beyond what students might interpret as a gay subtext. Sure, cultural commentators who thought themselves awfully clever might glibly proclaim that Ken and Dave clearly harboured a latent desire to get inside one another's tight jeans/chunky cardigans, but in truth, this reading of the relationship between Starsky and Hutch is way too simplistic.

Whether it was the intention of the writers or a product of that immense chemistry between the two lead actors, *Starksy & Hutch* was a captivating study of true love and affection between two straight men. Culturally, it probably marked the point at which the action hero first attempted an evolutionary step away from his Dirty Harry forebears and morphed into a more emotionally three-dimensional archetype, less constricted by the rigours of machismo and permitted to rehearse a little vulnerability and even – dare I say it – femininity.

The opening titles are a brilliantly concise mission statement for the show, depicting a dizzying montage of action moments, persistently undermined by subtle comic touches and hints of an almost husband-and-wife closeness between the lead pair. It opens on the famous 'striped Tomato', a scarlet Ford Torino with a white flash on its wing, careening through the litter-strewn streets of LA. We then see our heroes grab a perp each and roughly bend them over the hood of a car (you can see why a media student might get so excited). Then, as if to dispel any thoughts of rough bum sex, we find them in a strip joint as Ken Hutchinson is hypnotised by a gorgeous exotic dancer, who is pumping her hips at him seductively.

The seemingly nonplussed Starsky blows into his partner's ear to get his attention, demonstrating emphatically that these guys are into girls but have more important things to do with each other. We then hit the beat and see them doing those all-important things: Hutch eagerly walks alongside the Tomato, gun drawn, as Starsky drives with the door open, suggesting collaboration and partnership; the duo emerge drenched from a swimming pool, partly a pre-Mr Darcy demonstration of soaking wet masculine cool but also evidence that they are prepared to go through shit together as a team. We then see them having a laugh in Captain Dobey's office, while dressed in undercover costumes. Hutch is a cowboy, Starsky a Travolta-style disco dancer; both outfits are slightly camp but acknowledge the guys' innate sense of fun.

Next, the pair separate into singles for the build-up to their respective title cards; we oscillate between them running and jumping and shooting and doing all sorts of crazy man stuff, although hinting at their fallibility as they bounce off walls and land arse first on the roof of a car. The dramatis personae then unfolds, introducing not only David and Paul but also Antonio Fargas as Huggy Bear and Bernie Hamilton as Captain Dobey, two supporting but nevertheless principal characters both of whom were black which, despite them being somewhat stereo-typed, remained a progressive move. The titles end with a vignette in which Starsky saves a bemused Hutch using a shopping trolley – a traditional signifier of feminine domestication – to break down a door at which moment an explosion blows Starsky into Hutch's arms, forcing them into a momentary embrace. Brilliant.

I'm not suggesting the programme-makers were as rigorous in their devising of this title sequence as that analysis suggests, but there is no doubt it represents a cleverly constructed semiotic narrative that tells us everything we need to know about the show, most importantly that Starsky and Hutch have a deeply co-dependent relationship.

It was another ten years before John McClane arrived on the scene and truly cemented the vulnerable action hero in the cultural subconscious, starting a process of cultural dominoes that led to audiences accepting ordinary schmoes as heroic protag-onists in films such as, well, *Shaun of the Dead* and *Hot Fuzz*. In fact, it could be convincingly argued that Nicholas Angel and Danny Butterman are partly the product of a fictional union between Starsky and Hutch; fictional because men can't have babies and they wouldn't have had sex anyway. Although Danny and Nicholas might.

It is also arguable that the last spurt of absurd masculinity represented by the muscle-bound, superhuman and sometimes non-human action heroes of the eighties could be attributed to a knee-jerk response to the slight feminising of the male characters acutely demonstrated in *Starsky & Hutch*. The show was certainly one of the first examples of what would in the future become known as the 'bromance'. Sure, we had seen male bonding before in everything from Laurel and Hardy's bed-sharing to Tony Curtis and Sidney Poitier's handcuffed fugitives in Stanley Kramer's 1958 prisoners-on-the-run classic *The Defiant Ones*, but *Starsky & Hutch* took the notion of male affection into the mainstream. When Starsky is strafed with bullets in a drive-by shooting that leaves Hutch potentially partnerless, we feel for him because he is losing someone he not only cares about but also most probably genuinely loves.

This relationship always appealed to me, perhaps because of the closeness I developed with my father as a result of his departure or just because I am not frightened of expressing love for boys. The relationship I have played out with Nick Frost both on and off screen has been hugely indicative of this. We are dear friends and I have no problem expressing that physically or emotionally. I can look him in the eye and tell him that I love him without feeling weird or fearing him recoiling and shouting 'Get off me, you bummer', although he sometimes does, we both do.

Our relationship heavily influenced the relationship between Tim and Mike in *Spaced*, Shaun and Ed in *Shaun of the Dead*, Nicholas and Danny in *Hot Fuzz* and most recently Graeme and Clive in *Paul*. Tim and Mike, together with Shaun and Ed, have an almost parent/child relationship with each other, Tim/Shaun being the father to the innocent/mischievous Mike/Ed. I am a few years older than Nick and have a more thorough academic history, and although I have learned as much from him as he has from me, at the outset of our friendship, I all but adopted him.

He was entirely complicit in this and came along of his own free will and with a voracious desire to discover new things. I fed him cinema and comedy and provided something of a cultural education, while he opened my eyes to realities my previous existence had kept me cloistered from. At first, I did have something of a paternal relationship with him. I encouraged him to pursue comedy because he impressed me immensely and his success has filled me with nothing but admiration and pride. The relationship between Danny Butterman and Nicholas Angel reflects this symbiosis completely. Angel represents everything Danny aspires to, whereas Danny represents everything Angel needs to understand in order to be a more rounded human being. I'll talk more about my relationship and work with Nick Frost later, but there is no doubt in my mind that the male closeness I witnessed as a child, watching *Starsky & Hutch*, informed my attitude towards such relationships in later life. Ken and Dave taught me that man love was not something to fear but rather something to embrace and then pat heavily on the back.

A Princess and
a Guy Like Me

The arrival of *Star Wars* didn't just bring excitement and adventure; it brought romance. There was something so gorgeous about Carrie Fisher's Princess Leia; she was beautiful but also slightly boyish in her tenacious attitude, which made her easy to relate to. When re-enacting scenes from *Star Wars* in the playground, we found ourselves with a constant dearth of female candidates to take the role of Princess Leia, so the role was almost always taken by Sean Jeffries, who would delight in running away from me and Stuart Clegg (Han Solo), shouting 'Shoo, shoo' to fend off our amorous advances. A few years later while being held hostage by the rough boys in the swimming pool changing rooms, I mentally told myself to remember Sean as Princess Leia if they actually went through with their threat of enforcing lewd interaction between us, as it probably would have helped.

Sean wasn't particularly feminine, he was just tall and happy to double as Leia and Chewbacca whenever we played *Star Wars*. Despite that tomboy edge, Carrie Fisher was definitely feminine, with her glossy lips and flowing white dress which acquires a little smudge on the breast area during her escape from the Death Star, serving not only to draw attention to the boobs George Lucas tried so hard to downplay, but also demonstrating a willingness to get grubby, which I, for one loved. In *The Empire Strikes Back*, Han Solo even seduces her while rubbing her oil-smudged hands, essentially saying, 'You LOVE it!'

She was a princess but a princess you could relate to if you were a seven-year-old boy, and I related to her every night before I went to sleep (I really didn't intend that to sound quite so unseemly). In 1977, I was a full four years shy of taking up that particular favourite of male pastimes, despite being aware that my penis had uses other than doing wee-wees (although I had no clear idea of exactly what they were). The relationship I had with Carrie Fisher was far more innocent and involved placing a nightly kiss on her photographic lips, on the picture of her I had torn from *Look-in* magazine which was blue-tacked on to the wall next to my bed. I did it with such frequency that the picture began to deteriorate, and the area around her mouth became whitened as my saliva broke down the paper. It's not as if I was 'film-star kissing' her. I hadn't done that with anybody since Kyle, and wouldn't do it for another year when I would find myself on a bed with a girl called Claire at a friend's party, again surrounded by clapping children.

Claire and I had decided to 'go out' with each other because we were the fastest runners in the school and as such represented perhaps the most formidable power couple at Castle Hill Primary. We were the Posh and Becks of the day, which is approximately how long the relationship lasted (one day). I seem to remember kids running in and out of the bedroom turning lights on and off and screeching with laughter as Claire and I sucked face amid the teddy bears. It wasn't particularly sexual – how could it have been? Those breathless, dizzying encounters of genuine early passion wouldn't take place until the bacchanalian teen parties of the early eighties. This was more like a cross between the exhibition kissing of my smooches with Kyle and a rehearsal for the more serious facilitative embraces of later life. Whatever it was, it was a lot more than I bestowed upon my precious picture of Carrie. These kisses were far more tender and infused with a sense of longing that was at once exciting and slightly depressing.

It inspired me to fantasise about what I would do if I met her or how her character's relationship might progress with Luke Skywalker, unaware at this point that they were siblings, which would have utterly soured my fancy, despite being from Gloucester. Although the sensation was slightly heartbreaking, I enjoyed it. There was something pleasurable in the predicament of hopeless love; I found it inspiring and would continue to do so as I grew older. Much of the comedy poetry that formed my early stand-up shows at university was about being in love with the actress Diane Keaton, itself a euphemism for the love I had for Eggy Helen, the girl who inspired me to commit window-cide, an emotional cataclysm I would eventually mine for my romantic contributions to *Spaced*.

We are never more creative than when we are at odds with the world and there is nothing so artistically destructive as comfort. Princess Leia taught me that. Twenty-seven years after I had to replace the picture of Carrie Fisher with a picture of Lou Ferrigno (not for kissing) due to lip damage, I lined up to meet her at the 2004 San Diego Comic-Con, with all the other *Star Wars* fans, despite being there to promote my own movie and having just completed an autograph signing of my own. Carrie had no idea who I was. Why should she?

I'm sure she still doesn't and I have total comprehension of the depth of personal interaction that takes place at these events. It means something to the person that has queued up to meet the signer but it is usually as forgettable and fleeting for the person doing the signing as it is exciting for the signee. Nevertheless, she was there and for the sake of my seven-year-old self I paid my fifteen dollars and got in line. When my turn came I stepped up and confessed everything.

Me: I used to kiss your picture every night before I went to sleep.
Carrie: Do you feel better for telling me that?
Me: Much. Thank you.

As beautiful as ever, she smiled at me and I smiled back. I'd like to think we had a connection, or at least I had amused her with my candour. I'm pretty sure the latter was true because I played it supercool, with all the British dryness I could muster, something the Americans often get a kick out of because they find our repression amusing. The connection, though, was entirely mine. To her I was yet another of the millions of fanboys she has encountered over the years for whom her portrayal of the ass-kicking galactic princess was a formative moment in their sexual awakening.

For me, though, it was the achievement of an ambition I had harboured for many years – to breathe the same air, to look into her eyes and have her look back at me – and it was very nearly everything I had hoped for. I felt lighter than air as I walked in a daze across the convention floor, going nowhere in particular and not needing to wear a mask. I slightly regretted not getting a photograph with her but I was pleased that I hadn't overstayed my welcome and pushed my luck. I got lucky with Tom Baker in 1978, Carrie might not have been so patient. I did manage to get a picture of me with Lou Ferrigno, so the day wasn't a complete photographic bust.

I attended a *Star Wars* panel later that day in one of the large convention halls. Carrie was making an appearance and I was also curious to hear the title of the third prequel announced, despite my agonising disappointment at the other two. She walked out onstage to rapturous applause from the partisan crowd. As the clapping settled into a fading crackle, someone shouted out, 'I love you!' She smiled broadly and replied, 'I love you too.' 'I know!' I shouted, as the crowd swelled into a collective roar of appreciative laughter. She found me amid the throng and smiled, recognising me from our earlier encounter. She gave me an impressed conciliatory nod and winked with genuine affection. I blew her a kiss, which she snatched out of the air and placed into the left cup of her gold-trim bikini which she was wearing that day. Of the thousands of kisses I had bestowed upon her over the years, it was the first she had actually received and something told me it would not be the last. OK so not all of the above story is true. In fact, I went off-piste at the point where she said, 'I love you too.' I thought of saying 'I know' but stopped myself for some reason. I think it would have got a laugh and I think she would have found it funny but I hesitated and the moment passed.[10]

[10] While writing of my childhood love for Carrie Fisher, I remembered that I follow her (@CarrieFFisher) on Twitter and broke mid-flow to check out the list of people she follows, on the off chance she might be following me (@simonpegg) now that I'm more well known in America. She's an intelligent and culturally savvy woman, I felt certain she would have a penchant for British comedy. Turns out I was absolutely right, except that she doesn't follow me, she follows fucking Russell Brand! As if that immaculately scruffy Lothario doesn't get enough love from the ladies, without snaffling the affections of my boyhood paramour. Damn you, Brand, with your charming and charismatic comedy stylings, damn you to hell!

Little Things

After three years of waiting, *The Empire Strikes Back* arrived, heralding a darker, more adult vision of the world I had grown to love. The tone and feel of the movie had an immediate effect on the ten-year-old me, and my writing at school took on a darker edge, with characters not always surviving to the end of stories, or suffering great losses along the way, usually their right hand.

Of course, these stories were still only ever about a page long but their mood changed significantly. I could dive into the socio-cultural implications of *The Empire Strikes Back* and what it meant to America – basically an exercise in self-reflexive re-evaluation in the wake of the confidence-boosting first instalment – but I won't. It's a great sequel and widely regarded as the best film in the entire series. Lucas reputedly told publicist Sid Ganis that *The Empire Strikes Back* was the worst of the *Star Wars* films,[11] which seems odd, particularly as Lucas tried so hard to recreate *Empire*'s most effective beats in the vastly inferior prequel, *Attack of the Clones*. He would most likely refer

[11] http://www.slashfilm.com/2007/02/11

to this as poetic, although it seems more likely an attempt to emulate the success and admiration the original had earned, particularly in light of the critical drubbing received by *The Phantom Menace*.

Return of the Jedi, released in 1983, was immensely enjoyable, but, on more critical reflection, seems to be a rehash of the first two, with the addition of an army of fighting teddy bears, a wrong step most of us chose to ignore. As a metaphor for America's involvement in Vietnam, *Jedi* is perhaps the most blatant and paradoxical in that the audience allegiance is clearly positioned on the side of a group of primitive jungle fighters, attempting to fend off the usurping might of a technologically superior force. Here the Empire is America, being punished for involving itself in a war it could not and did not win.

The Phantom Menace presented us with barely disguised oriental bad guys in the shape of the Trade Federation, although these were more likely manifestations of George Lucas's business demons, since the whole film is a veiled whine about having to pay taxes. In 1977, Lucas was Luke, a young idealist, obsessed with adventure, excitement and going really fast; in 1999, his concerns are more financial and out of touch, although going really fast still figures. The prequels, though, are ostensibly a justification of evil. An account of how even the best people can go bad if exposed to certain circumstances. The three films work towards us pitying the 'big bad' of the first three films, namely Darth Vader. This faceless murderer, whose grip on the galaxy represented the outdated imperialist mentality America wanted to shed, became a spurned lover and tragic widower, lumbering around the Emperor's secret laboratory melodramatically shouting the word 'no' and expecting us to empathise with his decision to become a homicidal intergalactic despot.

The war in Iraq had been raging for two years by the time *Revenge of the Sith* was released, a film that told us that sometimes even good people do terrible things. One of the most interesting expansions of this theory is demonstrated in the recent *Star Wars* video game, *The Force Unleashed* which takes place between Episodes III and IV (the last and the first film) and deals with the foundation of the rebellion through a morally ambiguous protagonist called Starkiller (Luke Skywalker's originally intended surname). Starkiller, who seemingly works for Darth Vader, attempts to hunt down the remaining Jedi. However, in so doing, begins to feel sympathy for the opposing team. The game is brilliantly realised and for my money is the most enjoyable incarnation of the saga since *Return of the Jedi*. As Starkiller (and initially Vader), you travel from planet to planet, laying waste to a variety of 'enemies' including Jawas, innocuous little sand scavengers, and Wookiees, the race of bear-like humanoids that gave us one of the most beloved characters in the *Star Wars* universe, Chewbacca. It feels strange playing this character, basically killing anybody who gets in his way, irrespective of their moral stance. However, these actions are ultimately justifiable as they lead to the formation of the rebellion and the eventual destruction of the Empire. As elsewhere in the world, it was impossible to conceal the huge civilian casualties in Afghanistan and Iraq, and the message of the game is essentially a rallying justification for the reality of actual world events, this being 'Hey, sometimes you just gotta fuck up a Wookiee.'

Before I let *Star Wars* go (and it's unlikely that I ever truly will), it's worth mentioning how the films affected me emotionally, if only to demonstrate how deeply its influence ran.

It was 2 June 1983 and *Return of the Jedi* had arrived in cinemas in the capital. After much planning, Sean and I were due to travel to London to see it. However, a last-minute change meant that I was unable to make the trip as early as Sean due to my being admitted to Bristol Children's Hospital to have a birthmark removed from my forehead. The birthmark, an oval of darkly pigmented skin on the right side of my forehead about the size of a ten-pence piece, became troubling to me as I grew into my teens whereas before I had assumed it to be cool. I developed a habit of constantly smoothing my hair down to conceal it in order to avoid hurtful comments from people who hadn't seen it before, the most common of which was, 'Why have you got as leaf stuck to your head?'

When my mother realised the birthmark had started to bother me, she took me along to our GP who identified it as a 'hairy naevus' and assured me that he could 'have it off in no time'. I was put on an NHS waiting list and in a matter of months I was booked into Bristol Children's Hospital where the procedure was to take place. On 2 June, as Sean Jeffries was travelling to London to see *Return of the Jedi* before me, I was getting into my pyjamas and climbing into my bed on ward 34 of the BCH, being looked after by a number of delightful nurses, all of whom I fell in love with. I watched the original *Star Wars* on the ward's video cassette player as a consolation for missing the fun in London, and Mum and Richard went into Bristol and bought me a Biker Scout action figure, one of the new *Return of the Jedi* range, released in conjunction with the opening of the film. Even now, I can still feel the thrill of studying the packaging before ripping it open to get inside (would have been worth a fortune today if I'd left it in the box, stupid child). The smell of the fresh plastic and the sophistication and newness of the mould compared to the older, now well-used figures in my collection filled me with a wonder and excitement that completely dispelled my nerves about the operation.

When visiting hours ended I said goodbye to Mum and Richard and settled down for my first night alone in hospital. At 6 a.m. I was woken by the nurse and asked to put on one of those embarrassing gowns that leaves your arse exposed. I was then given a small plastic cup containing two pills, which I duly swallowed. Nine hours later, I became aware of a familiar whistling coming from somewhere in the distance and struggled my way back to consciousness as though from the bottom of a swimming pool. The first person I saw when I opened my eyes was Mum, sat by my bed looking anxious. Actually, it's perhaps more accurate to say I opened my eye; the other one was already open and had been since the operation, despite Mum's frequent attempts to close it. The procedure had entailed cutting the naevus out of my forehead, then pulling the skin together and stitching it up. This resulted in my right eyebrow being pulled up into a quizzical Spock-like expression, where it remained for a few months until the skin was stretched back to normality. Fortunately I was a teenager and frowned a lot, which helped pull the skin around my eyebrow down to a less surprised height. In the hours after the operation, though, the stretch was at its maximum and however many times Mum gently closed it, the lid would open, settling me back into an unnerving one-eyed stare.

Mum called the nurse who came over and welcomed me back to the land of the living. She was a bit surprised that I was awake and seemed impressed, if slightly concerned, that I had come round from the anaesthetic an hour or so early. I remembered the whistling and realised the culprit had been R2-D2. Some of the other children on the ward were watching the *Star Wars* video a few beds down and the sound of robots and lasers and spaceships had brought me out of my heavily induced sleep prematurely. Mum immediately noted this down in her 'things to do if ever Simon is in a coma' book before cracking open the grapes.

I recovered very quickly, unlike the boy in the bed next to me who had had his ears pinned back. He could only manage half of *Star Wars* later that evening, before projectile vomiting Ribena into a kidney dish. The nurses hit him up with a few more painkillers and sent him off to his bed, while I was allowed to watch the video all by myself, the TV stand pulled up intimately to the end of my bed.

A few weeks later, now fully recovered, I travelled to London with my babysitters, Paul and Fay, a young couple who often looked after my sister Katy and me when Mum and Richard were out at the theatre. I loved Paul and Fay. They were cool and loved movies as much as I did. Whenever they came round, they would allow me to stay up just that little bit past my bedtime, so we could discuss our favourite films and television shows. They had no children of their own at the time and they felt more like friends of mine than friends of Mum and Richard's. When the marketing campaign for *Return of the Jedi* began, we hatched a plan to see the film in one of the big theatres in London, where the screen was four times as big as Screen 1 in the ABC and the sound system consisted of speakers that encompassed you in a siege of blaring, crystal-clear sound. I was extremely excited; not only was I going to London to see the film I longed to see more than any other, I was going with my friends, who treated me like a grown-up and laughed when I swore.

I had only been to London once before, as a birthday treat in 1977. We had visited the Natural History Museum and Madame Tussaud's, then gone to see Harry Nilsson's musical *The Point!* at the Mermaid Theatre. On the journey from South Kensington, where I had marvelled at the huge dinosaur skeletons in the museum, we stopped on Wood Lane to look at the BBC building. We actually stopped the car and got out to look at it, the famous concrete doughnut where so many of my favourite programmes were made. Eighteen years later I called Mum from my dressing room inside the building, before recording my first appearance on the BBC's *Stand Up Show* and reminded her that we had once stood outside and just looked, like Victorian orphans outside a cake shop. It says a lot about the level of mystique retained by television at the time that it could make a grey, ugly building seem enchanting. In the early eighties I would experience the wonder again, when I went to see daytime magazine show *Pebble Mill* being recorded in Birmingham and met Don Maclean from *Crackerjack*. I also met Greek crooner Demis Roussos but he was a bit of a knob. I knocked on his dressing-room door and asked for his autograph, which he grudgingly scrawled in an illegible dribble of ink into my autograph book. To this day, if ever I sign an autograph, my internal monologue is singing 'Forever and Ever', to remind me to put some effort into it, lest anyone walk away, look at their spoils and think, 'What a knob.'

Anyway, in 1977, we clambered back into Richard's Opel Manta and set off for the famous house of wax. In 1995, I was fantasising about stepping out of my ESTB and striding across Wood Lane towards the awestruck little boy gawping at the building where they made *Doctor Who*. In 1983, I was sat in the auditorium of the Dominion, Tottenham Court Road, and as the lights dimmed, the curtains parted and the Twentieth Century Fox fanfare blasted from the circle of speakers, London's potential to amaze seemed boundless. It was a truly amazing experience and when the film came to an end, we left the theatre, dazed and thoroughly entertained. Paul has often recalled the moment he looked over to see if I was enjoying the film and witnessed my slack-jawed awe at the imperial speeder bikes, careening through the forest of Endor at breakneck speeds. I remember sensing Paul clocking my expression and nudging Fay in amusement. Rather than look back at them and break the moment, I continued to gawk at the screen, happily making a performance of my genuine wonder. This wasn't to show off or get attention, more my way of demonstrating to them how grateful I was that they had brought me there. Besides, it's not like I really had to act: the speeder-bike chase was and still is a hugely exhilarating sequence, pissing on anything else that came afterwards, helped along perhaps because I care(d) so much about the individuals riding the speeder bikes in the first place.

The effect of the film upon us was so strong that, even a full year later, Sean and I would cycle every morning the four and a half miles from his house in Little Whitcombe, up the same steep hill where I had been visually punished for fondling Meredith Catsanus's budding boobs, to my house in Upton St Leonards. We would then climb over the fence at the end of my garden into the small area of woodland that backed on to our house and play with our *Star Wars* figures, re-enacting the forest scenes from *Return of the Jedi* with a host of new characters and vehicles collected since the release of the film.

And then one day, 25 May to be precise, a friend of mine by the name of Chris Dixon was hit by a car while out running and was subsequently rushed to Frenchay Hospital in Bristol, where he remained unconscious for ten days. Chris lived in the same static-home park in Little Whitcombe, Gloucester, as Sean Jeffries and in truth was more Sean's friend than mine. There was even a slight antagonism between Chris and myself as we jostled for Sean's attention. I was Sean's best friend at school but at home, with the benefit of proximity, Chris and Sean became very close. Whenever I visited Sean at the weekends, Chris would join our fun and games, and though there was a proprietorial tension between us, we got on well most of the time. The thing that bonded Sean and me specifically was a love of *Star Wars*, which had started six years before and been maintained as the saga continued.

After Chris's accident, our sojourn to the woods became a way of keeping our minds off the battle Chris was fighting in Bristol against his injuries. Towards the end of the week, Sean pulled into my driveway on his racing bike as he always did and said, in a tone of voice I had never heard him use before, 'Chris is dead.' I had stepped out of the side door of the house to get something from the garage as Sean had arrived and now stood in my socks, staring at him blankly, trying to process the information he had just imparted.

His eyes were red, and although I didn't see him cry, I knew he had not long stopped. This in itself was alarming. I had never known Sean to cry, not even while being terrorised by sadistic bullies in the changing rooms at Gloucester Leisure Centre. Unable to truly comprehend the idea that someone so young, someone I knew, could have died, the idea that Sean had been crying seemed somehow more terrible. We walked numbly over to the large Safeway supermarket near my house and bought drinks and *Return of the Jedi* themed biscuits, then went back home to do what we always did. We played *Star Wars* in the woods behind my house. Perhaps not as vocally or even as enthusiastically as we normally would, but play it we did and it helped us enormously.

Escaping into that world which we so loved enabled us to cope, at least initially, with the shock of losing Chris. I hadn't been bereaved since the night Mum had interrupted *Fabulous Animals*, but this time the implications were so much more serious and shocking. I suddenly understood the dazed look of bewilderment on my mum's face that night as I felt it creep across my own, eight years later, as Sean delivered the news. That evening, lying on my bed, the tears came and I was able to articulate my grief freely; but for those first few hours in a world where I suddenly and shockingly found myself one friend down, I had coped in the only way I knew how: by going into my imagination where, in death, you simply disappear and become part of a greater world. I can still see Chris in my head, a robust young bruiser with a scruff of blond hair and an infectious, cheeky smile. I'm sure Sean can too.

7

'What are you doing 'ere?' whispered the Scarlet Panther throatily, a thin film of sweat glistening on her amazing knockers, as she lay in Pegg's muscular arms.

'I would have thought that was obvious,' quipped Pegg, his dwindling member resting on his lower chest.

The mysterious beauty (the Scarlet Panther) looked at the inert figure of Canterbury standing nearby, still wearing his burka. She frowned, a delightful wrinkle appearing between her eyes like the one Meg Ryan used to have.

'Are you sure ee cannot see us?' she asked suspiciously.

'If the virus you implanted to disable his early-warning sensors performed a temporary memory wipe, then he'll need time to recompile his storage platters. Trust me, he is in the robot equivalent of snoozetown, USA. He didn't see a thing.'

'Zhat's a relief,' smiled the Panther, arching an exquisitely plucked eyebrow. She was unspeakably beautiful. Tall and slender with alabaster skin and a shag of wavy copper hair. Born and raised in Paris, France, her American Ivy League education had not fully rid her of her Gallic purr. She was tough, tenacious and wily, but possessed an innate sophistication that hinted at a deep intelligence. Pegg always felt slightly hypnotised

by her perplexing charisma, feeling clumsy in her presence, forever cursing himself for saying things before
he had properly thought them through.

'Believe me,' said Pegg, 'if he had been watching us,
there's no way he wouldn't have achieved major droid wood.'

The Panther let his crude remark go with an admon-
ishing smirk that only made him blush with regret for
an instant.

'I'll repeat zee question,' she furtherised. 'What
are you doing 'ere?'

'Looking for you, of course,' said Pegg, 'although I
didn't have to look far. How on earth did you know I
was in Morocco?'

'Zee flag was up over zee riad,' stated the Panther
plainly.

'What?' coughed Pegg.

'Zee flag zhat lets everyone know zhat you are in.'
The Panther was finding it hard to conceal her amusement at Pegg's frustration.

'Damn it, Canterbury, I told you not to put it up!'
Pegg spat, jamming a fist into his palm.

'Eet has been up for months actually,' said the
Panther.

'Damn it, Canterbury, I told you to take it down!'
Pegg jammed the other fist into the other palm.

'I am teasing you,' purred the Panther, tracing a
fleeting white strip down the valley between Pegg's
diamond-hard pecs. 'I saw zee jet come in to land last
night. I 'appened to be taking tea at Ali Ben Hassan's
Old-Fashioned Tea Shop and Internet Cafe in the square,
when you arrived.

'It's supposed to be a stealth jet,' grumbled Pegg
through his teeth.

'Yes, but you put all those lights on zee side and painted "Pegg Jet" on the fuselage in reflective paint.'

Pegg cursed internally with a bob of his head and muttered something as his lips tightened into a sphincter of regret. He became lost in thought.

'Looks pretty good though, doesn't it?' Pegg eyed the Panther hopefully.

'Hell, yes,' she said in a comedy African American voice that wasn't racist. She smiled, sensing his moodiness dispersing. 'Why were you looking for me?'

'Oh, come on, Murielle,' Pegg said affectionately to his old lifeguarding colleague, for it was she from earlier. The two had chosen different sides of the moral highway after leaving Gloucester Leisure Centre and had been on a perpetual collision course ever since. 'I know you lifted the Star of Nefertiti from the Museum of Egyptian Antiquity in Cairo, with the express intention of selling it to the highest bidder.'

'Oo told you?' Murielle enquired, half furious, half impressed, half amused.

'Who do you think?' Pegg was enjoying having the upper hand.

'Needles!' It was Murielle's turn to jam her fist into her palm. 'Le petit twat!'

'I love it when you talk French,' chuckled Pegg, only to be met with an angry glance from his nemesis/fuck buddy.

'I knew I shouldn't have invited him over for zhat tour of zee local minarets.' Murielle cursed her decision to holiday with a known informant.

'He is a known informant,' said Pegg echoing her thoughts, 'and besides, if you hadn't, we would never have had all that amazing sex. Now let's return the diamond to its rightful place in Cairo, then get a suite at the Marriott Hotel and Omar Khayyam Casino and have some more —'

'Eet's too late,' said Murielle, already regretting selling on the Star of Nefertiti and, in doing so, missing out on at least a month of shagging and blackjack. 'I stole it to order, eet's already been delivered.'

'Who to?' urged Pegg, rising up on to his elbow to indicate urgency.

Murielle avoided Pegg's gaze; she seemed reluctant to divulge the identity of the buyer, although Pegg sensed this was more from regret than any misplaced loyalty to her employer. Pegg intensified his glare so that Murielle could almost feel it burning into her pale, flawless skin, which she clearly moisturised regularly.

'Lord Black,' she whispered shamefully.

'What?' Pegg leapt up, his body flexing with tension. Things had suddenly become very serious. He didn't even have a semi any more. 'Lord Black is a notorious criminal and nobleman, Murielle; I've lost count of the amount of times I've foiled his attempts to commit massive atrocities in the name of needless financial gain!'

'I know,' pleaded Murielle, 'but this was simply a case of interior design and zee fee ee offered me was really good considering the current economic climate. Eet was more than enough to keep my deaf brother Etienne at the Institut National de Jeunes Sourds de Paris.'

Murielle became unfocused momentarily as her thoughts drifted to her gifted, but sadly deaf younger brother, for whom she committed most of her non-violent crimes, thus giving her illegal activities a moral justification only intensified by the fact that she always made sure there was never a direct victim.

'Murielle, I need you to focus,' enforced Pegg, pulling her face towards his with a gentle yet firm insistence. 'What do you mean, interior design?'

Murielle shook her head several times, trying to clear her thoughts, her fiery red hair scattering across her swimmer's shoulders.

'Ee said ee was doing up his town house in Hendon. Ee was collecting artefacts to go round his pool and said zhat zee Star of Nefertiti would make a wonderful addition to ees collection.' Murielle frowned as she searched her memory.

'There's no way he's decorating that room with antiquities,' said Pegg emphatically. 'That pool's tiny! — I saw it in *OK!* — it would be way too cluttered.'

'Ee said it would go nicely with some of the stuff his great-uncle Barney left him in his will,' Murielle recalled. 'Ee did seem to have a few design ideas, even if eet wasn't for the pool area.'

'Oh, he had a design all right,' seethed Pegg, 'and if by Uncle Barney he means Colonel Barnabus McCartney, then his design is to hold the entire world to ransom by threatening to fire an ancient Egyptian laser beam into the sun.'

'Fuck er duck!' said Murielle.

'We have to get to Hendon and stop Black before he puts his plan into action,' said Pegg, punching a series of numbers into a wall-mounted control panel.

'I am sorry.' Murielle hung her head in shame, her hair forming a curtain across her coral-pink areolae, so that Pegg could no longer officially see her boobs. 'Eet's so hard to tell what ee's thinking due to the mask.' Lord Black famously insisted on wearing a mask, reminiscent of Doctor Doom from *The Fantastic Four*, despite having to settle out of court with Marvel for the privilege.

'Don't be sorry,' said Pegg, checking to see if he could see them from a different angle. 'You had no idea and I know your judgement is often clouded by your love for your deaf brother.'

'Not just my deaf brother,' she said honestly, lifting her head, much to Pegg's relief.

'We'll leave immediately,' said Pegg. 'It will take fifteen minutes for the jet to power up and perform its auto-check cycle — I've just activated it remotely via this pad I had installed last year.'

'What shall we do until zhen?' asked Murielle, noticing Pegg's penis had inflated and was rising into threat pose like a one-eyed pink cobra.

Pegg smiled and walked towards her slowly, wiggling his hips.

'Actually, I am on,' admitted Canterbury.

The Benefits of Failure

I owe most of my professional achievements to an earlier monumental cock-up: I failed my eleven-plus exam and as a result was unable to attend the local upmarket grammar school.

Instead, I attended Brockworth Comprehensive and set about the process that would eventually lead me to the heady show-business world of this glass office at the Random House Publishing building. It's close to London's fashionable Victoria and provides me with such luxuries as an electric fan, a chair and access to my editor, Ben who occasionally peers through the window at me to make sure I'm not using the Internet to masturbate or tweet, which are essentially the same thing.

However, I almost didn't make it to Brockworth Comprehensive. The Gloucestershire education board wanted to unload me into a secondary modern that didn't even allow its pupils to sit O levels and instead fobbed them off with CSEs, which weren't as difficult or as impressive on a CV. However, Mum was determined that I have the full spectrum of choice and fought a passionate stand-up battle with the local authority to get me into

Brockworth, despite my failure to get into the more auspicious Tommy Rich's Grammar School.

My stepdad had attended Tommy Rich's in Gloucester and it only seemed right that I should be given the same opportunity. I was a bright and lively pupil and what I lacked in mathematical acumen, I more than made up for in creative writing and general enthusiasm. My Class 6 teacher, Mr Miller, had told my mother that I was potentially a candidate for the auspicious Rendcomb College in Cirencester, a magical institution where kids levitated bricks and bent spoons with their minds, recognising that reality as they knew it was simply a construct of their own subconscious and as such could be manipulated beyond the basic laws of physics.

Actually, it probably just had posher teachers and better sports equipment, but it was cool to be considered worthy. Whether Mr Miller genuinely had faith in my academic ability or he just fancied my mum (all my teachers fancied my mum, even the female ones), I was accepted to Tommy Rich's on the proviso that I pass a single examination.

The eleven-plus exam was compulsory until the mid-seventies at which point it was used only to determine transfers from state primary schools into more selective secondary establishments, like Tommy Rich's. Previously it had been part of the old tripartite system of filtering children into secondary, comprehensive and grammar levels of education, and although this practice had been scrapped, it is exactly what happened to me. I was taken out of class one day and led to a small room off the assembly hall and given an hour to complete the test, which consisted of various exercises in verbal and non-verbal reasoning. There were lots of shapes and word games and the whole thing made my head spin. When I finished I had a sick feeling that I would not be receiving the racing bike I had been promised if I made it into Tommy Rich's, and that inclination was one of the only things I got correct that day.

When the results came in, my scores were so low that the education board recommended me for a school on the bottom rung of the tripartite ladder, whereas if I hadn't taken the test at all I would have automatically transferred to the school on the middle rung. My mum went bananas and went in to bat for me at the education authority. So it was, in September of 1981, I walked into the sports hall of Brockworth Comprehensive to join my friends from Castle Hill Primary, all of whom were somewhat surprised to see me, having assumed I would be starting my first day at Hogwarts or wherever the hell I was supposed to be going (as mentioned earlier, Warner Brothers did indeed use the interiors of Gloucester Cathedral for certain scenes in the Harry Potter movie, the same windy cloisters I walked down every day during my brief stint at the King's School, so technically I did go to Hogwarts for a while).

My time at Brockworth Comprehensive School was extremely important and formative in terms of my eventual career path. I appreciate that's a somewhat trite sentence – doesn't everybody's school career affect their career path? That's what it's for. What I mean is, I can pinpoint specific moments that contributed to my becoming a professional actor and comedy writer, which perhaps would not have occurred in the more staid, all-male environment of Tommy Rich's. Fate or not, I can't help feeling pleased that I failed that exam. I'm not a superstitious person but it's fair to say that my entire career as I know it now depended upon the outcome of that one little test. I would no doubt have had some kind of career but it would not have been this one. Chaos theory dictates that small events can have massive ramifications; the old flap of a butterfly wing leads to a storm in China, or as I prefer to see it: a gunner on an Imperial Star Destroyer decides not to shoot a tiny escape pod and consequently an entire regime remains impervious to the efforts of a rebellion, lacking the information necessary to bring down its ultimate weapon. Who's to say what I would have done if I had attended Tommy Rich's. I might have followed my early dreams of becoming a vet or a professional athlete.

Now, you most probably just spat your hot beverage all over the pages of this book in amused disbelief, but as a youngster I was an extremely fast runner. Unbeatable in fact. Even when I graduated into a more crowded and diverse secondary school, I continued to take the 100- and 200-metre titles for my year on sports day (apart from one occasion, when a slip early on in the race forced me to overexert in order to gain ground and I pulled a muscle in my groin). Perhaps in a more sports-orientated environment, surrounded by the peer pressure of teenage machismo, I would have eschewed the arts in favour of the track and remained friends with Matthew Bunting.

Whatever path I had taken it would not have been this one and this one has given me so much. Not just in terms of the friends I have made and the experiences I have had. If I had passed that exam I would never have met Nick Frost or Edgar Wright, let alone the mother of my beautiful daughter. Those relationships and the product of those interactions were, for my part at least, determined entirely by my ability, or rather inability, to take one letter from one word and add it to another word to make two new words. Maybe I'm wrong; I might not believe in fate but I do believe in causality and who's to say fate isn't just a sort of social mathematics that brings like-minded people together. I have a theory about this, which I'll get into later. For now, let's stay in childhood and the decade that taste forgot: the 1980s.

At the age of eleven, I entered Brockworth Comprehensive, slightly shame-faced that I hadn't made it into the clever boys' school, and as well as my snazzy new briefcase (which I quickly swapped for a more generic sports bag due to cloakroom ridicule), I carried the baggage of having something to prove with me into the sports hall that morning in September 1981. My boundless enthusiasm to please drove me to volunteer for every single task my new form tutor, Mr Calway, threw out to the class. My hand would shoot into the air if someone was required to fetch the register or relay a message to another teacher. I'm sure my other classmates, even the ones I knew from Castle Hill, a few of whom had joined me in 1 Coopers, thought I was trying a little too hard.

The school was divided into five houses, Gryffindor, Slytherin . . . no, wait, it was Coopers, Painswick, Birdlip, Leckhampton and Crickley, all hills that surrounded and enclosed the valley in which Gloucester was situated. During World War II, Gloucester had escaped the severe bombing of dockland cities due to its ability to disappear in the dark. When the German bombers were detected and the lights went out, the city vanished into the darkness of the valley, making it a difficult target. Consequently, whereas the docks of Liverpool and Bristol sustained heavy damage during the war years, Gloucester's remained intact and operative. The lack of modernisation in the post-war era meant that Gloucester Docks were the go-to location for TV companies producing maritime period dramas. The BBC's long-running nineteenth-century shipping drama, *The Onedin Line*, although set in Liverpool, was filmed on location in Gloucester and called upon many members of the GODS to be extras, including Richard Pegg. In 1982 a mass casting call went out to the company for extras to fill out the background of a German film production. The entire Pegg clan, with the exception of my sister Katy who was only three years old, made the trip down to the docks and dressed up in Edwardian period costume to spend the day as biological scenery. This was effectively my first film. I played the part of a young German boy at the back of the shot. It wasn't a massive stretch for me. I've never seen it, in fact I can't even remember what it was called.

It's not listed on my Internet Movie Database Page either, but I am positive that it happened. I distinctly recall my costume fitting, in a makeshift wardrobe room in one of the empty warehouses down at the waterside. The seemingly endless racks of musty period costumes being distributed among the excited amdrammers, my mum being delighted at getting the prettiest dress. What with the free lunch and the twenty-pound note I received at the end of the day, I made a mental note to try and be in a film again some time.

Back in Mr Calway's classroom, that initial burst of eagerness sustained me for quite some time, despite David Kyle making a 'swot' gesture at me by thrumming his nose as I returned from completing my fifth voluntary chore in one day. I told my joke in front of the class every Monday morning and learned my first lesson about social responsibility from Mr Calway after delivering one of Jim Davidson's Chalky routines, and, towards the end of the year, performed my first self-penned stand-up comedy set to the rest of the school to varying degrees of success.

Before the teachers' strike put paid to any extra-curricular activity, the pupils of Brockworth Comprehensive were treated to two outward-bound excursions in their first and third years at the school. The first-year trip was to youth hostel in Welsh Bicknor, the third-year one was to a campsite called Biblins in the Wye Valley. We never made it to Biblins due to industrial action and boy, were we bummed! Bummed in the American sense of course, although rumour had it, a boy was bummed in the British sense by a loony in the woods at Biblins. On reflection, I am certain that story was as apocryphal as the ones about the kid who had his balls crushed in a vice or the boy in the fifth-year who had two cocks.

The teachers' strike became such an annoyance to the students of Brockworth Comprehensive (due mainly to us having to remain outside in the cold during breaks) that the pupils themselves decided to strike. One lunchtime, during a particularly snowy winter, a rumour went round the school that we were not going to return to lessons after break in protest at staff action. Sure enough, when the bell rang, a sizeable chunk of the school population remained on the tennis courts to some amusement from the staff. News of the demo spread to neighbouring schools and soon copycat protests were playing out across the area.

By day two, the local news companies were on the scene. However, by this time, a deep schism had split the protesters down the middle. The problem was mainly one of credibility, due to the ringleaders of the strike being those pupils least likely to take any interest in school whatsoever. The most disruptive, delinquent and apathetic pupils became suddenly politicised and passionate about student welfare, simply because it enabled then to legitimately skive.

It was hard to present a tenable manifesto to the staff and media when our main spokesperson was a notable glue sniffer and cat murderer. By the time the local correspondents started interviewing the children involved, the Brockworth Pupils' Front had spawned a breakaway front, the sceptical and less militant Pupils' Front of Brockworth, a group of students who agreed with the fundamental tenets of the original action but were quite cold, didn't want to get into trouble and, if they were honest with themselves, wanted to get on with lessons because exams were coming up.

I was in the latter camp and admitted as much when the regional news show, *Points West*, interviewed me outside the school gates. Unfortunately, my blistering polemics were deemed too controversial for teatime television and instead they went with the more measured comments given by Mark Simpson, the boy standing next to me. Nevertheless, that evening I appeared on television for the very first time; not all of me, about 50 per cent if I remember correctly; but it was enough to qualify as an appearance – you can see my face just before I look sullenly at my eighties slip-on shoes and white socks, allowing my dirty-blond hair to fall into my eyes in case any girls were watching. By the time the ringleaders had nobly marched the four and a half miles to lay their protest at the Gloucestershire County Council building, securing another day away from the classrooms all in the name of fairness, everyone else was back indoors. It was quite exciting, although nowhere near as exciting as a camping trip to Biblins would have been, bummers in the woods or not.

Welsh Bicknor was intended as a bonding experience for the first-years at Brockworth Comprehensive. The school was a nexus for a number of junior schools in south-east Gloucester and the classes were only sporadically populated with familiar faces. So, in an effort to integrate us, we were taken away from the comfort of our families and delivered to a sort of manor house in the countryside, supervised by a couple of teachers and a number of sixth-form girls, one of whom I fell hopelessly in love with.

Laura was blonde and buxom and won my affection by holding my hand as we hiked to a place called Symonds Yat. She can't have been older than sixteen but to me she seemed like a woman. She smelled fantastic and there was something exotic about her big chunky jumper, tight jeans and pixie boots. I stayed by her side for the entire trip and became her devoted fan.

As part of the last-night celebrations at Welsh Bicknor, the students put on a cabaret, a mixed bag of songs and poems and sketches. To impress Laura, I decided to draw on my experiences as a racist comic at the Salvation Army and class entertainer back at school, performing a stand-up comedy routine comprising observational material I had written myself. It was a concept I didn't entirely understand, assuming the trick was simply to mention things that the audience could relate to. The jokes were mainly about children's television programmes and relied on members of the audience being familiar enough with them to find the memory of them funny. For instance . . .

Do you remember *The Wombles*? They were pretty funny, weren't they?

It didn't occur to me to make any particular funny observations about them to qualify the set-up. Not quite grasping the notion of observational comedy at this point, I neglected the crucial process of developing a comic take on familiar reference. I didn't use the touchstone of well-loved children's entertainment to launch into an amusing analysis of sexual politics beneath Wimbledon Common then segue into some topical stuff about the difficulties of puberty. I'm sure the question of which Womble Madame Cholet was sleeping with would have brought the house down with the kids and teachers alike. Of course, what I should have done is step out in front of the assembled throng, lit a cigarette and said . . .

Do you remember *The Wombles*? They were funny, weren't they? Which one do you think was fucking Madame Cholet? Anybody? I mean, I'm just going by personal appearance here but surely Tomsk has got the biggest penis. He's all muscles and confidence, isn't he? Sure he's a little slow but then what does that matter when you're packing trouser grams. Am I right, ladies?

Mind you, as an unintelligent bodybuilder, chances are he's using anabolic steroids, in which case (wiggles little finger) knob tax!

Could be Tobermory, I suppose. He has a porn-star moustache and a backless apron. He does seem to put a lot of his energy into making stuff, though. Maybe he lost his balls in a workshop accident involving a lathe and a tin can.

It sure as shit isn't Great Uncle Bulgaria; I mean, he was

probably an absolute fuck machine in his day but the dude is never out of his slippers.

I don't think it can be Bungo because no one gets laid wearing tweed and it definitely isn't Orinoco because he is clearly gay. Come on, the big hat, the way he wears his scarf over the shoulder, just off the neck? He has way too much style to be straight.

Which means it can only be Wellington. Who'd have thought that little pipsqueak would be capable of boning such a hot French chick? I'm amazed. Actually, I'm not, it's always the nerdy-looking guy who whips his pants off in the changing rooms to reveal what appears to be a German sausage in a bird's nest. I see it all the time in the showers after rugby. One week the guy next to you is a fly half, a week later he's a prop forward. Not that I'm looking . . . oh, who am I kidding? Of course I'm looking. It's like a vintage-car rally in the boys' changing room. Everyone's checking out each other's junk and pretending not to be impressed.

It just seems to me the change happens so quickly. But when? I'd like to know, because right now mine still looks like something you'd find on top of a seafood cocktail (close your ears, Laura). Do you wake up in the morning like David Banner in the woods, to discover your shredded pants next to you? I mean, puberty's insane, isn't it? Am I right, guys? Girls, I can't speak for you, I've never even seen a vagina. Well, I have but it was about five years ago and I don't really want to get into that now. Which is coincidentally what I said at the time . . .

What I mean is, I don't get to see what goes on in the girls' changing room. Not since they blocked up that hole in the boiler-room wall. I'm kidding, I'm kidding . . . It's still there!

Waiting for puberty is like waiting for the postman to bring you something fun. Every morning you leap out of bed and check if it's there, only to be disappointed. Difference is, it's not the *Incredible Hulk Weekly* you're waiting for, it's body hair, a deeper voice and a hairy little monster, and no, I'm not still talking about the Wombles.

You've been a great audience, thanks so much for listening, we've got a great show lined up for you this afternoon. Next up, Erica and Meredith will be singing 'Frère Jacques'.

I've been Simon Pegg, thanks for listening . . . goodnight!

Mr Calway would have removed me from the makeshift stage and exacted swift justice before I'd even got into the stuff about Tomsk's tiny cock, and he read the *Guardian* (Mr Calway, not Tomsk. Tomsk would probably have read a tabloid. I should tour this stuff round schools, it's golden!).

Despite the lack of any substance, my nostalgia routine played well with my peers, probably due to the cocksure delivery and the fact that the mere mention of Wombles brings a smile to anyone's face. In fact, we were so pleased with our little revue, we decided to transfer it to the sports hall where it would be performed for the rest of the school.

The Monday after we returned from the wilds of Welsh Bicknor, all bonded and different as if from combat, the school assembled in two shifts to witness our variety show. First up were the second- and third-years (or Years 8 and 9 as I believe they are called now). This was what comics often refer to as a 'tough crowd'. The second-years had just advanced into a position of power, having spent an entire year as the most vulnerable and disrespected group in the school's social infrastructure. It's the way of every school and no doubt always will be. No longer the weakest in (micro)society, the newly promoted second-years, empowered by their status, replicate the disdain heaped upon them as first-years and inflict it on those who have replaced them.

This would actually later backfire on me in a karmic fashion once I had made it to the heady heights of the second-year, when I selected the wrong whelp to push around in the corridor. While lined up outside a classroom, a caterpillar of sheepish-looking first-years filed past us, clearly worried and uncomfortable, much to our smug, old-hand amusement. I singled out one skinny little candidate and shoved him against the wall as he shuffled past. He resisted me slightly, which I didn't expect. First-years were supposed to automatically kowtow to their superiors – it was the law of the blackboard jungle and resistance was rare. I laughed it off and just about hung on to my dignity as my victim stalked away, scowling.

Over the next few years, puberty hit this boy like a freight train. He literally doubled in size, and not just in terms of height. A time-lapse film of his physical development over just twelve months would have been a ghastly spectacle, reminiscent of Jekyll and Hyde. He became muscular, almost misshapen, and sprouted so much hair, it looked as though he had been covered in glue and rolled in the dog basket. Even more worryingly, he grew in status. He became one of the hardest boys in the school.

It was only a matter of time before my former victim decided to act out his revenge on his one-time tormentor. It started quietly enough in the corridors between lessons, where he would often go out of his way to shoulder me into the wall, pretending he hadn't seen me but making it very obvious that it had been intentional. His recollection of my unprovoked shove had not been lost amid the swelling folds of his brain as I had hoped. I was clearly being dished up a revenge that, after three years, was still being served ice cold.

The shoves soon became more and more frequent and I began to plan my passage between classrooms specifically to avoid him. In the end, he exacted his final vengeance under the fabricated pretext that I was hanging around with his girlfriend. It's true, I was friendly with the older girl he was dating, but there was nothing going on. I had hoped her friendship might have eased the tension between Bigfoot and me, but in the end it was used as an excuse for violence.

I was sat in the cloak bay at lunchtime with a couple of friends when he rounded the corner, immediately cutting off my escape from the cul-de-sac of hooks in which I had trapped myself. He asked me if I had been having it away with his missus, to which I responded in a panicky negative. He then walloped me, rebounding my skull off the wall behind me. I remember feeling a vague sense of disappointment that he had initiated his assault with such a flimsy accusation, even as his fist slammed into my forehead. A furtive little henchman encouraged his boss to finish me off, but the big kid said it was pointless because I wouldn't fight back. He was absolutely right, there was no way I was going to enter into physical combat with this behemoth – it would have been suicide.

I'd only had one fight before and that was when I was nine, with the boy who turned out to be my second cousin, and it had thoroughly traumatised me. I had called him out after a dispute over a game of rounders and met him on 'the green' after school. During the scrappy struggle, it occurred to me that we weren't just trading blows in some noble pugilistic ceremony, this boy was actually trying to hurt me, any way he could. My eyes filled with tears at the sudden horror of it all and I called a halt to proceedings, conceding defeat.

He was tougher than me, from a more physically oppressive background (his mother had once punched the headmaster), so he was more equipped to deal with the situation, although I think he was as relieved as me to see the skirmish end. Four years later, there was no way I was about to reprise the experience with somebody twice my size, so my long-time persecutor stalked off scowling, leaving me humiliated but relieved that it was over. He met me outside a classroom later that afternoon and asked if I was going to report him. I mustered up courage enough to say 'no', even managing to add a grumpy disdain, although in truth I just wanted the trouble to end.

A few months later he got into an altercation with Martin (the other school nutter) about who was the hardest in the school and found himself on the end of a punch so forceful, it dislodged his eyeball. I experienced only a glimmer of *Schadenfreude*. Eventually, relations between us thawed, although we never became friends. I was walking towards the sports hall in my fifth year and felt a hockey stick slide between my legs, threatening to pull back against my plums. I spun round with a tremendous 'fuck off' and found myself face to face with my old enemy. He laughed and didn't take offence. By the time I left Brockworth Comprehensive, we had even exchanged semi cordialities, something of a relief, since the threat of his physical presence had never fully gone away.

Anyhow, I had all this to come as I stood before the daunting audience of second- and third-years about to deliver my children's TV routine that had had them rolling in the aisles at Welsh Bicknor. The routine was met with a bemused silence from the audience who regarded me as if I was nuts. The biggest laugh I got was when I panicked and activated my new digital watch so that 'Scotland the Brave' rang out from behind my back, signalling it was time for me to leave the stage.

Only slightly disheartened, I stepped out before an even more intimidating audience of fourth- and fifth-year students but luckily found them to be far more appreciative. The social gulf between us was such that I appeared small and cute and eligible for the sort of affectionate patronising that children are so quick to level at their juniors. Their appreciation spurred me on and the performance went really well – I even improvised a little and scored extra laughs. As a result I found an 'in' with a group of fourth-year boys for whom I became a sort of humorous pet.

I would find them at their hang-out spot during lunch break

and make them laugh with various impressions and silly improvisations. One of them in particular seemed to relish our comic sparring sessions and would set me up and encourage me. He became a friend who I later missed; he seemed to get me, where the others just found me a bit weird and annoying.

The faint disdain I had experienced from the second- and third-years stayed with me for a while. I decided to reinvent myself as a cool, stand-offish type who didn't get involved in school drama productions and pushed younger kids around in corridors, a decision I eventually regretted on both counts. The annual school production rolled around a few months into my first year at Brockworth and, rather than sign up, I decided to contemptuously dismiss it as the stuff of poofters and girls and hang out with other boys for whom disdain was a badge of honour. Lee Beard didn't. Lee had finally shaken off his Perthes' and burst from his calipers like Forrest Gump, becoming one of the most enthusiastic and active boys in the school.

Lee and I had been separated by the house system at Brockworth Comp and didn't hang out as much as we used to. I had retained Sean Jeffries and a few other boys from Castle Hill in the sorting and made new friends who had come from other schools in the area, like Nick May, who eventually became my best friend after we had both left Brockworth behind, and Darius Pocha, a curiously androgynous, highly intelligent boy who professed to being bisexual and was given to rampant fantasism. Darius and I had bonded over a love of cinema at Welsh Bicknor and it wasn't until a few years later that I realised he hadn't seen half the films he had claimed to have seen. He did, however, elaborately reinvent the plot lines of films such as *Mad Max* and *Mad Max 2*, piecing together details he had read from various magazines and the back of VHS boxes. I seem to recall being suspicious of his knowledge and matching him with a made-up film of my own, which featured a werewolf squashing a human eyeball between finger and thumb. I thought it sounded pretty cool.

In our third year, Darius sombrely informed me that he had a month to live, having swallowed some toxic waste which was slowly poisoning him. It sounds outlandish but I'd actually been with him at the time. We were playing near my home on one of those legendary rope swings that inhabit almost every young boy's childhood. The rope was originally suspended by some brave soul on a thick branch, ten or so feet above a brook, in an area referred to by the local children as 'the bunker'. The area was so called because of a large brick structure, with sealed iron doors, engaged in some purpose that remained ever a mystery to us. A thick concrete wall extended from its side, tall enough to step on to from one side, a sheer drop to the brook on the other. The rope hung just within reach where the wall crumbled away down the bank, so that a swinger could launch himself off at speed into a fifty-foot arc, with the option of letting go at three points of differing difficulty. The buzz was particularly keen when the waters of the brook rose and churned with great force after a heavy rainfall, and it was on one such occasion that Darius fell off.

It happened in the sort of slo-mo with which one can so often recall misfortune. It is similar to the acute presence of mind that slows time during the actual event; allowing you to comprehend what is about to happen, to brace for impact, to duck, to reach out. Unfortunately, I was unable to help for two good reasons. Firstly, I was on the opposite bank to Darius so there was simply nothing I could do, and secondly, I was laughing my arse off.

Now, I wouldn't say Darius was dyspraxic at that age, but he was definitely very gangly. He had that teenage physicality of someone not entirely adept at inhabiting his own shape. As if put in charge of a vehicle he wasn't qualified to drive, Darius was plainly still getting used to his new, taller, fuller form and did not yet have all the controls down pat. He let go of the rope at the most treacherous point, where only seasoned swingers were able to negotiate the awkward drop on to the small bank. Inevitably, he landed badly and, with an expression of extraordinary concern, toppled into the brook, disappearing beneath the swirling currents. I was spastic with laughter on the other bank; doubled up with helplessness.

I wanted to assist in his rescue, I genuinely did, but I was worried that if I uncrossed my legs I would wet myself. He surfaced almost immediately, gasping for air, and scrambled up on to the bank. Meanwhile, I was still rolling around on the floor in fits of hysterical giggles, my throat hoarse, my vision blurred by tears. It was by far the funniest thing I had seen since Mr Miller fartsploded the table in Class 5, and I felt awful. I actually kicked myself, physically drove one foot into the side of the other leg to try and curb my mirth in the face of Darius's misfortune.

Later that day, having got Darius dried, dressed in some ill-fitting clothing and sent home, I cried, unable to contain my guilt at finding my friend's misfortune so funny. I felt genuine and heartfelt remorse and in retrospect could not locate the 'funny' in his extreme panic and discomfort. A few weeks later Darius summoned myself and Nick May into the boys' toilets and delivered the news of his impending death. He told us that the water he had ingested as a result of his fall had contained a number of lethal toxic chemicals that were to be his undoing.

A month passed and Darius remained chipper, and for some reason we never asked why he wasn't dead. He still remains chipper as far as I know. I'm sure he contracted some sort of parasite or stomach upset, the possible conclusion of which may have been terminal, in the same way that flu or asthma are terminal, but I don't think his life was ever really in any danger.

Given to the occasional Walter Mittyesque tales, I'm pretty sure
Darius was just exacting revenge on me for the humiliation he
felt in the face of my cackling hysteria, and I don't blame him.
We remained close until I left school. He was excellent company,
and a shared love of modern music nourished our friendship
through hours of sitting in his bedroom reading *Smash Hits* and
playing his Casio VL-Tone keyboard.

He possessed an acute natural intelligence, which informed
his undeniable wit and inspired me to try and match him. He
wrote the word 'coitus' in biro on the wall next to his desk as a
sly dig at the crass graffiti that adorned the desks, walls and text-
books, and in a moment of uncharacteristic laddishness had once
impressed me no end with this exchange with an attractive female
teacher, attempting to shoo us out of the cloak bays.

Attractive Teacher: Can I have you outside please?
Darius: You can have me anywhere you like, Miss.

Crude, I know, but he was thirteen and political correctness was
barely even fashionable in the early eighties, let alone common
practice. It was the speed at which he processed the comeback
that impressed me. Also, and importantly, it was Darius who
introduced me to the comic *2000 AD*, for which I will always
love him.

So it was that I developed new friendships away from those
I had cultivated at junior school, and although Lee Beard and I
would end up being friends into our forties, I didn't see him
much that first year. I heard about him though. Lee, being the
outgoing and confident young boy that he was, had auditioned
for the school play in our first year and won the part of a band
conductor, which he apparently performed to much appreciation all round. Lee's glory pricked at the impulses I had attempted
to suppress with my reinvented cool and I resolved to give apathy

the heave-ho and audition for the next production. This turned out to be in the inter-house drama competition, which was an annual event, pitting house against house in a one-act-play festival, staged over the course of a school day and adjudicated by a local luminary.

Coopers' effort that year was a reworking of the Greek myth concerning Telemachus and his search for a family. A third-year boy called Wayne (who eventually became known for being able to execute a particularly difficult break-dancing move called the helicopter) played the eponymous hero. The story revolved around a young man on a quest, trying out various possible families along the way. I played one of the parental suitors, a sort of upper-class military type with a comically plummy voice. The role required me to wear a fake moustache, which I ended up having to hold on with my finger when the spirit gum I had borrowed from my mum's theatrical make-up kit proved ineffective.

The character got a laugh and I had fun with the role, but when the adjudicator made his comments at the end of the competition, he focused on the failure of my moustache to remain on my face rather than on my efforts as an actor, which was hardly constructive, I mean, come on, tell it to Screen Face.[12] Nevertheless, it was a heady time for me, and the thrill of the extra-curricular activity was made all the more intense by the presence of my sixth-form crush, Laura Bot, who as luck would have it was playing my wife.

There was something so exhilarating about hanging out with my fellow pupils in the dining halls, getting ready to perform. The buzz was palpable and the usual barriers that separate the year groups, creating the traditional social hierarchies, were nonexistent. Theatrical types often wax lyrical about the familial

[12] Popular manufacturer of spirit gum etc.

nature of theatre but there's definitely something in that hack-neyed gush. Even the hard kids who had opted for the drama competition as a skive became approachable, almost affectionate, as we pulled together in the name of our designated local hill. Just to be hanging out with Laura again was reason enough to participate for me. She had vanished back into the impenetrable sixth-form block on our return from Welsh Bicknor and I only saw her now and again, between lessons or during breaks, when sometimes she would blow me heart-stopping kisses or admin-ister sweet-smelling hugs. To her I was the little first-year boy/puppy who offered her limitless adoration and loyalty; to me she was a woman, an exotic goddess to be worshipped and desired. That is, until she did something that shattered my opinion of her forever and gave me a sensation I understood to be some-thing like heartbreak.

After the competition was complete, the entrants were given the opportunity to perform their plays in the evening to an audi-ence of parents. This involved the hugely exciting process of returning to school after hours and hanging out in the brightly lit dining halls, waiting to perform in an atmosphere even more exciting than the competition. This felt like proper grown-up theatre and there was something infinitely thrilling about coming to school in the dark, out of uniform. The play went down well, a feeling of achievement made sweeter by the fact that we had come first in the competition despite my rubbish tash, and as we bundled back into the dining hall after our curtain call, the euphoria was total and my good mood indestructible. That is, until I saw Laura produce a packet of Silk Cut cigarettes from her coat and place one in her mouth. I don't think I would have felt any less betrayed if I had seen her kissing the headmaster. If anything, that would not have been nearly as bad since I had no illusions about actually having some kind of relationship with Laura; it was a crush. Nevertheless, to see her smoking sent her tumbling from the pedestal I had placed her on and I never felt the same way about her again. I had oddly high standards for a twelve-year-old.

The next production I participated in was *Tom Sawyer*, which further cemented my passion for acting and proved an even more thrilling experience than the house drama contest, not least because of my new crush on Libby 'Aunt Polly' Cox. This was a lead role in a large-scale production, staged not in the makeshift studio theatre of the dining hall but in the cavernous interior of the sports hall for three whole nights. It proved to be enormous fun and ended with an unforgettable after-show party at which I drank half a cup of cider and thought I was drunk. The imaginary high gave me the audacity to persuade Libby Cox into giving me a reluctant peck on the cheek, which I regarded as a massive victory. This acting business was just becoming more and more fun.

The following year we staged a revue show instead of the usual dramatic production, due to it being less labour-intensive for the staff who had begun their strike. My contribution to the show was to be part of a robotics display, which I performed with Darius and a boy called Glenn. We painted our faces white and our lips black, wore baseball caps, wrap-around shades and wore our shirts backwards in order to look futuristic. Thinking about it, Darius eschewed the backwards shirt trick and wore an 'envelope' shirt he'd bought from a fashionable boutique (he was the only boy I ever knew to own a jumpsuit who wasn't in the air force).

Glenn chose to be double different and painted his face gold as well as pinning a circuit board to his chest for extra roboticness. Glenn was a late addition to our planned display, having finagled his way into our clique by doing a passable moonwalk in the dining hall. It wasn't as impressive as the one I had seen a New York street kid do on *John Craven's Newsround*, but he presented it with such confidence and pride, Darius and I couldn't really say no. I remember looking at my fellow robotics expert after Glenn had tiptoed backwards on his kung-fu slippers and seeing my 'What the fuck was that?' reflected back at me in his eyes.

Nevertheless, Glenn joined us onstage as we moved our bodies in a mannered jerky fashion to Shannon's 'Let the Music Play'. I still get a tingle of nerves if I hear the hissing rat-a-tat of the intro on the radio. I am instantly transported back to the echoing sports hall, the smell of white panstick and the ache in my arms from attempting to do my buttons up behind my back.

After the robotics,[13] there were no more big productions during my time at Brockworth. The inter-house drama competition

---

[13] My love of robotic dancing eventually gave way to an interest in body-popping and break-dancing, after a item on *John Craven's Newsround* left me gobsmacked by this new wave of urban street dancers who took the jerky movements of the robot dance to all-new levels of mesmerising fluidity. It wasn't long before this dazzling means of easing tension in the American inner cities reached the lanes of Upton St Leonards, and although we perhaps lacked the tensions of habitu-alised gang culture, we did have a few spare bits of linoleum and a couple of 'ghetto blasters' between us. I spent many an evening down at Safeway car park, spinning on my back and rocking my body to whatever breakbeats we could record off the radio. We even formed a posse called the Galaxians, which consisted of me (Retroshock) and Sean Jeffries's older brother Gavin's best mate and fellow *Star Wars* nut, John Guy (Gizmo), who would occasionally throw down in the dining hall at lunchtime but mainly just sit around at John's house during lunch breaks, watching the brilliant *Arena* documentary 'Beat This' from 1984, then attempt to do the 'helicopter' in John's dining room where there was a small area of floor space. I buried my skills as a body-popper as I went through the intense goth period of my late teens during which I was much happier spending my leisure time listening to Sisters of Mercy and searching for the perfect leather jacket from the Oasis Centre in Birmingham. Eventually, as I realised that aligning myself with one subculture at a time was unrealistic (and when it became sort of cool again), I re-embraced my childhood dance skills and put them to use at work. My signature move, an arm wave, kicking off a double body wave, termi-nating with a reverse wave through the other arm and developing into a three-point float, can be witnessed frequently throughout my work, including the sketch show *Big Train*, *Spaced*, *Shaun of the Dead* and an appearance on the American chat show *Jimmy Kimmel Live*. I really need to get a new routine.

continued sporadically, although I actually wrote a play for my final year there, a loose pastiche of *E.T. The Extra-Terrestrial* called *G.J. Three Million Light Years From Home*. The G.J. of the title was an alien called Gunky Jam who visits Earth and is befriended by a young boy. *E.T.* had an enormous effect on me as a kid and temporarily eclipsed *Star Wars* in the gap between *The Empire Strikes Back* and *Return of the Jedi*. I had heard of the film from my stepdad, a regular viewer of Barry Norman's film programme, which ran an item on the huge fuss about the movie in the States. We were on holiday in Devon when he started talking about how the film was by the same man who had directed *Raiders of the Lost Ark* and how people were getting as excited about it as they had done about *Star Wars* five years before. We were walking from the lighthouse at Start Point at the time. It's funny how I can remember that and yet struggle to remember what I had for breakfast yesterday. I guess it has to do with emotional significance. (That or early onset dementia.)

When the film was released, I went to the ABC to watch it on my own and pulled the hood of my parka up towards the end as the tears began to flow. It was during that first viewing of *E.T.* that I experienced a little epiphany of understanding about the potential for interaction in art, which I have often used to justify some of my own decisions. There is a moment when E.T. is out and about on Halloween, dressed as a ghost, and spies a small child dressed as Yoda from *The Empire Strikes Back*. As E.T. spots this apparently kindred spirit, he lifts his arms in greeting and cries 'Home'. In scoring the moment, John Williams uses a phrase from Yoda's theme from *The Empire Strikes Back*, creating a moment for viewers to make a connection for themselves. I got it immediately, having listened to that particular soundtrack over and over again, and found myself looking around at my fellow audience members to see if they had spotted it too.

What thrilled me about the moment was that it wasn't

telegraphed and explained. It was there to be discovered. It credited me, the audience, with the intelligence to join the dots and I felt privileged and trusted by the film-makers, and was suddenly possessed by an urge to let them know, to tell them that the device succeeded and that I'd got it.

A more cynical commentator might dismiss the moment as a shameless exercise in brand sharing, but I happen to think it was more affectionate than product placement. Years later, George Lucas secreted a delegation of E.T.s amid his galactic senate in *The Phantom Menace*, confirming that E.T. had indeed witnessed a familiar face that Halloween night, although the moment felt somehow less magical. Perhaps it was the context. Back in the early eighties, I found the moment thrilling and never forgot the sense of communication I felt between the film and my twelve-year-old self. It taught me that the viewing experience could be made even more fun with the addition of interaction. This collaborative approach was something I would use a lot in my work, particularly in *Spaced*, which often relied heavily on the audience's cultural awareness to get all the jokes. I never forgot the sense of empowerment I experienced in that cinema, like someone had thrown me a ball which I had not only caught but thrown back.

G.J. Three Million Light Years From Home was never staged at Brockworth, due to industrial action, and eventually got lost amid a mass of paper I destroyed in celebration of leaving my comprehensive education behind. I'd be interested to read it now. I remember G.J. had a robotic arm and a Mohican haircut, looking more like a refugee from a *Mad Max* film than a cute little alien, but then this was 1985 and *Beyond Thunderdome* had just been released and I'd been slightly obsessed with that particular film series since Darius Pocha had embellished it into oblivion at Welsh Bicknor. It is most certainly the case that my time at Brockworth Comprehensive encouraged an interest in writing as much as it did in acting, and in my first few years at the school that was entirely down to the efforts of one amazing teacher called Mrs Taylor.

Mrs Taylor was one of those teachers who seemed born to do the job. She had the capacity to make any pupil, no matter how reluctant, want to work for her and she did this without ever really raising her voice. Her method was a simple and irresistible wave of positive reinforcement, which made her impossible not to love. The scariest, most dangerous pupils in the school became sweet-natured and attentive in her presence, and her lessons were always the highlight of any day.

She was attractive and mercurial and a cloud of grey hair seemed to have arrived prematurely on top of her head. Her comments in the margins of stories and projects were always emphatically positive; even when she was offering constructive criticism they sat there happily emblazoned in bright red pen. She would add positive comments throughout, rather than reserve her opinion for the end, and she would congratulate the smallest flourishes in your creative writing with ticks and stars.

Looking through a project on the movies I completed for her in 1983, there are frequent examples of her technique. She compliments artwork with superlatives, but then adds a recommendation to draw on plain paper, as it will look even better. After a short chapter on censorship and some hilariously hypocritical moralising on the subject of pornographic films which, I write, will 'soon hopefully be banned', she added the question 'Have you seen any?', challenging my preconceptions even on such a sensitive subject and no doubt sensing my decision to somewhat toe the PTA party line, rather than formulate my own opinion.

Concluding a protracted chapter about *Star Wars* (the real reason for me starting the project in the first place), I wrote the words 'May the force be with you', under which she added the rejoinder, 'And to you, brother.' At the end of this lovingly crafted piece of coursework, which came bound and illustrated, I had left a page with the word 'Comment' written at the top, on to which she wrote the following, in her usual scarlet ink:

A+

Another outstanding piece of work, Simon. Very interesting indeed and fascinating to look at. You certainly have a good eye for visual detail. This kind of book could go on and on. How about continuing it? One day you may use it in some form, when you go *into print* that is. Others have published far less interesting and absorbing material. You could capture the 'teeny boppers' market. Well done, Simon. Colour would add a new dimension, though I do like your black-and-white effect.

There was never a homework assignment more exciting than a creative-writing piece for Mrs Taylor, knowing that every flourish of the imagination or descriptive metaphor would be picked up on and noted in the margin. A somewhat significant story I remember getting good marks for was written in the same year as my 'Movies' project and concerned a simmering obsession of mine at the time: zombies.

Zombies

B
ack in 1983 and technically a zombie virgin, I was nevertheless able to write a zombie story for Mrs Taylor, pieced
together from stuff I'd read and heard, long before I
became an authority on the subject.

The story concerned a young boy who awoke one morning to
discover the world had been overrun by the living dead. Realising
he is the sole survivor of the outbreak, he attempts to escape
from the bloodthirsty ghouls by running up a local hill, where
he falls through the ground to find himself in a forgotten muni-
tions dump.

This might sound far-fetched, but there were several military
installations on the hills around Gloucester, left over from
World War II. On our frequent walks to Brockworth, over Nut
Hill, we would pass an old air-raid shelter and anti-aircraft gun
mount. Drawing on Robert Westall's famous children's novel *The
Machine Gunners*, the story of a group of wartime kids who take
possession of a German machine gun, the hero of my story finds
a similar weapon among the forgotten ordnance and uses it against
the zombie horde who have followed him up the hill (at a slow,
stumbling pace). Part of the appeal to me as a kid was the bizarre

lolloping threat that zombies presented, a critical handicap which enabled survivors to take stock of their surroundings and regard their attackers with fascinated disgust as much as fear as they staggered towards them. In the story, as the zombies' heads become visible over the brow of the hill, my little survivor opens up with the machine gun, aiming for the head, the only way to effectively stop the walking dead.

Mrs Taylor's response to the story was typically enthusiastic; whereas some teachers might have dismissed it as schlocky and overwrought, she offered a volley of bright-red encouragement and genuine glee at all the gore. This definitely stands out as an ESTB moment, if only to go back and give Mrs Taylor a VHS copy of *Shaun of the Dead*. I think she'd be rather chuffed, that's if the whole time-travelling student thing didn't turn her grey hair white. If you're reading this Mrs T, I'd love to know what you think.

Although I'd never actually seen a zombie movie when I was thirteen, I knew all about them. In the early eighties, as the popularity of home video grew, a number of small UK distribution companies started up with the express intention of cashing in on the sudden interest in affordable home entertainment. Video rental libraries began to appear everywhere, offering an extensive catalogue of older titles although little in the way of new releases.

The larger studios, somewhat myopically, held on to their content, choosing to generate revenue from repeat theatrical presentation, assuming video to be something of a fad. This led to a dearth of content for video distributors who, in response, took advantage of certain censorship loopholes and imported a variety of low-budget, foreign exploitation films that had never been seen theatrically in the UK. Although unregulated by conventional cinematic classification, the videos did fall under the remit of the Obscene Publications Act 1857, which rendered the distribution of any material which 'tends to deprave and corrupt' as a statutory offence.

Eventually, these titles drew the attention of the media and subsequently a whole army of crusading moralists on a mission to eradicate this filth from our high streets. Smart, well-made horror titles, such as Sam Raimi's *Evil Dead* and George A. Romero's seminal zombie flick *Dawn of the Dead*, were lumped in with the likes of *I Spit on Your Grave* and *Last House on the Left* and as a result lost to a generation.

Obtainable only on grainy pirate video after the ban, these films became the stuff of legend, often far more horrifying in description than they were to actually watch. The film that fascinated me the most amid this censorship massacre was *Dawn of the Dead*. Romero's star was sufficient that the film already had a certain amount of credibility, particularly within the horror community. The film had been released unrated in the US so as to avoid the porno tarnish of an X and had done good business in America as well as non-English-speaking territories, where Romero's friend and collaborator Dario Argento had final cut. Argento's version concentrated on the more visceral aspects of the film and is likely to have been the version that found its way to the UK on VHS, further bolstering the case for the National Viewers' and Listeners' Association's decision to consign it to the video nasty sin bin. Several images from the film featured in The *Encyclopedia of Horror* I received as a Christmas present in 1983 and I became fascinated by this tale of a shopping mall that becomes awash with blood.

I would stare at the image of David Emge's zombified flyboy character, trying to make sense of the apparent gaping hole in his neck, or the shocked face of the zombie with a machete embedded in his cranium. The film became something of an obsession for me. I quizzed friends who had seen it and would get them to tell me in as much detail as they could exactly what went on this blood-soaked mall, listening open-mouthed as they regaled me with gleeful reports of helicopter decapitations and graphic disembowellings. I read everything I could about zombie movies, dwelling on the more extreme descriptions of unfortunate individuals being forced to regurgitate their insides or suffer eyeball impalements on wooden splinters. Not including John Landis's groundbreaking video for Michael Jackson's 'Thriller', I didn't actually see a zombie movie until 1985 when Romero's third instalment of his *Dead* trilogy came to home video and I experienced *Day of the Dead*. I saw Dan O'Bannon's comical *Return of the Living Dead* before I finally got my hands on a copy of the elusive *Dawn* and actually saw Tom Savini's remake of *Night of the Living Dead* before I saw the Romero version.

Audio Gold

Of course it wasn't all videos, videos, videos – before the advent of sell-through VHS, there was a sizeable market for album versions of films, just as there was for stand-up comedy and musical theatre. As a very small boy, I would avidly listen to my father's Bill Cosby albums and still recall his routine about Noah building the ark despite not having heard it for thirty-five years; the 'shru-baa shru-baa shru-baa' of Noah's saw is still audible in my mind.

Owning a piece of spoken entertainment and then listening to it at will seemed awfully novel at the time. Today, comedians define their entire careers by making themselves available to watch at home and comedy DVDs are everywhere. Back then, only a select number of highly regarded and established comics were able to commit their musings to vinyl. Another audio comic delight I recall enjoying at this time was the more musical styling of the Bonzo Dog Doo Dah Band. Both Cosby and the Doo Dahs were a little sophisticated for a five-year-old, but I distinctly remember enjoying Cosby's vocal gymnastics and crazy characterisations and the silliness of Bonzo songs such as 'Mr Slater's Parrot' and 'Jollity Farm'.

I would often sit in the corner of the room wearing Dad's

massive headphones, carefully replaying the records time after time. It was something I did frequently throughout my childhood with music, comedy and film, inspiring my own creative imagination, the headphones rendering the experience intensely personal, as though it were all happening inside my own head.

One of the first long-playing records I ever owned was a Wombles album, called *Keep On Wombling*. *The Wombles* was a hugely popular, animated children's TV series, about a family of diminutive creatures living on Wimbledon Common in south-west London, 'making good use of the things that [they] find, things that the everyday folks leave behind'. It was essentially a show about recycling, thirty years before it became fashionable. It became so popular that Merton council, which presides over the borough of Wimbledon, had to deal with a sharp increase in littering, after children desperate to catch a glimpse of these little eco-warriors began wilfully discarding rubbish across the common.

The theme tune became a hit and composer Mike Batt went on to produce further singles and albums under the guise of the Wombles, one of which marked my first foray into studious vinyl appreciation. Side one of *Keep On Wombling* was a sort of concept album, which gave way to more generic fare on side two, a bit like *Sgt. Pepper*. Everything on side one fell under the banner of 'Orinoco's Dream (Fantasies of a sleeping Womble)' and encompassed the most popular Womble's dreams of being an astronaut, a cowboy, a jungle explorer, etc.

I spent many hours in my nan's front parlour (one of those silent front rooms, seldom entered) listening to this album and imagining I was Orinoco living out these diverse fantasies. Predictably, my favourite track was 'Womble of the Universe', in which Orinoco travels into space in a clockwork rocket ship with only Madame Cholet's cucumber sandwiches for sustenance. Space travel appealed to my imagination even before *Star Wars* arrived, and the possibility and potential contained in the dark void that surrounded us always filled me with enormous excitement.

My vinyl collection eventually grew to include two films, which I would listen to repeatedly, happy in my headphone cocoon. The first was Mel Brooks's *Young Frankenstein*, whose purchase coincided with my mum marrying Richard Pegg.

When Mum married Richard, not only did he take on a ready-made family in Mum and me but I took on new grandparents, John and Pam, who I loved very much, and also a new uncle called Greg. Greg was a something of an AV enthusiast, and around Christmas time, the Peggs would gather to view 16mm movie prints, chosen and projected by Uncle Greg. It was always incredibly exciting, not just because it felt like we had a cinema in our house but because we never knew what we were going to watch.

At the time, the notion of home cinema was an absolute luxury; prints were expensive and complicated to screen, and the appeal was rather specialist. This made it all the more thrilling as our annual movie nights approached and speculation would mount as to what film it would be, information Uncle Greg proudly held back until the last moment.

When home video erupted in the early eighties, Uncle Greg's film nights evaporated somewhat. It's odd that I can go into a Blockbuster or increasingly visit a LEGAL download facility on the Internet and stare blankly at the endless choice, only to give up in the face of so many options. I never felt disappointment when Uncle Greg announced the title of that year's film, only intrigued and excited. Invariably, I hadn't heard of the film anyway. Lovingly projected on to the kind of screen used to look at holiday snaps, were Richard Lester's *Royal Flash* (1975), *Sky Riders*, a James Coburn, Robert Culp hang-gliding actioneer from 1976, and Mel Brooks's *Young Frankenstein* (1974). I have dim memories of enjoying the first two, but it was Mel Brooks's loving parody of the old Universal horror films that really captured my imagination. It made me laugh, totally freaked me out and left me desperate to see it again. Fortunately for me, the film was available as an album, which my stepfather purchased from a record shop on St Aldate Street called Hickies. What is it with that street?

I listened to it again and again. Poring over every word and musical cue, replaying the film in my head. Closing my eyes I was able to clearly visualise the events of the film – Gene Wilder and Peter Boyle stomping out their hilarious version of 'Putting on the Ritz', or sexy Teri Garr playing the violin to lure the monster back to the castle. I must have listened to it hundreds of times.

It's interesting that, years later, my first foray into film-making would not only be a horror/comedy but would similarly achieve its aims by employing a beloved horror staple and placing it within a comedic context. I'll talk more about *Shaun of the Dead* later, but it occurs to me there is a correlation between my love of Brooks's movie and the film that would mark the beginning of my big-screen career. I certainly poured real-life experiences into my contribution to the film, not least Shaun's relationship with his stepfather. My own relationship with Richard Pegg was complex and problematic, as are the majority of step relationships. It basically boiled down to a power struggle for my mother's affection that caused a certain amount of tension between us. We're friends now but at the time we most certainly weren't.

I was already six when I met him and he, at twenty-four, had no prior parenting experience. It was a learning curve for both of us and it wasn't a particularly smooth arc. As much as I saw him as an interloper and he saw me as the physical manifestation of another relationship, when we did bond, we did so enthusiastically over films and music. We were the opposite of best friends, in that we were generally at odds, but occasionally we did enjoy bouts of welcome unity.

In the summer of 1980, he made a promise to take me to the fair that annually camped out on Gloucester city's parkland. On the day of the proposed excursion, I visited him in Debenhams, where he worked at the time (Richard was another frustrated creative, venting his urges with the GODS), and he offered me the choice of either going to the fair or going to see a new film called *Raiders of the Lost Ark*. I'd seen the trailers on the television, and duly noted its credentials as being 'from the producers of *Jaws* and *Star Wars*', and decided I'd forgo the dodgems and the waltzers in favour of another trip to the ABC. With hindsight, I did it as much for Richard's sake as for my own ends. I did it because I sensed it was what he really wanted to do, and I knew if I agreed, it would not only soothe the tension between us but win me some approval. I was ten years old at the time.

Looking back, the decision I made on the third floor of the Gloucester branch of Debenhams (the back entrance of which was on St Aldate Street, opposite where our music shop used to be) was absolutely key. I didn't realise it at the time but I was quite possibly at a metaphorical fork in the road. One path led away to easy superficial fun – all bright lights, loud noise and sugar – the other led to the movies. Now, I know *Raiders of the Lost Ark* isn't Fellini but, crucially for me, it represented choosing substance over stimulation, mental interaction over a more fleeting sensory gratification.

My reason for doing this wasn't a noble embracing of the humanities over the more base pleasures of the senses, it was an attempt to ingratiate myself with my stepdad; but, like *Star Wars* before it, *Raiders* served to further inspire my love of cinema and my interest in the film-making process. I have no doubt I would have seen it eventually, but something about making that specific choice resonates with me even now. Twenty-eight years later the man who made that film asked me to be in one of his films and one of the first people I shared that information with was Richard Pegg.

Have We Got a Video?

I perfected my Rick impression very quickly, widening my eyes with glee and training my top lip to pull back across my teeth in a simpering grin, sending every 'r' to the front of my mouth to be flattened into thin-lipped pomposity. When *The Young Ones* burst on to our screens in 1982, it was so wildly different from anything that had been on before, its effect on the country's young was seismic. The characters were so instantly brilliant, and classrooms across the land were suddenly populated by Ricks, Vyvyans, Neils and Mikes (although mainly the first three), all competing for the honour of best impersonation. Vyvyan required you to screw your lips into a perpetual pucker, set your head abob with a subtly aggressive bounce and shout every word you said from the raspiest part of your throat, whereas Neil, often intoned by the less extrovert, required a slow, nasal drawl and use of words such as 'wow' and 'heavy'. Mike seemed to be the least popular character, probably because he was an interloper from a different world: an adult scamming a student grant he was not entitled to. He was clearly the patriarch of the unit, and every self-respecting *Young Ones* fan knew dads weren't cool.

A new wave of alternative comedy had already started with the arrival of *Not the Nine O'Clock News*, but, 'Gob On You' and 'I Like Trucking' notwithstanding, the show had always felt more like the preserve of grown-ups. The comedy was wicked, smart and often driven by a sly cynicism that somewhat sailed over the heads of the under-fifteens. The show's contribution to the changing comedy landscape is unassailable, but its effect was far subtler than that of *The Young Ones*, which yelled and spat its way into all of our minds. I, like most, found *The Young Ones* utterly mesmerising, not just because it was so bold and daring and the characters so clearly defined they could be identified simply by their silhouettes, but because it seemed to speak directly to me. I wasn't watching a simulation of some adult life I had no mental or spiritual connection with, I was watching something that was meant for me, and that, crucially, was specifically designed to alienate the older generation.

Every break time, and even during lessons much to the fury of teachers to whom the show was complete anathema, our school would echo with lines such as 'Oh, have we got a video?' and 'Neil, Neil, orange peel, if only I could see you again.' On lunchtime visits to John Guy's house – he whose dining room became our break-dance rehearsal space – we would watch the one episode he had taped from the TV over and over again, to the point where I remember asking myself if I would ever tire of it, genuinely believing I would not. In truth I never did. I could watch it now and enjoy it just as much. *The Young Ones* taught me that comedy did not belong to other people, it wasn't governed by grown-ups in rooms I was allowed to enter only if I behaved. It also taught me that the silly, childish, weird things I found funny weren't a sign of peculiarity, alienation or a cause for alarm but that loads of other people found them funny too!

Over on Channel 4, a slightly more grown-up exercise in redefining the comedy landscape was taking place with Peter

Richardson's *The Comic Strip Presents* . . . Using many of the same faces that appeared in *The Young Ones*, producer Jeremy Issacs had, with an extraordinary amount of balls and foresight, commissioned this troupe of untested actors and comics to create a series of one-hour films that varied from genre pastiches to original and surreal flights of fancy. It amazes me that so much effort and expense was ploughed into what was essentially a hunch; a hope that this fledgling ensemble could come up with the goods. Despite being a highly inventive and hugely talented group, they were an unknown quantity in televisual terms. Their freshness and sheer force must have felt like something of a gold rush for Channel 4, a network initially committed to producing challenging and alternative television. Indeed, the Comic Strip's *Famous Five* parody, *Five Go Mad in Dorset*, formed part of the line-up for the channel's opening-night entertainment and this spirit certainly powered things along for some time.

One night, planted in front of the TV with my snacks and drinks, I witnessed a group of people having a lot of fun with a budget. *A Fistful of Travellers' Cheques* was, as you might expect, a pastiche of the Sergio Leone spaghetti westerns, following the misadventures of two cowboy wannabes who find themselves living the dream in Almeria, Spain, with a number of other travelling misfits. Rik Mayall and Peter Richardson play Carlos and Miguel, the two role-playing students who drop their drawling affected accents only once, during the build-up to an apparent duel. While arguing about who should start the row that provokes their pretend gunfight, Mayall asks in timorous, plummy tones, 'Sorry, have we started yet?' To which Richardson replies in a thick, West Country burr, 'Course we have, you great tosser.' I laughed so much I wept. Fortunately I had decided to tape as much of *The Tube* as I could, determined to get some souvenir of my night alone with the TV. As soon as the show had finished, I wound it back and watched it again, making much use of the review-search option to continually replay the specific exchange between Richardson and Mayall.

Another moment that I replayed obsessively was Adrian Edmondson's first line as Billy the homicidal matador. As Nigel Planer's stoned rocker tries to steal a beefburger from his plate, Edmondson lunges at him with a fork and grunts, 'Fuck off!' It was the first time I had ever heard the word 'fuck' said on television and it was a genuine shock. I felt a sudden jolt somewhere in my abdomen, which took me by surprise, almost as much as hearing the word itself. This wasn't right. People weren't allowed to say things like that on TV. They didn't even say it on *The Young Ones*. Suddenly, comedy had become even more exciting and dangerous and I desperately wanted to see more.

I continued religiously taping the shows whenever they were aired and would recreate them endlessly at the back of lessons with my old friend Lee Beard, whose friendship I had rediscovered. Knowing the scripts and being able to recite moments from the shows became a badge of honour for us and an annoyance to people not in on the joke, just as I'm sure *Python* fans had delighted in doing the same some fifteen years before. Indeed, my love of modern comedy led me to rediscover *Monty Python's Flying Circus*, which according to my dad I enjoyed immensely as a youngster, although I don't remember it first time round. When the BBC repeated the series in the eighties, I realised that alternative comedy did not begin with the Comic Strip but rather regenerated through the ages like Doctor Who, the mantle being passed on to the next generation of subversives (often directly): Spike Milligan (*The Goons*) appeared in *Monty Python's Life of Brian*, Terry Jones (*Monty Python*) appeared in *The Young Ones*, Ben Elton (*The Young Ones*) introduced Vic Reeves at *The Secret Policeman's Ball*, Steve Coogan (*The Day Today*) was a guest on *The Smell of Reeves and Mortimer*, Chris Morris (*The Day Today*) directed the pilot of *Big Train*, etc. The connections are many and varied, and although the style of comedy evolves and mutates, the desire to undermine the norms of comedy remains constant and a new incarnation will emerge as the older version is assimilated into the mainstream and disempowered.

In 1999, just after completing the first series of *Spaced*, I landed the role of Mr Nice alongside Rik Mayall and Adrian Edmondson in *Guest House Paradiso*, a cinematic outing for their *Bottom* franchise. Shot at Ealing Studios, where four years later I would shoot *Shaun of the Dead* with fellow cast members Kate Ashfield and Bill Nighy, the film was a typically grotesque comic take on the bad hotel set-up, with Richie and Eddie as the feckless proprietors. The whole thing culminates in an incident with radioactive fish, which leads to many of the characters, including myself, projecting fountains of green vomit across the walls and floor. I leapt at the chance to work with my childhood comedy heroes. It meant a lot to me to be able to chat about *The Young Ones* with Rik between takes (director Ade Edmondson was less available although no less friendly).

It is an extraordinary thing to meet your heroes and find them to be everything you hoped they would be. Despite the high pedestal I had placed them on as a child, Rik and Ade appeared to be very normal with no superpowers or bad attitudes. Rik even seemed a little insecure, relishing the crew's laughter at the end of a take and worrying if it was not forthcoming. Here was a man whose comic talents had inspired me enormously as a youngster, who had created one of the most enduring characters in alternative comedy, who had even appeared briefly in *An American Werewolf in London*, and I was sat next to him chatting about silly things, as if we were friends. Suddenly, the world I had scrutinised for so long was all around me, as if I had leaned forward and climbed into the television like Alice through the looking-glass. I had no idea just how deep the rabbit hole would go.

8

Hendon spread out beneath them like a big map of Hendon. The twinkling lights of north London seemed deceptively peaceful from the solitude of the jet and yet Simon Pegg knew what lay ahead and shuddered internally, before becoming distracted by Chiquito's Bar and Grill, Staples Corner, and experiencing a powerful yearning for a single fried chicken chimi with cheese.

'What are you looking at?' enquired Murielle.

'Hendon,' Pegg said, banishing all thoughts of Tex Mex cuisine from his brain. 'You will never find a more wretched hive of scum and villainy. We must be cautious.'

'You 'ave a wonderful way wiz words,' whispered Murielle, from beneath the silk sheets.

'Thanks,' said Pegg, sideways glancing at the French beauty.

They had spent the flight from Marrakesh analysing the schematics of Lord Black's town house, which they had downloaded from the Foxtons website. Although they were barely able to keep their hands off each other, they knew there was work to be done, so they had compromised by working in the nude. Of all Pegg's plans and schemes over the years as a crime-fighting adventurer, this was probably the least thought through.

'You should try to get somesing published,' said Murielle, stretching with feline grace.

'Funny you should say that,' scoffed Pegg. 'I'm supposed to be writing a book right now but instead I'm jetting round the globe, having primo bunk-ups and trying to prevent the destruction of all life on Earth.'

'Oo's your publisher?' enquired the French beauty.

'Ben Dunn at Century, a subsidiary of Random House Publishing,' Pegg replied bitterly, busying himself with his portable info-hub so as to distract himself from the fact that he hadn't finished his book.

'Ee sounds like a bastard,' said Murielle, her naked body clearly defined by the gossamer film that sheathed her perfect shape, defining every curve, every protrusion.

'Someone's smuggling peanuts!' said Pegg.

'Pardon?' Murielle replied, drawing the sheet around her midriff in a soft swathe.

'A multinational crime syndicate is moving cheap peanuts into Guyana and undercutting the local farmers. It's all here,' said Pegg, indicating his info-hub. 'I've got to stop them!'

Murielle's hands were suddenly clasped around either side of Pegg's face. She looked deeply into his eyes, bringing him back into the room before she spoke.

'One thing at a time, mon amour,' she said firmly/gently. 'You cannot be everywhere at once. Eet's impossible, even for you. We need to get back the Star of Nefertiti or there won't be any peanuts left to smuggle.'

Pegg nodded sombrely and said something Murielle could not make out due to her hands squashing his mouth shut.

'Pardon?' she half laughed, trying to fathom the gorgeous enigma that sat in front of her. She released his face and brushed the hair that had fallen delightfully into his eyes, giving him the appearance of a young Hugh Grant with more conventional teeth.

'I was just saying, you're really squashing my face and I can't talk properly,' Pegg offered sheepishly.

A broad grin spread across Murielle's face, her wide mouth bending into an irresistible bow, revealing her dazzling white teeth. Her beauty was truly breathtaking. She made Betty Blue look like Hughie Green, and staring at her for too long could lead to disorientation and mild arrhythmia. Pegg broke into a similarly devastating smile, which developed into a chuckle. Murielle laughed in response, her infectious chortle building in the back of her throat, before escaping her lips. Pegg reciprocated, releasing the ball of tension in his gut as a hearty cackle, which burst from his diaphragm like big hiccups. Murielle's own titterances became a fully fledged giggle which vibrated her shoulders violently and forced her head back, exposing her soft neck and giving clear passage for her deep throaty yuks. Pegg's laughter intensified into silent shuddering, turning his face bright red, the veins in his forehead protruding with alarming prominence as Murielle whooped in an enormous gulp of breath to facilitate the next wave of hilarity. At this point, Pegg let go a tiny squeak from between his muscled buttocks. It was a barely audible toot but it was enough to send both of them into convulsions of breathless, screaming guffaws, which propelled both of them off the bed on to the floor in an undignified heap, and reduced Pegg to a screaming cramp of convulsive sobs. At this point, it was difficult to tell whether it was laughter or tears, such was the level of self-pissing.

The door suddenly splintered inwards, silencing the

helpless pair as they spun round to face whatever had interrupted the hilarity. Canterbury stood in the doorway, his robotic eyes glowing deep red, his chest plate open to reveal a mini Gatling gun, which had already started to rotate in anticipation of its spitting a deadly report. Both of Canterbury's hands had retracted into his cuffs and been replaced by razor-sharp blades which glinted in the dim light of the in-flight boudoir. His shoulders too had flipped open to reveal two epaulettes racked with deadly mini rockets, three on each side, swivelling in response to some silent subroutine emanating from the robot seneschal's silicon synapses.

'What the fuck?' said Pegg in a voice higher than he thought he was capable of.

Canterbury didn't respond; instead he simply stared, rocking slightly on the spot, the whirr of the Gatling gun increasing in intensity.

'Canterbury!' Pegg shouted, clapping his hands together.

Canterbury's fearsome armoury gave no sign of disengaging. Lights atop the shoulder-mounted rockets changed from red to green, as Canterbury's body tensed as if bracing itself.

'Mon dieu,' whispered Murielle in French.

'CANTERBURY!' Pegg barked. 'Cessation code roger, roger, charlie, zero. Engage!'

Canterbury's red eyes flickered momentarily before he straightened, shaking his metal head like a guest on the Paul McKenna show who had just spent ten minutes farting around like a chicken.

'Forgive me, sir,' stumbled Canterbury. 'I heard screams over the intercom and assumed you were in distress. I thought perhaps the jet had been infiltrated and you were in need of some assistance. Combat mode initiated involuntarily, sir. It wasn't my choice.'

Pegg got up from off the floor, composing himself, which was difficult considering he had tears in his eyes and a DVD stuck to his face.

'Murielle and I were just laughing at something,' explained Pegg awkwardly.

'What was it?' asked Canterbury, hoping to distract from his faux pas.

'You had to be there really,' muttered Pegg, still stunned.

Canterbury sagged slightly. If he were human, one might have taken the gesture for shame.

'I'm sorry, sir. I did not mean to intrude.' The cybernetic concierge didn't leave; instead he stood, as if awaiting retribution.

'It's OK,' said Pegg softly, 'although I am worried that you somehow self-enabled full combat mode without my authorisation. There might have been a nasty accident. I trust you completely but I think it would be best if we implemented a voice-activation procedure to prevent it happening again. From now on, the trigger for multiple-attack deployment will be the word "toast".'

'Won't that make breakfast treacherous, sir?' Canterbury faltered.

'I'LL JUST HAVE ALPEN!' Pegg roared, surprising both the robot and the nude French lady.

'I'm sorry.' Canterbury hung his head.

Murielle looked from the android to the master then back again, aware that Pegg had been overly harsh but unsure whether or not she should intercede.

'There was one other thing, sir,' Canterbury said quietly.

'What?' said Pegg, not looking up.

'We have touched down in Hendon Park as you instructed. Lord Black's town house is less than a mile away. Might I suggest we take the Peggcycles and make our way to the rear entrance? The property is guarded by a number of henchmen who get tougher and more dangerous the closer you get to Lord Black.'

'Very well,' said Pegg. 'We'll leave in fifteen minutes.'

Canterbury seemed about to say something but stopped himself. He moved off, leaving Murielle and Pegg alone.

'Why were you so hard on eem?' asked Murielle. 'Ee was only trying to 'elp.'

'That's not the point,' said Pegg. 'He's a lethal weapon in that state. If anything had happened to you, I —'

Murielle pushed her finger to his lips, crushing them gently against his teeth.

'Don't,' she said. 'I don't know eef I could willingly go into this situation knowing exactly what I 'ave to lose.'

Pegg nodded, without looking at her. She removed her finger from his lips.

'Let's go get the Star of Nefertiti,' he said, finding the strength in his voice once again. 'There will be time for proclamations when we return.' Pegg strode towards the door. He was energised, charged with a determination that made all previous missions seem somehow trite. He wanted to tell Murielle how he felt but knew he must resolve the matter of the magic diamond first. His motivation to foil Lord Black was now greater even than the desire to save the world. He was going to end this and nothing was going to stop him.

'Wait!' said Murielle, a hint of desperation in her voice. 'We should get dressed first.'

Summer of '83

In 1983, I fell in love with a French girl called Murielle Burdot. She was an exchange student who had come over to England to stay with Ann Tickner, the girl I was snogging on the floor when my friend's dad walked in on the bacchanalian teen party many chapters ago. Ann and I had dated briefly in a kissing-in-the-cloak-bays fashion but had split up after a massive two weeks, as one does at that age – I seem to remember her getting a controversial perm but I'm sure it had no bearing on the breakdown of our relationship – and after a similarly brief period of post-relationship grumpiness, we became good friends again.

Ann lived in the old part of Upton St Leonards, near a farm property where she kept a white horse called Boots. I first met Murielle at the gate to a field where Boots grazed and impressed her no end by falling off the handsome steed and splitting the crotch of my jeans wide open from knee to knee. I sat chastened on the ground, next to an indifferent Boots, a pair of bright purple Mark & Spencer's briefs on sudden shocking display between my legs.

Word had spread that Ann was taking custody of a genuine French girl, so myself and Nick May, who lived conveniently close to Ann, wandered up to the top field to see if we could catch a glimpse of her Gallic mysteriousness. We were in luck, and she was everything we had hoped for: tanned, chic, fragrant, exotic and unspeakably beautiful, with a pidgin English and hypnotic accent that immediately elevated her to the status of Most Amazing Girl I Had Ever Met, more amazing even than the blonde Finnish girl who had visited a year before and spoken frankly about masturbation. Murielle was smart and funny, with a touching note of affection in her laugh that filled me with a curious warmth.

I would ride up and down past Ann's house on my red Raleigh Grifter, hoping that the pair would emerge and see me cycling past, as though by sheer coincidence. If they didn't appear, I would knock and casually ask if they wanted to come out and loiter in the warm evening air, since I just so happened to be passing. Murielle became my obsession that summer; she made my entire being ache with longing. I hadn't felt anything like it before, not with Laura or Libby, my sixth-form crushes, nor with Ann or her best friend Allison who followed, not even Meredith Catsanus. This felt more like Princess Leia, bottomless and painful in the most exquisite way.

On one particularly balmy, magical evening, a party was being held in a barn on the other side of the village for purposes I have now forgotten, possibly a rich kid's birthday. The event was fully catered and featured a sound system and disco lights and promised to be a lot of fun. King of the swingers, Darius Pocha, who for some reason had not been around that summer (maybe encephalitis), was joining us at the party and I was excited for him to meet Murielle. I had taken great pleasure in telling him about her, making sure I said her name in a Charles Aznavour voice, *Murielle*.

The night was electric and I relished the chance to hang out with her for a few hours in an environment more conducive to socialising. Fences and fields are fine but nothing beats a paper cup full of warm Coke laced with cider. She seemed to get on well with Darius, which pleased me immensely, although a couple of times I noticed her making faces behind his back. At the end of the night, tired and psychosomatically tipsy, we clambered into Ann's mother's car and headed back to our part of the village. Huddled in the back seat, Murielle shifted her weight and put her arm around my shoulder, her hand drooping down over my chest. Her head nodded forward as exhaustion overwhelmed her and she slept next to me.

I became more awake than I had ever been in my thirteen years. My heart rate doubled and my breath became shallow and shaky. I slowly closed my fingers around hers and shifted my weight to make her more comfortable. She didn't wake or protest, so I held my position as though balancing a priceless vase on the tip of my nose. Her head lolled on to my shoulder, and in a moment of semi-consciousness, she felt my hand clasped around hers and snuggled into me, purring slightly as she drifted back off to sleep.

I didn't want the journey to come to an end. I wanted Mrs Tickner to just drive round until dawn, so that I could prolong this moment of closeness to the object of my affections. Eventually we reached our destination and Murielle stretched and yawned out of the embrace, giving me a tired smile, within which I desperately searched for some meaning. Were we going to kiss? Was it possible in front of Ann and her mother? Would I be able to stay upright if we did? Her lips were a perpetual pout of softness and I had imagined many times the feeling of actually kissing them. Was this it? She kissed me on both cheeks, as was customary in her part of the world, and it was enough for me. I can still feel the sting of her cool saliva on my face and the smell of her spiky eighties hair as it brushed passed my ear. I walked home in a daze of intoxication, my clothes infused with the smell of her. This was it, I was in love.

The next day I discovered her and Darius in an amorous embrace outside Ann's house and my world exploded. I could barely contain my shock as I saw them sat snuggled together, planting tiny kisses on each other's lips. With sudden clarity, it dawned on me that the faces she had been making behind Darius's back had been expressions of attraction and approval, and her affection towards me in the car had been nothing more than friendly – we had, after all, become close over the summer and her actions denoted nothing more than her sense of ease and comfort in my presence. Somewhere inside me, something lurched and snapped and I stumbled towards my Raleigh Grifter, making the hasty excuse that I suddenly had to be elsewhere, the first time that entire summer I had wanted to be somewhere other than near her.

As I rode away, my eyes clouded with tears and I released a torrent of anguish that forced me to pull over and give in to its weight. I sat against a blackberry bush and wept openly, tears mixing with the grime and sweat on my face as I tried to make sense of the situation. He had known her for one day, one single day. I had been her friend for weeks, I knew her better, liked her more, how dare he appear out of nowhere and destroy everything. The truth pricked at my despair, threatening to deepen it further. Darius was very cool in an androgynous, slightly self-conscious way. He was tall and beautiful, a perfect mix of his pretty English mother and smart, exotic Indian dad. His fashion sense was avant-garde, which definitely appealed to Murielle's European sensibility over my own jeans and T-shirt simplicity. He was novel and fresh, a newcomer to our little summer clique. Just like she had appeared as a breath of French air to invigorate our familiar surroundings, Darius had made a timely entrance into the ranks of pasty English boys that had turned out to get a look at this exotic beauty, and without even meaning to, he had swept her off her feet. After a while I realised I was going to have to go back. As painful as it was to see them together, the idea of not seeing her at all was far worse.

I rounded the corner on the faithful metal steed I had owned since I was eight, simply raising the saddle and handlebars every time I noticed I had outgrown it. Darius and Murielle sat together on the grass verge outside Ann's house, arms draped over each other; Ann sat slightly apart from them, no doubt almost as pissed off as I was. Not because she was jealous, but because she had found herself custodian of the summer's main attraction and as such became the conduit to Murielle, rather than a person in her own right. I climbed off my bike, flipped it upside down and threw it into a hedge, overwhelmed by a fit of impotent demonstrative emotion.

'Are you hungry?' Murielle enquired, chewing her words for clarity.

'What?' I said, betraying my disgust at her betrayal. She made a face and continued.

'Why are you hungry, Simon?'

It took me a few seconds to realise that what she was actually asking me was if I was 'angry'. She seemed genuinely oblivious that her actions may have upset me, which frustrated me even more, as it meant the unspoken sexual tension which I assumed existed between us was a myth of my own construction. We were just friends, that's how she saw me. Not as a potential boyfriend or an object of desire, just a friend whom she nevertheless cared for very much.

She seemed perplexed and upset by my reaction, which left me with little recourse but to take it out on him. Even that was hard. I loved Darius, he was one of my best friends and someone with whom I felt an enormous affinity. He was aware that I had feelings for Murielle but he had no idea how deeply they ran because he hadn't really been around that summer. I did not extract myself from our social summer huddle but instead became the wounded martyr, wearing my pain on my sleeve. I noticed a bloody purple splash across the back of my T-shirt later that day, where I had leaned against the blackberry bush, and made some vague comment about it being evidence of Darius stabbing me in the back. Melodramatic, yes, but I was thirteen and in love with a French girl.

When the time came to say goodbye to Murielle, I had just about got used to the idea of her and Darius and managed to get a little angst-ridden mileage out of being the spurned lover. Murielle realised that I had feelings for her and seemed apologetic and genuinely concerned about my moods, often pleading with me not to be 'hungry'. The night she left, Nick, Darius and I gathered on the lane leading up to Boots's field and lined up to give her our goodbyes. The tears spilled down her cheeks and I remember being pleased that she was hurting, not in a sadistic way but because it was some indication at least that she was going to miss me. I didn't cry, perhaps buoyed by the validation of her tears; I smiled and said I would see her again next year. As we walked away, my mind raced with the implications of the goodbye and I realised that I could not possibly end things there, I could not permit that to be the last moment we shared. I ran back over the brow of the hill, calling her back, sprinting towards her, full of something I couldn't contain. She opened her arms as her face once again crumpled into an expression of sadness and I wrapped myself into her embrace.

'Kiss me,' she said through her tears.

'A proper one?' I heard myself say dumbly.

She nodded and I leaned in without a second's pause. It was a long, slow, passionate kiss, which required both of us to breathe heavily through our noses, squeezing our eyes shut as we pressed our mouths together. I could taste her tears as they gathered at the sides of my mouth and felt something strange in the very pit of my stomach which I assumed was love but now know was simply profound infatuation. I became aware of an echoing rhythmic slap some way off and realised it was Darius walking back over the crest of the hill slowly clapping his hands. He wasn't angry, or being sarcastic, in fact he seemed oddly happy.

We walked back down the hill together with our arms clasped round each other's shoulders, our friendship tightened by his graciousness. There was no regret, no feeling of betrayal. We came to the silent understanding that, in the end, Murielle had liked us both and was sad to be saying goodbye, and this simple truth suited Darius and me just fine, since neither felt undermined. We were oddly grown-up about it really, which was surprising given our age.

I corresponded with her regularly over the next year and looked forward to her letters, which always smelled faintly of her floral scent. She returned to the UK the following summer but it wasn't quite the same. She and Darius weren't speaking after their relationship faltered in the face of the distance between them. I asked her out while waiting for Ann to buy perfume in Boots the chemist but she insisted she wanted us to be just good friends. Whether this was because she had already lost one British friend in Darius or because I was wearing a cagoule tucked into a pair of pinstriped jeans, I will never know, but truth be told I wasn't terribly heartbroken. She was still as beautiful and exotic as ever. Something, however, was definitely missing. The summer of '84 wasn't as hot and seemed somehow less magical, and perhaps we both subconsciously knew it would be pointless to try and top the previous year. We resolved to be friends and enjoyed another few weeks hanging out, although sitting in fields and on fences had somewhat lost its appeal in the intervening year, a fact we accepted without nostalgia. We were, after all, growing up.

To this day, whenever I smell horses, I am taken back to the summer of 1983; not that Murielle smelled in any way horse-like, it simply evokes the atmosphere of the time we spent in frequent proximity to the pungent beasts. Murielle smelled of sweet flowers and dizzy promise, and whenever I find myself on a farm or near a stable, I can locate the phantom of her aroma amid the acrid pong, even though it isn't there, such is the indelibility of her presence in my memory.

You might wonder why I bothered to include this story. It has no real bearing on my professional life. I didn't eventually find myself acting alongside Murielle in *L'odeur d'un Cheval*, an Anglo-French production from Studio Canal about a cross-Channel love affair set in the Cotswolds. Tenuously, I might suggest that I tend to relish the drama of heightened emotion and have channelled it into my writing. I definitely enjoyed contributing to the romantic interplay between Tim and Daisy in *Spaced*, appreciating through experience how compelling the will they/won't they relationship can be. Playing the victim of unrequited love certainly formed an important part of my early persona as a stand-up comic, but that was born out of desire for someone other than Murielle Burdot. Truth is, it's a story I have always had a hankering to write down, recalling the heady emotions as keenly as I do, and there's always room for a little nostalgia. You don't need an ESTB for that.

Everything I Learned from VHS

*B*asket *Case*, *Lemon Popsicle*, *Inseminoid*, *King Frat*, *Screwballs*, *Porkies* and *Class of Nuke 'Em High* – every one of them an enticing proposition of illicit thrills and mild titillation. The auditorium for the viewing of such school-holiday delights was usually the front room of a friend whose parents worked during the day and couldn't afford childcare. Their absence meant the top-loading video player was open to anything the boys at Astrovision permitted us to rent, which was usually anything.

Not every classic horror film suffered alienation at the prim whim of Mary Whitehouse and her brigade of knee-jerk crusaders. The numerous pre-Blockbuster video rental shops that appeared in the mid-eighties were a veritable treasure trove of fascinating titles, yet to be eclipsed by a continual wave of new releases. These cinematic emporia were more akin to vintage bookshops in their appeal and were a ready source of cultish and low-budget entertainment. For a single English pound, one could spend an entire day with Chuck Norris or a bunch of horny, Popsicle-sucking

Israeli teens, pausing the action to study a particularly grisly act of violence or flicker of nudity.

Maybe there was a small amount of validity in the moral panic that ensued after the arrival of VHS. I certainly wouldn't want my teenage child watching a film that made violence titillating, promoted misogyny or featured truly disturbing imagery. It's just a shame these self-appointed guardians of decency lacked the guile and intelligence to distinguish between smart, cinematic genre pieces and witless exploitation. We were permitted access to films we would not have stood a chance of seeing theatrically, due to our being under age. This was most likely due to video shops being run by nerdy guys who relished introducing youngsters to a variety of mondo video rarities for vicarious thrills.

It started with films such as *Porkies* and the slew of imitators and sequels that followed. Me and a few close chums discovered an early Stallone picture called *The Italian Stallion*, a softcore porn flick from 1970, re-released after the success of *Rocky* as a cash-in on the actor's sudden stellar status. Whether it was a genuine mistake on the part of the store owner or indeed a sly gag, we opened the video box back at my friend's house to discover the film we had rented was John Badham's *Whose Life Is It Anyway?*, starring Richard Dreyfuss as an artist paralysed from the neck down after a horrific car accident who questions his right to die voluntarily. We didn't know this at the time, we just assumed that *The Italian Stallion* had previously been called *Whose Life Is It Anyway?* before it had been rebranded for the post-*Rocky* audience and for some reason had retained its original title on the cassette. A tenuous denial, sure, but we were porn drunk and very optimistic.

We slotted the tape into the chunky VHS player and settled down to watch. Our excitement at seeing the guy from *Jaws* and *Close Encounters* was tempered slightly by the creeping realisation that this wasn't the film we had intended to hire. It didn't say anything on the box about Dreyfuss being in the film and surely it would have, he was a huge star, not as big as Rambo but still worth a mention. It wasn't until after at least twenty minutes of watching Dreyfuss be grumpy in a bed, getting no action whatsoever – not even from his own arms and legs – that we suspected a duping. There was also the distinct lack of a sexually active Sylvester Stallone to consider and eventually we threw the cushions from our laps and conceded that an error had occurred, requiring us to go through the whole nervous, sweaty process of hiring a bluey again.

Hire it we did, though such was our teenage fascination with sex, it eclipsed all fears of dignity loss. We watched most of the film and found its poorly shot, grainy action to be about as arousing as a quadriplegic Richard Dreyfuss and nowhere near as sensitively penned. This says a lot about the film's failure to engage our penises, considering we could all achieve erections just by thinking about the bath and shower section of the Littlewoods catalogue.

Not all the films we watched were low-quality deposits into our wank-bank of sexual imagery to be recalled on the bathroom floor. I witnessed some of the films that became personally important to me in the darkened front rooms of local work orphans. I was initially timid about horror as a youngster. Despite regularly poring over my *Encyclopedia of Horror*, I found the static images alone were enough to give me nightmares, and the prospect of witnessing one of the new contemporary American horror movies felt like a step I was not quite prepared to take. I had watched the old Universal horror films despite a youthful fear of Frankenstein that sent me screaming back through the entrance of the Haunted House at Gloucester Fair in 1975. I had seen a few Hammer movies and had no fear whatsoever of monsters and dragons, I just found the wave of brutality emerging from underground American horror cinema to be very unnerving, as though it were real.

The nastiest expressions of this new wave of brutality – Wes Craven's *Last House on the Left*, Michel Gast's *I Spit on Your Grave*, Tobe Hooper's *Texas Chain Saw Massacre* – found themselves on the list of banned films in the UK drawn up by the National Viewers' and Listeners' Association, along with other far less deserving titles. Although I can appreciate why Hooper's classic account of serial murder in rural America was singled out, it suffered more due to the effectiveness of the film's scares, rather than simple moral reprehensibility. The images and ideas are horrific, but then it is a horror film, and whereas it does adhere to the dubious convention of punishing sexually liberated teens,[14] its nastiness is more a condition of its success, rather than it being purely a worthless titillating or exploitative device. In that respect, it is far more worthy than either Craven or Gast's schlocky, unpleasant efforts.

It's true that most of these titles were no great loss to the shelves of Astrovision and its ilk, but freedom of choice was as much our right then as it is now. As a result of its prohibition, *The Texas Chain Saw Massacre* became one of those films that circulated in school bags and beneath desks on so-called pirate video. A friend of mine's father worked for an oil company in Saudi Arabia and would often bring home snide copies of films to compensate for his frequent absence. On one such occasion, my friend was given a copy of *The Texas Chain Saw Massacre* and came to my house furtively to ask me if I wanted to watch it.

This possibility had been on the cards for a while and I had

---

[14] *The Texas Chain Saw Massacre* is a particularly juicy text for the film theorist, since the principal terroriser is Leatherface, a hilariously stroppy matriarch dispensing his/her punishments like a flustered fifties 'mom'. 'Hacked off' probably being the most suitable description of his/her mood.

mentally prepared myself for the experience by talking about it constantly, as if it was a forthcoming sports event in which I was competing; psyching myself up for the experience with deep breaths and short exhalations. When the time came, I couldn't do it. I looked at the unmarked cassette in his hands and made my excuses. I just wasn't ready to watch something that had apparently made people violently sick in cinemas across America.

Looking back, I think I made the right decision. When I finally watched it while at university, I had to marvel at its grungy effectiveness, at the brilliant use of sound and tension, the terrifying contrast between the ghastly organic bric-a-brac of the 'family's' living space and the shiny metallic door to the killing floor, as it slides violently shut on a twitching victim. As a twelve-year-old boy I would have absolutely shat my pants. I had a vivid imagination and this masterpiece of horror would have sent it spiralling into recurring nightmare. I still find it hard to watch now.

The film that popped my modern horror cherry was to have a huge influence not only on my career but also on my personal life, in that I would eventually be lucky enough to call the director a friend. Of course, I had no idea this was to be the case as we once again drew the curtains of my friend's front room and slipped *An American Werewolf in London* into the video player. What I witnessed over the ensuing ninety-seven minutes changed me forever.

From the very beginning, the film draws the audience in, adeptly establishing sympathetic characters thanks to a winning combination of writing and performance, lulling the audience into thinking it to be a warm buddy comedy about two Americans on holiday in rural England. The tension builds quickly to a horrific and devastating animal attack which resets the film as something entirely different. Even as the horror of David's situation comes to light, amiably explained to him by his dead friend

Jack, the light comic touch established early on persists, so that the extraordinary transformation effects, which win out even today in the face of CGI and continue to beg the question 'How did they do that?', are counterpointed by a charming levity which makes it all the more memorable.

I felt as though I had advanced in some way, as the credits rolled on *American Werewolf*, as if I had successfully performed some rite of passage. I had watched a modern horror film and not only had I survived with my disposition intact, I had actually enjoyed it. Not just enjoyed but loved it, to the point that it was all I spoke about for days afterwards. I quickly sought out other similarly visceral monster titles such as Joe Dante's *The Howling* and John Carpenter's *The Thing*, which I consumed with avid appreciation.

The Thing was a particular favourite of mine, in that it represented the darker aspect to my love of science fiction. It had been released in the same year as *E.T.* and presented a polar opposite version of the human-meets-alien story. This was no cute, friendly soulmate from the cosmos, this was an aggressive and relentless shape-shifter, hell-bent on assimilating every living organism on the planet via a process of slimy replication and violent death. It remains one of my favourite films to this day.

These films became my teenage obsession. As the original *Star Wars* saga drifted into the infinity of my eternal admiration, my new preoccupation became the horror movies I was given access to, thanks to permissive video-shop clerks. Years later, Edgar Wright, the co-writer and director of *Shaun of the Dead* and also a teenage horror aficionado, and I found ourselves surrounded by a support network of our childhood heroes. As our low-budget zombie movie was released in the States, Romero, Landis, Carpenter, Dante, as well as more recent heroes such as Peter Jackson and Quentin Tarantino, all made positive noises about the film, enabling us to cover our poster with impressive quotes.

It was a moment of extraordinary circularity that no doubt would have required extensive use of the ESTB to fully exploit the ironies at play, although we would have reprimanded the time traveller as he appeared in front of the TV in that darkened front room for preventing us from properly seeing Jenny Agutter's top bollocks.

Perhaps the most joyous circularity was the support and eventual reciprocation Edgar and myself received from the man who inspired us to make *Shaun of the Dead* in the first place. I couldn't help but recall my fascination with *Dawn of the Dead* as a youngster as I paced the floor of my kitchen, waiting for George A. Romero to call me. At the same time, somewhere in Florida, accompanied somewhat ironically by a Universal Pictures security guard (as if George was going to steal OUR film), George was watching *Shaun of the Dead*, a film which is in every way a paean to his own groundbreaking contribution to genre film-making and his single-handed reinvention of a horror-movie staple.

George Romero was born in New York in 1940 and, twenty years later, graduated from Pittsburgh's Carnegie Mellon University, intent on becoming a film-maker. In the late sixties, he and a number of collaborators, including screenwriter John Russo, formed Image Ten Productions with the express purpose of making what would become one of the most influential horror movies of modern times, *Night of the Living Dead*. The film tells the story of a mixed group of survivors, fending off a relentless attack from an ever growing number of walking cadavers, intent on devouring them.

As with most of his subsequent films, the story was laden with social subtext and made comment on notions of collectivism, the civil rights struggle and America's involvement in Vietnam. Romero was one of the first film-makers to feature a black protagonist, Duane Jones's Ben, who is subversively permitted to survive until the end of the film, rather than serve as a sacrifice, providing the white male lead with the motivation to complete his journey. Indeed, the two main characters in *Night of the Living Dead* are a black male and a white female, both of whom last longer than any other character in the film. Eleven years later, film theorists would celebrate Ridley Scott for doing the same with *Alien*, when it is Romero who deserves plaudits for breaking with convention so many years before. The film's climax is bleak and unforgettable, cementing its status as serious and credible cinema, despite its roots in a genre dismissed as schlock.

A decade later Romero returned to the zombie genre to create his masterwork, *Dawn of the Dead*. Picking up from where the original left off, we join the film as the crisis is reaching critical mass. A small group of survivors escape Pittsburgh in a news weather helicopter and seek sanctuary in an abandoned shopping mall. *Dawn* strikes a perfect balance of horror, comedy and sharp satire as it makes sly comment on the nature of modern consumerism and the ingrained social rituals that determine our behaviour. At once funny, tragic, heart-warming and terrifying, the film is a mesmerising take on the end-of-the-world fantasies that most of us at some point indulge in and stays with the viewer long after the brilliantly counter-scored credit muzak has ceased.

When I was twenty I finally got to see *Dawn of the Dead*. I watched it alone in a media-viewing suite at Bristol University and found it to be everything I had hoped for as a young child. The moments recounted by the lucky few who had seen it on pirate video were all there: the helicopter decapitation, the screwdriver in the ear, great chunks of flesh bitten out of shoulders and legs, all realised in glorious crayon red.

The images I had stared at in my *Encyclopedia of Horror* came to grisly, shuffling life – the machete in the head, Stephen's gaping neck wound. Even as I experienced the closure of finally

Helping out with the Shaun make-up tests in early 2003. Ealing Common was crowded with the dead that day.

Me and Nick Frost trying our very best to look as cool as Bill Nighy.

Lord of the Rings director and part-time Santa Claus, Peter Jackson, delighted to have stabbed me through the hand on the set of *Hot Fuzz* in 2006.

Looking like a badass. I bloody loved that uniform. It made me feel whole.

Me onstage with Coldplay in front of 18,000 people at the O2 Arena in December 2008. I left the band shortly afterwards but then rejoined for a short appearance at Wembley Stadium the following year. My on/off status as a member of the band is ongoing.

Sweatily trying to blend in among the throng on the convention floor in San Diego, 2008.

Me with my best friend Lou Ferrigno at Comic-Con 2004.

Edgar Wright, Kevin Smith, Jessica Hynes and I doing promo for the US release of *Spaced* on DVD in LA, August 2008.

Me and Nick Frost escaping a stampeding herd of iron cattle in Dallas, Texas.

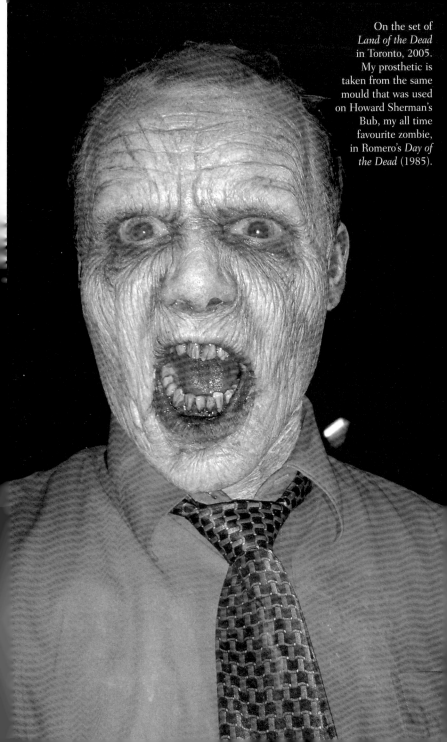

On the set of
Land of the Dead
in Toronto, 2005.
My prosthetic is
taken from the same
mould that was used
on Howard Sherman's
Bub, my all time
favourite zombie,
in Romero's *Day of
the Dead* (1985).

Me, George Romero, Edgar Wright and Greg Nicotero – two of the happiest zombies ever to walk the necropolis.

Me, Greg Nicotero, Ken Foree and Edgar Wright at Comic-Con in 2004. Ken played Peter Washington in the original *Dawn of the Dead*. I believe the popular term is 'Squeeeeee!'

Edgar and me hamming it up for the camera in the *Land of the Dead* principle make-up truck.

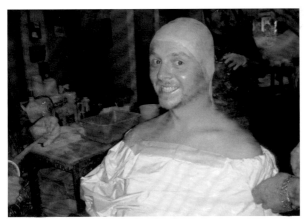

Getting my head cast at the KNB Workshop in Van Nuys in 2004. The mould was later used to create my make up for *Land of the Dead*.

Me and F/X guru Greg Nicotero. Greg gave Edgar and I this bust of Bub. I treasure it to this day.

Small world. Me and David Walliams meet George Lucas at the *Revenge of The Sith* premiere in little Britain.

San Diego Comic-Con 2004. It took him a while to track me down but eventually my luck ran out. He was actually quite apologetic and friendly.

seeing the film, I could sense its influence making further headway into my psyche as I sat in silence afterwards. I was completely and utterly hooked.

I had already seen *Day of the Dead* by this time – the third and most gruesome instalment in Romero's zombie series. Released after the moral panic of the early eighties had subsided, it had no problem securing a mainstream video release in 1986. *Day of the Dead* follows a group of soldiers and scientists trying in vain to coexist in an underground bunker, long after the walking dead crisis has consumed the globe.

This time Romero addresses the dangers of unchecked militarism and moral questions surrounding vivisection, as the zombies are experimented on and, in one case, even tamed. Howard Sherman's 'domesticated' zombie, Bub, is perhaps the greatest mobile cadaver in the history of the genre, proving far more sympathetic and likeable than many of the human characters. We cheer him on at the end as he breaks free of his shackles and delivers ironic justice to his prime tormentor. Although slightly talkier and arguably less affecting than Romero's first two zombie films (mainly due to budgetary issues and hurried rewrites), *Day of the Dead* remains one of my favourite zombie movies, if only for providing such memorable moments as evil Captain Rhodes's literally gut-wrenching bisection, the conscious severed head discovered in Dr Logan's lab still hungrily flexing its jaws and, of course, for one of the most sensitively played anti-heroes of all time. Bub stayed with me ever after and if you watch the scene in *Shaun of the Dead* when Shaun and his friends attempt to evade the undead horde by pretending to be part of it, it is Howard Sherman's Bub that I am channelling as Shaun makes his attempt at zombie play-acting.

One of the key attractions for me of the zombie myth, particularly Romero's interpretation, is the zombies' fascinating ambiguity. They are without any moral imperative or visible emotion and as such cannot realistically be defined as evil. They are simply 'us', driven by our most basic impulses. They cannot be blamed for the atrocities they commit because there is no agenda or culpability, only the same ingrained instincts that motivate the living ungoverned by morality. They are the evolutionary or perhaps devolutionary extension of that old maxim of the philosopher Descartes, *I think therefore I am* – in the case of the zombie, *they eat therefore they are.*

Crucially, their tragedy and moral ambiguity is demonstrated by their being ultimately weak and ineffectual. Crippled by the tragic disability of death, their approach is slow, pathetic, even temporarily avoidable. I have written about this on several occasions, particularly in light of a new wave of 'fast zombies', which, I feel, forgo the winning subtleties of the genre in favour of less cerebral scares. Suffice to say, Romero's films turned me into a very particular type of nerd, for whom such details become of massive importance. If you can't relate to that obsessive fascination with something ultimately so silly, you're probably shaking your head right now and thinking 'What a prick'. Well, I say this: 'Who is the bigger prick? The prick who writes the book or the prick who reads it?' (Well, it's the prick who writes it, obviously.)

Time to Act

Now in my fifth year at Brockworth Comp, and despite a lifelong interest in the performing arts, it hadn't really occurred to me to actually try and make a living from it. People from Gloucester just didn't go into professional acting. Such destinies only befell people who lived in London and could walk to the BBC from their house, rather than drive there on very special occasions.

I had considered a number of potential career paths, including veterinary practice and physiotherapy. I have no idea what possessed me to consider the latter. I think I took a leaflet away from one of those vague careers meetings, in which a tired, disillusioned teacher casually raises the question of what you are going to do with your life and you shrug and leave with the first leaflet you see.

As a subject at Brockworth, although masterfully represented by Mrs Brooking, drama was somewhat underestimated in terms of importance, by students and school governors alike. Pupils were given the option of studying drama at A level, but only as a third option, having elected to pursue two other more academic modules. The first two brackets offered subjects such as English, maths and sciences, whereas the inauspiciously numbered 'third bracket' in the three-part group contained subjects like media studies, art and baking. Supposedly bereft of any real application, drama was relegated to this Vauxhall Conference League of educational advancement and as such didn't feel entirely credible.

Barbara Luck, leader of the Gloucester Youth Theatre, had enlisted my help in fleshing out the cast of an outdoor production of Shakespeare's *Taming of the Shrew* at Hidcote Manor just outside Gloucester. As the still sole male member of our drama club, I was a valuable vein of testosterone, a unique thing in similar short supply at Barbara's own society, the Gloucester Drama Association. Also, I'd like to think she thought me worthy of the production, having enjoyed my robotics and swearing during the evening workshops I had now been attending for over a year.

Barbara, who was playing the female lead, Kate, would pick me up in her Austin Maestro and drive me out to Hidcote, where we performed the famous comedy for three consecutive nights. During our conversations to and from the manor, Barbara must have gleaned that I harboured a desire to follow acting professionally. She had certainly always been very encouraging during sessions at the youth theatre, apart from an occasion where I pretended to be Vyvyan from *The Young Ones* (taking a break from my usual Rick impersonations) and headbutted a stack of chairs over, making a lot of mess and noise, and making her tut and raise her eyebrows.

On one evening, she brought along a leaflet for South Warwickshire College of Further Education, and asked me to share it with my mum, of whom she was an old friend. One of the major attractions for me was that the college had been attended by none other than Ben Elton, co-creator of *The Young Ones*, and as such promised a tried and tested educational path to success in the arts. Not just success but snot-soaked, bottom-burping, alternative-comedy success, something that had until that moment appeared to be nothing more than a dream.

The theatre studies course wasn't free, however, and Mum agonised at being unable to afford it on her own meagre wage, after we found ourselves outside the catchment area for a grant from Gloucester County Council. Fortunately, and with almost creepy serendipity, our house, although technically outside Upton St Leonards, still fell within the parish and as such made us eligible for an educational fund called the Lady Downe Trust which had been specifically set up to assist young people living in the area to pursue a career in the arts. As far as we knew this was the only fund of its kind in Gloucestershire, and, by a series of events triggered by me failing my eleven-plus exam, we had found ourselves living within the bounds of its influence.

Assuming I would pass the eleven-plus in 1981 with flying colours, the Peggs had upped sticks even before the results were in and moved from Brockworth to Barnwood, so as to be nearer Tommy Rich's Grammar School. However, when I flunked out, I found myself having to commute all the way back to Brockworth on the bus. After a few years living in Barnwood, the house proved a little too costly and the family decided to move. A new development on the outskirts of Upton St Leonards offered reasonably priced housing within the catchment area for my school, even offering free bus travel there and back for the kids in the village. So four years later and by a somewhat circuitous route, we found ourselves in reach of this independent fund that would enable me to attend the South Warwickshire College of Ben Elton.

Mum insists that it was all meant to be and puts it down to something she calls cosmic ordering. I tend to regard it more as a coincidence but an undeniably fortunate one nevertheless. Mum and Barbara both wrote to the trust, explaining why they thought I deserved its assistance, and a few weeks later we received a lovely handwritten letter, agreeing to part fund my education in Stratford. It wasn't a huge amount, but it was certainly enough to prevent my mum from having to eat cardboard or become a high-class hooker, which I'm sure she would have done, such was her unfailing and heartening support of my decision to enter the precarious world of acting. Actually, it's preposterous to imagine her going to such lengths; there is no way my mum would ever eat cardboard.

9

The hover-bikes sped across Queen's Park at an alarming rate, silently skimming the recently cut grass as they hurtled on towards their destination. For the riders, it was more than just a destination, it was a destiny, although destiny is technically less than destination because it's a smaller word, but its figurative implication is massive, particularly in comparison to Lord Black's town house, which was tiny. He conducted most of his nefarious ill-doings from a secret hideout in the North Sea, a disused oil rig which had been renovated and made to look a bit like a spider. It was an awesome and impressive spectacle, but in constructing his dastardly headquarters he had gone slightly over his budget and had to downsize his plans for a second house in the capital. It was big but it wasn't huge.

'Ow much furzer?' whispered Murielle Frenchly into Pegg's ear. The jet had been equipped with only two hover-bikes, one for Canterbury and one for Pegg. Thus the handsome adventurer and crime fighter had to give his sometime adversary a backie.

'Not long,' said Pegg, trying to ignore the warmth of her embrace around his midriff and the whisper of her warm breath against his cheek (he was too cool to wear a helmet). 'Canterbury, status report.'

Canterbury knew that his master was still mad at him for having a spaz attack with his weapons systems in the boudoir. He had no explanation for the malfunction; presumably something deep within his neural network had kicked in and overridden his safety protocols. He would have to run a diagnostic on himself when all this was over, that is, if they made it back at all. Something bothered Canterbury, something gnawed at the very base of his synthetic neurocortex. His programming was impeccable and subject to constant updates transmitted from the hub; bugs and malfunctions were telegraphed by bursts of predictive code that enabled him to anticipate and remedy glitches before they occurred. It was almost as if his apparent error had been nothing of the sort and instead had been the product of a perfectly constructed artificial brain, operating at full capacity.

'Canterbury,' said Pegg impatiently, 'what the fuck?'

Canterbury cursed himself for ballsing up yet again and pushed his ruminations to the back of his processor.

'Five hundred and sixty-seven metres sir,' said the likeable robot with efficient accuracy. 'Five hundred and forty-seven, five hundred and twenty-seven ...'

'We'll stop two hundred metres before the target and proceed on foot,' decided Pegg out loud.

'Can't you make eet fifty? I'm wearing eels,'

protested Murielle with a hint of Gallic bluster.

'Don't you have a pair of flats in your handbag?' enquired Pegg, 'I know I have.'

'What?' shouted Murielle above the rush of air.

'Nothing,' replied Pegg. 'Fifty sounds good to me. The park's dark enough and there's no way the perimeter sensors can extend further than thirty metres, not on his budget.'

'Very well, sir,' said Canterbury, 'powering down in five, four, three, two, one . . .'

The bikes hummed to a stop and the silence of the night closed around them as they dismounted and prepared to make their approach. Pegg zipped up his combat suit and checked his various knives and guns, which made him look like a complete badass.

'Canterbury, I want you to run interference, OK?' ordered Pegg. 'Strictly hand to hand. I'll deal with the bulk of it. You just make sure the fight stays even.'

'But, sir . . .' protested Canterbury.

'I can't risk a friendly-fire incident, Canterbury,' insisted Pegg. 'I saw your eyes back there, it was as though you were possessed by robot satan aka, B.L.Z. Bub.'

'Yes, sir, I will initiate an artillery escalation only if I hear the activation word. I have triple-checked my subroutines and installed a fail-safe.' Canterbury projected his intended efficiency with an eagerness to please that seemed almost human. Pegg had to make a real effort to maintain his moodiness, but maintain it he did, giving his robot sidekick a cursory nod in reply. He looked over to Murielle who was staring at him, an odd expression on her face.

'What is it?' Pegg enquired, with a note of concern.

Murielle seemed conflicted for a moment, an inner struggle pulling her beautiful brows into the slight frown he himself had worn the night Canterbury caught him reading *The Twilight Saga*.

'Nothing,' she said eventually. 'Let's do this.'

Pegg approached her and stroked her cheek (upper right) with a tenderness his rugged exterior suggested he was incapable of.

'Listen,' he said quietly, 'if anything happens, I just want to say —'

'Don't.' Murielle once again flattened her finger against Pegg's lips, squashing them into an unflattering pout.

Before Pegg could respond, a blinding beam of light illuminated the area, flooding the park with a stark glare.

'Shit, he bought new sensors!' exclaimed Pegg as he struggled with the Velcro on his leg holster. 'Murielle, run!'

A sharp pain shot through his neck as if something had bitten him. His hand flew to his carotid artery with a slap and he felt something foreign beneath his fingers, embedded deep in his skin. He plucked the invasive object out and looked at it; even as his head clouded and his vision began to blur he could see the familiar fluffy head of a tranquilliser dart.

'The word, sir!' Canterbury chirped frantically, clanking over to his faltering master. 'Say the activation word! I can't say it myself, sir, it's restricted.'

'Hmmm?' said Pegg absent-mindedly.

'It's something you have for breakfast,' urged Canterbury.

Pegg's mind dulled and folded in on itself as he struggled to remember the word that would transform Canterbury into a lethal weapon, resembling Iron Man if he'd been on the Atkins for a few months.

'Murielle knows what the word is,' mumbled Pegg, barely coherent, 'but I told her to run away.'

'She didn't run, sir,' said Canterbury.

Through the haze of his intoxication, Pegg noticed an odd resigned sobriety in Canterbury's voice but ignored it. He threw his head sideways on his limp neck and saw Murielle standing nearby.

'The word, Murielle, say the word.'

But something was wrong. Murielle seemed relaxed, almost distracted. A flicker of guilt registered across her face, and as the last vestiges of consciousness ebbed out of Pegg's body, he realised the awful truth. This was a trap. She had betrayed him. He wanted to punch a window until it smashed, which it would have done after the first punch, but he was succumbing to the tranqs and by now could barely lift his own arms. As his heavy lids drew closed, the figure of Lord Black striding across the grass towards him blurred and expanded into darkness.

'Oh bollocks,' he thought.

The Undiscovered County

I left Brockworth Comprehensive in the summer of 1986 and the following term began a two-year course at SWCFE, living five days a week with Anne and John Mallins, a wonderfully nurturing couple who along with their Weimaraner Misty and moggy Bailey became my de facto family for two whole years.

My time at Stratford was incredibly important to my growth as a person. I was living away from home for the first time in my life and getting to participate in almost constant dramatic endeavour; performing in various shows and plays and loving every second of it. I became something of a theatrical type and my obsessions drifted away from the science-fiction staples of my youth, drawing closer to Shakespeare and Marlowe.

The college was a five-minute walk from the Royal Shakespeare Theatre, and for a time my ambition was to perform Hamlet in the main auditorium, rather than man the dilithium chambers of the Starship *Enterprise*. Thus stories of nerdiness and circularity from this time are scant, although I could fill an entire memoir with my adventures at Stratford, since they include virginity relinquishment of varying kinds, not just sexual.

My initial forays into more grown-up comedic performance definitely occurred at Stratford. Our first production was a revue show, for which I performed several *Monty Python* skits with my friend Andy, an impossibly cool young man whose influence transformed me into a goth. Before the end of the first year, we had formed a band called God's Third Leg & the Black Candles, after I discovered I could play the drums (a latent skill acquired while messing around among the stock at the music shop in St Aldate Street).

We had one song but never performed it live. We did perform a few Half Man Half Biscuit[15] numbers at the Edinburgh fringe Festival which drew favourable comments from a three-piece Australian musical comedy act called the Doug Anthony All Stars, who were a fixture at the festival for a time. I'm pretty sure they thought the songs were ours, and in the face of praise from professional comics, we didn't ever correct them.

The ethos behind God's Third Leg & the Black Candles was mainly about being *in* a band rather than the actual composing and playing of music. The line-up – Andy Harrison (vox), Simon Pegg (skins), Steve Diggory (axe), Ruth Adridge and Gab Starkey (backing vox) – represented an amiable clique of teenage hedonists: we smoked cannabis resin and crimped our hair with abandon.

It was a heady and formative time for me and I eventually paid tribute to God's Third Leg in *Spaced*, as the band my character Tim designs a record sleeve for. We had a reunion recently, all of us in our forties and seemingly changed beyond recognition; one of us had a grown-up son; another had recently beaten

[15] Brilliant if short-lived eighties indie music satirists responsible for such gems as 'I Left My Heart in Papworth General', 'All I Want for Christmas Is a Dukla Prague Away Kit' and 'Trumpton Riots'.

cancer. It wasn't until we were a few drinks in and gathered around a drum kit and a guitar that our younger selves revealed their presence and our black candles appeared not to have burned down that far after all.

My time at Stratford wasn't solely theatrical in pursuit. I witnessed a number of key inspirational movies during that period, including *Withnail and I* and *Evil Dead II*, which I believe I watched as a double bill at Gab Starkey's birthday party, shortly before going upstairs and losing one of my virginities (the main one). I also developed a love of Woody Allen which I would carry with me ever after, so impressed was I with this diminutive one-man production machine. The film that sparked off the obsession was, predictably, his 1973 science-fiction romp *Sleeper*, which sees Allen playing Miles Monroe, a health-food store owner from Greenwich Village, New York, who wakes up two hundred years into the future having unwittingly been frozen in cryogenic stasis. The film is one of Allen's silliest and owes much of its slapstick appeal to silent-comedy greats such as Chaplin and Buster Keaton. Allen himself is on hilarious form as the man out of time and Diane Keaton puts in a beguiling performance as Monroe's hedonistic hostage, Luna.

I actually fell in love with Diane Keaton having seen her in *Sleeper*, an obsession she only compounded with her Oscar-winning portrayal of Annie Hall, a film I latterly sought out while on my mission to consume everything Allen had ever done. My love for Keaton eventually became a key factor in my early stand-up routines, borne out of weekly viewings of *Sleeper*, which my friend Jason Baughan had on video. Every Thursday after college, I would stay at Jay's parents' house. We'd eat Marmite on toast and watch the film, never tiring of its perfect blend of smart and silly.

Living away from home in Stratford-upon-Avon enabled me to experience something very close to the freedom of adulthood while essentially still a child. Anne and John Mallins acted as guardians but never assumed the role of parents and as such I was able to get away with far more than had I still been at home. As a consequence, I chalked up a lot more life experience than I would have done under the constant watch of my liberal but concerned mother. (Although at the Mallins' we did always eat together at the dining table with our puddings on our laps, and I did once get told off for coming home drunk and covered in make-up, so perhaps it was just like being at home.)

Dramatically speaking, my two years at Stratford also saw me participate in far more productions than I had in five years at Brockworth. In my first term, as well as the revue show, we devised a pantomime called *Not the Wizard of Oz* in which I played a very Rik Mayallish Prince Charming. The following term, we staged Federico García Lorca's *Blood Wedding* in which I sparkled as 2nd Woodcutter. The next year was busier still for me, including a production of Peter Nichols's *A Day in the Death of Joe Egg* and a production of *Hamlet* in which I appeared as the ghost of Hamlet's father. I had hoped to play Hamlet but a slump in my coursework, due to an increased social life, led to a little karmic payback elsewhere. Word got back to Gordon Vallins, the inspirational patriarch of the drama department, that I had burst into an English lesson twenty minutes late one summer Monday, having returned from my first Glastonbury Festival but not from my first acid trip.

Elsewhere, my work suffered due to a habit of spending much of my time in the Green Dragon pub watching the video jukebox and smelling of patchouli oil. Gordon called me into his office and gave me a stern talking-to about potential and the importance of education and how if I continued along the same trajectory, I wouldn't get into university. I clearly needed this kick up the backside, as Gordon called it, and pulled myself back from the brink of teen abandon on which I teetered.

I remained gothy and faintly rebellious in appearance, but buckled down academically in an effort to get the requisite grades and progress into higher education. I even started going to art classes, much to the surprise of my teacher who claimed not to recognise me. It was all too late in terms of me securing the role of Denmark's stroppiest prince – that honour went to Dale Crutchlow. I had to make do with playing his dead dad, which I did to the best of my ability and got singled out in the *Stratford Herald*, so stick that up your arras, Dale Crutchlow. Not that I'm bitter. The last production before the end of the final term was Kander and Ebb's timeless musical satire, *Chicago*, in which I took the role of smooth lawyer Billy Flynn, having bucked up my ideas since the *Hamlet* fiasco. I got to sing classic numbers such as 'Razzle Dazzle' and 'All I Care About' and had probably the most fun I had ever had onstage.

My time at SWCFE was magical from beginning to end both socially and academically. I grew as a person and as a budding actor and, by the time I left, was absolutely certain that I wanted to pursue a career in theatre. I learned as much about life as I did about Bertolt Brecht and Tom Stoppard, and even wrote my first play for the practical part of my theatre studies A level, a predictably sci-fi-tinged tale about a tribe of post-apocalyptic teenagers who worship a bedside table with a light in it. The play was called *Shadowland* and was essentially Mad Max vs the Wombles. As I've always said, write what you know.

As much as I loved returning home at weekends from Stratford, leaving SWCFE forever to return to the relative solace and isola-tion of home took its toll on me emotionally and I fell into a depression. The malaise was sparked by the vague irrational fear that I might suddenly turn gay, despite having no impulses in that direction. I also had a very beautiful girlfriend called Caroline at the time, who I had pursued for months with a relentless charm offensive that eventually paid off. The sexuality confusion most likely occurred in the wake of leaving college and the sudden uncertainty of my future.

The results of my A levels would determine my next move, and despite having chosen Bristol University as my intended place of higher education, my tenure there would not be confirmed until late August when the A-level results came in. The limbo I found myself in after leaving Stratford could best be described as post-dramatic stress disorder. I felt isolated and misunderstood, having no one around me who had shared the experience. I kept feeling the urge to fall to my knees and scream, 'You weren't there, man!' It was in a very pure sense a case of culture shock, compounded by my having to work a number of manual labour jobs in order to earn money when what I really wanted to do was act. I had spent the last two years being Prince Charming, Billy Flynn and Hamlet's dad. I was the 2nd Woodcutter, damn it! Why am I lifting boxes? *What happens if I turn gay?*

I worked as a packer and loader in different warehouses, including a mouse-infested animal-feed factory, this one being at the height of my depression. The job required me to lift big sacks of grain on to pallets and break down huge eight-foot clusters of expired Sugar Puffs to be bagged and sent to farms as horse food. Break times were a bizarrely disorientating affair for someone in my delicate state. The facility seemed to be staffed entirely by gruff, sullen old men, all on the verge of retirement. During downtime, they would sit themselves in various chairs and sleep soundly as hundreds of mice swarmed around their feet, and I would sit among them, wired on my own endorphin deficit. There was a perpetual haze of grain dust that hung in the air, defining the scant light that leaked into the room through the filthy windows as churning, visible shafts, making the whole environment fantastic and nightmarish. I would sit bolt upright with my sandwiches on my knee, my eyes darting from oblivious, sleeping men to the hundreds of grey blurs flashing across the floor, all the time wondering if it was really happening. Wasn't I just onstage singing 'All That Jazz'? I lasted eight days before I told the temping agency that the grain particles were aggravating my asthma. Fortunately for me, they didn't ask for a letter from my doctor.

When my results finally arrived, I had started to feel better and was fairly happy, working in a double-glazing warehouse, assembling packs of parts and moving boxes around. There were a few younger guys there and I had even made a few friends. The foreman approached me one morning smiling broadly and let me know that my mother was on the phone. I took the call in his office and was excitedly told that I had met the entrance requirement for Bristol's placement offer and would be starting in October. I walked back on to the warehouse floor with a spring in my step and assembled some of the neatest double-glazing packs of my career, buoyed by the knowledge that I had managed to scrape a B and two Cs and thus ensured my continued presence within the education system. My dreams of becoming an actor were alive again and I was about to take one step closer. I had no idea that Bristol, for a time at least, would take me in a completely different direction.

Student Union

I felt prepared for Bristol University, having already served some serious hard time in Stratford – playing pool, smoking other people's weed and making five pounds last seven days. I was well versed in living away from home, although the whole idea of preparing my own food was initially baffling now that I was bereft of Anne Mallins's weekly set menu, and for my first year I conducted an experiment to see how long a human being could subsist solely on toast and Marmite (163 days).

The difference between going to drama school and studying drama at university is that drama school is almost entirely practical, whereas university is predominantly theoretical. That's not to say Bristol was just about theory; the drama department put on a number of productions every year, as did the drama student body know as Studiospace. Students were also encouraged to put on their own productions, ranging from traditional plays to ten-minute theatre pieces performed at lunchtime. We also learned about all aspects of theatre, film and television production, not just performance, the idea being that we graduate with a broad spectrum of skills that would enable us to work in the industry in a variety of capacities. Some of the most successful

Bristol University Drama Department alumni have been directors, producers and writers. It certainly changed my outlook in terms of my future involvement in the arts. If anything, it engendered in me a healthy wariness of convention and encouraged me to develop self-reliance, rather than simply become an actor beholden to the swirls and eddies of fate. After all, as Sarah Connor told her son John, there's no fate but what we make, and who are we to argue with *Terminator 2*?

It was at Bristol that I discovered the joys of critical analysis, which eventually inspired me to pick apart my beloved *Star Wars* as part of my final-year exams. Lectures and seminars on populist cinema were hugely interesting, since they enabled me to consider what I had previously assumed to be a disposable art form as a rich source of academic study. I was able to watch my favourite films again then address them as historical 'texts', reflecting a host of psychoanalytical complexities. *Alien* became a treatise on genital terror and fear of the mother, *Terminator* became a tale of Oedipal obsession and mutations in received notions of masculinity, and *Top Gun* became about . . . well, we all know what *Top Gun* is about. The process was fascinating and enlightening. At the beginning of our first film studies lecture, Professor George Brandt informed us that after that day, we would never be able to view a film in the same way again. By developing and engaging our critical faculties we would effectively be given the ability to see through the artifice in three dimensions, able to detect meaning both intentional and unintentional, understand the intellectual mechanics at work in the narrative as well as identify temporal expressions of social neuroses and preoccupations, and thereby become boring cunts.

This is all very well when you're studying Jean-Luc Godard's *Numéro Deux* but slightly distracting when you're watching *The Jungle Book* and feeling irked by the use of infantilised anthropomorphic proxies as racial stereotypes, while everyone else is dancing around singing 'King of the Swingers' or finding your-self unable to enjoy a film because of the clumsy use of hastily written ADR[16] employed to disguise unwieldy transitions that join scenes not originally intended to be consecutive.

It's not totally debilitating, you can turn it down to a muffled complaint in the back of your head or even suspend it, if you're determined to enjoy something despite its shortcomings, which is sometimes entirely possible. It leaves you with slight multiple personality disorder since the little voice is impossible to silence completely, but you can ignore it, like you might ignore an annoying younger sibling or the sound of pigeons having sex on your windowsill or your best friend kissing a French exchange student.

Personally, I value this capacity since it can be enormous fun and comes in handy as a screenwriter, enabling you to deter-mine your film's hidden meanings and identify its social context before a frame has been shot. I was well aware of the psycho-analytical implications at work in *Shaun of the Dead*'s Oedipal subplot and exploited them as a dramatic device rather than them simply reflecting my and Edgar's own relationship with our parents. The 'father as enemy and rival' story is subverted slightly by a last-minute redemption for the dying Philip (Bill Nighy) that forges a crucial connection between (step)father and son, defined exclusively by their own (male) bond as opposed to their status as rivals for the mother's affection. Similarly, I was well aware of the symbolic significance of Shaun having to literally kill his mother, Barbara (Penelope Wilton). The drama of the moment lies in the son's rejection of his mother as the object of his affections, substituting her with a sexual partner. In order for Shaun to move forward, he replaces Barbara as his figure of

---

[16] ADR (automatic dialogue replacement) is the name for dialogue added to a film or TV show in post-production.

worship with his girlfriend, Liz (Kate Ashfield), and to that end, he shoots her in the head.

The situation arises because Barbara cannot survive this new phase of Shaun's life, unlike Liz who survives with him until the end. At the very end of the film, we see Shaun and Liz living in domestic bliss with Liz as mother, doting on Shaun. Yet even after this transformation, Shaun cannot fully reject his past and clings to his dead best friend, Ed (Nick Frost), his proxy father/son, whom he has concealed in the shed.

We always intended an ambiguity at the end of the film regarding whether or not Liz knows about Ed. If she does, she is complicit in Shaun's failure to evolve and as such is as reactionary as he is. If she doesn't, then Shaun's transformation from zero to hero has meant nothing, as he continues to cling on to his past by hanging out with his zombie friend. Also, there are numerous unintentional processes at work here, not least our fantasy female's ultimate acceptance of Shaun despite his being a bit of an idiot. Deep down, we all hope to be accepted despite our shortcomings and Edgar and I were effectively building an all-new bride of Frankenstein in Liz, a gestalt entity fashioned to satisfy both of our subconscious desires. We tried very hard to make Liz believable and have her protests be justified and not just needy and boring, but ultimately she is still a male fantasy: a beautiful girlfriend prepared to look past failings in the face of one's romantic gesture, maybe not a bunch of flowers but certainly extreme courage in the face of a zombie apocalypse (chicks love that shit).

The film is in some respects about human emotional consistency in the face of fantastic events. If a giant squirrel starts running amok in your city, it affects you only in a direct sense; you don't suddenly start liking broccoli or stop being afraid of spiders. All of Shaun's petty tendencies remain the same despite the zombie invasion – he still hates David and Dianne (Dylan

Moran and Lucy Davis) and likes peanuts; the bravery he displays has always been in him and the changes he makes in his relationships are all forced upon him. By the end of the film, it is clear that Shaun hasn't really been changed that much by his recent experiences, and although he has won the day by beating amazing odds, the fact that he remains unable to let go of his now literally toxic best friend hints that the final idyll will be short-lived. Or then again, maybe it's just a film about zombies . . .

I have to get off this tip, as I can feel myself being drawn back into old patterns. I'll be pulling an all-nighter with a bag of Murray Mints and a packet of Camel Lights next and we can't have that (I gave up smoking in 2001). What I will say, however (as I desperately search for my lighter), is that my early love of zombie cinema has persisted well into my adult life because the genre is so metaphorically rich and interesting. Edgar and I were certainly able to develop Romero's use of symbolism in his films and apply it to our own, specifically using the zombies as reflections of various social concerns: collectivism, conformity and the peculiar condition of modern city living. I believe it is this metaphorical richness that forms the cornerstone of their continued appeal. It's why I get miffed at all the dashing around in recent zombie films. It completely misses the point; transform the threat to a straightforward physical danger from the zombies themselves, rather than our own inability to avoid them, and these films are about us, not them. There's far more meat on the bones of the latter, far more juicy interpretation to get our teeth into. The fast zombie is by comparison thin and one-dimensional and, ironically, it is down to all the exercise.

Where was I? (Long exhale.) Ah yes . . .

First Man Standing

It was customary in the drama department at Bristol University for the departmental students' organisation, Studiospace, to throw a party at the beginning and end of every term. Being a drama department, the party also included a cabaret, during which students would sing songs, recite poems, perform sketches and generally feel pleased with themselves. However, almost nobody among our new batch of freshers was prepared to get up and risk humiliation in front of this collection of too-cool-for-school, bohemian intellectuals. The old school rules of social order applied even here, and although the second-years didn't push us up against walls, their knowing smirks were enough to worry our self-esteem, as was the almost total disregard of the third-years, who barely noticed our existence. Everyone seemed so at home and assured, the thought of performing for them was too terrifying a prospect to endure.

One of our number, however, seemed fearless in the face of all the newness, due to a healthy disdain for virtually everything. Dominik Diamond, a fop-haired, young dandy from Arbroath, Scotland, got up and delivered an assured stand-up routine which outraged the numerous feminists in attendance for its use of the phrase 'dolly birds'. This one incident set Dominik in permanent conflict with the moral elite of the drama department, whose rigid political correctness held inflexible dominion over artistic and social proceedings at the time. It was a period when the policing of language and behaviour was at its most draconian, and stories about a member of a feminist physical theatre group, ousted by his colleagues for offering to be 'mother' when pouring tea, seemed not only feasible but right. Dominik immediately became the Jeremy Clarkson of Bristol University Drama Department, a role that alienated him from and endeared him to his fellow students in equal measure.

I thought he was great. I felt a huge surge of admiration for him as he stepped up to the mike during that first Studiospace cabaret and a tinge of jealousy that I had not had the balls to do the same. I became aware of a sensation I used to feel when competing in athletics events with other schools or Cub Scout packs, finding myself pitted against their fastest runner or best bowler. Suddenly, the comfortable hierarchies of school seemed meaningless and the status you had worked so hard to establish was voided by someone who might actually be better than you. I had always been the funny one, at Brockworth and Stratford, and yet here was this ballsy young funny man in a big-shouldered jacket, doing pretty well in front of a not entirely partisan crowd. I clapped and I cheered and I was proud that one of our own was making a splash, but at the same time I was quietly hatching a plan for the next Studiospace cabaret.

I had dabbled with poetry while at Stratford and had even written a couple of comedy songs, one of which I wrote for the express purpose of seducing the girl whose heart I would successfully win. Caroline, a friend of a friend's sister, was a vision in gothic gorgeousness to the seventeen-year-old me. Dressed in flowing black skirts and fragrant leather, she sported the most impressive hair extensions I had ever laid eyes on and, wonder of wonders, she found me funny. I spent the best part of a year wearing her down by openly expressing my affection for her in the Green Dragon pub and other goth-friendly venues, including a Fields of the Nephilim concert in Coventry. During one flirty conversation she had told me she was celibate, which I wilfully misheard as halibut. I then wrote a song called 'Caz is a Fish Blues' and sang it to her at the Binton Folk Club where Andy (God's Third Leg) Harrison, Jason (*Sleeper*) Baughan and myself performed weekly as Blind Dog Harrison and the Dirty Gerbils.

The evening was supposed to be about folk music, but we had hijacked it and frustrated the regulars by bringing in a lot of much needed custom but somewhat muddying the point of the gathering. The evening became more of a free-for-all for drama students at SWCFE to indulge their musical fantasies in front of a friendly crowd. This loosening of parameters encouraged other acts and, before long, people were getting up and telling jokes and reading poetry. A chap whose name I believe was Mave, presumably short for Mavis, began reading his performance poetry and it greatly impressed me as a means of performing comedy without the need for a band and I started to write verse of my own, including the fish song, which I sang to a twelve-bar blues with the Gerbils, not quite ready to go solo.

Eventually, my persistence won out and Caroline succumbed to my dubious teenage charms. We stayed together for almost two years, eventually breaking up while I was at Bristol, a callous act of social evolution on my part which I still look back on with regret. Presumably I was too comfortable and chose instead to throw myself into an angsty pit of despair, which, while creatively productive, lost me a treasured friend and the first person I felt genuine romantic love for. The girl on to whom I transferred my unrequited affections provided dramatic impetus for me to fashion a brand of melancholy that formed my early efforts as a semi-professional stand-up. Finally we got together, and after five happy years, I found myself in the Hendon Garden Hospital with a smashed hand. I'm sure Caroline would call that karma.

I'm getting ahead of myself again here, or possibly behind. The point is, having seen Dominik Diamond perform a successful stand-up set in front of the student body, I decided I would do the same; styling myself as a performance poet, so as not to appear as though I was jumping on Dominik's bandwagon, and developing strengths I had already acquired in Stratford. I bought a notepad, stole a pen and began to write things down.

David Icke and the Orphans of Jesus

In our third and final year a small group of us with an interest in comedy banded together to form the recurring line-up for a weekly comedy club in Clifton, Bristol. We called ourselves David Icke and the Orphans of Jesus, after the BBC sportscaster who publicly unravelled, pronouncing himself the Son of God, extolling the virtues of wearing turquoise clothing and expounding conspiracy theories concerning a global cabal of shape-shifting lizards representing the true axis of world power. He made these proclamations with such equable rationale, it was hard to dispel the creeping dread that he might know something we didn't.

Whatever the truth of the matter, six Bristol University students took his name and the name of another much loved historical crackpot in vain and created a weekly showcase at the Dome restaurant in Clifton, which lasted for four weeks and much to our surprise drew in fire-officer-worrying crowds to every show. Dominik Diamond was the brains behind the enterprise, characteristically seeing it as a way to earn a few quid.

The six of us operated on a door split, with Dominik taking the lion's share of the 'box office' because he was the compère and it was his idea and he was a rampant capitalist. Joining Dominik and myself were Myfanwy Moore, Barnaby (Carrier Pigeons) Power, David Williams and Jason Bradbury. We mixed up the running order every week, working from the socialist standpoint that we were all equal and should share the burden of opening and the luxury of closing the show (a standpoint Dominik was never comfortable with, what with him being a money mad maniac).

I had developed my act a little by this stage; I was in my third year and had performed at a number of cabarets in the drama department and the student union. I had started using the some-what impractical gimmick of having a real live goldfish onstage with me. Rover, a fish I bought for my student house, became the central theme of the act. The idea being that he was a Marxist poet, using me as a proxy to deliver his blistering political invectives.

Luckily for you, gentle reader, I can't remember or find any of these works – I presume that they have been either lost or more likely destroyed by the government – but the premise worked well in a surreal way and enabled me to open my silly poems up to include daft anthropomorphic love songs and protest rants.

I was so committed to the idea that I would actually take the trouble of bringing the fish tank to gigs and placing it on a stool next to me so that the audience could witness the fish swimming around during the show. When I performed my Edinburgh show in 1995, I was unable to transport him up to Scotland and so opted for a plastic facsimile rather than buy a stand-in. Poor Rover died while I was away. He was five and, although he denies it, I'm sure it was Nick's fault. We will now observe five lines of silence in his honour.

I had also worked as a lifeguard at the Gloucester Leisure Centre by this time and channelled much of my poolside experience into my act, often performing actually wearing my lifeguarding uniform. My unrequited love shtick had developed specifically into a series of poems and jokes about being obsessed with the actress Diane Keaton. There was an agenda at work here. I had always felt that Eggy Helen (cast your minds back a few chapters – I punched a window – keep up) resembled the actress and my comic proclamations of love were a way of publicly expressing my affections for her in the face of her apparent indifference in the real world.

I Love You

I love you
I love you because
I cannot have you
Because I don't want to
Because you hurt me
Because I drown profound
In every thing that you do
In every thing that you say
In every thing that you are
In every single way
And because you look a bit like Diane Keaton

By the time the David Icke and the Orphans of Jesus shows started, Eggy Helen and I had finally got together, but I persisted with the Keaton routines because they were whimsical and effective and wound inextricably into my material, which had begun to expand, edging out the poetry into more anecdotal stand-up and silly stories. I only once strayed away from my obsession with Diane Keaton, with an ode to another gorgeous Hollywood actress, Sigourney Weaver.

Sigourney Weaver

Sigourney
You make me feel . . .

Like countless innuendo
You drive me round the bend
Oh Sig!
What will I tell Diane?

At the time of David Icke and the Orphans of Jesus, I had become obsessed with Vic Reeves and Bob Mortimer's surreal variety show *Big Night Out*, which I had accidentally taped when my VCR continued recording after Woody Allen's *Play It Again, Sam* (starring Allen and Diane Keaton, naturally). The show was a joyously surreal, wilfully obscure cabaret that somehow made you feel like part of an exclusive club made up of people who 'got it'. Endlessly quotable and always essential viewing (I eschewed live images of Thatcher finally leaving Number Ten to watch it), *Big Night Out* seemed brilliantly subversive proof that the minutiae of your own personal, very specific and silly sense of humour could translate into a performance that would appeal to a large audience, not just friends.

Encouraged by their lunacy, I began to introduce more absurdist concepts into my act, which sat well with the goldfish and the lifeguarding uniform. My stage persona took the form of a lovestruck, congenital liar who worked in a swimming pool, claiming that films such as *Close Encounters of the Third Kind* and *RoboCop* as well as comic-book characters such as Batman and Spider-Man had been ripped off from events in his own life, Spider-Man eventually becoming the basis of a later audition for *Six Pairs of Pants* and the sketch that won Jessica Hynes a place on the show.

The success rate of the erstwhile members of David Icke and

the Orphans of Jesus has been fairly impressive. Dominik Diamond went on to become an accomplished broadcaster, Myfanwy Moore moved behind the camera and became a highly influential producer at the BBC and was instrumental in bringing me and another member of the group to the attention of the Paramount Comedy Channel in the mid-nineties, Barnaby Power continues to work in theatre as an actor, Jason Bradbury is now host of the hugely popular *Gadget Show* on Channel Five, and David Williams changed his name to Walliams and joined forces with a young graduate called Matt the year after I left. Sadly, I have no idea what happened to them.

10

Somewhere amid the cotton-wool fog that was Pegg's consciousness, he became sensible of voices raised in confrontation around him.

One of the voices, a deep reptilian drawl, seemed to resonate in the pit of his stomach, as though he had swallowed a bee or a dildo.

Another gave him a different sensation that he couldn't quite decipher in the mists of his addled perception. As things became clearer, he realised the voice was that of Murielle Burdot and the sensation he felt was the sickening sting of betrayal. He tried to utter an expletive but discovered his mouth had been taped up.

He was, in some measure, relieved, as the words he was about to utter were a bit sexist. The first voice, he realised, was that of Lord Black.

Pegg opened his eyes. The tall masked figure of his arch-enemy stood directly across the room from him, next to a drinks cabinet, the doors of which, Pegg ruminated, were shaped like boobs.

'Aaahhh,' said Black, like a twat. 'Look who's decided to join us. I was beginning to worry you might remain unconscious forever and that would have been a distinct shame.'

Pegg flashed his eyes at Black, unable to deliver

the devastating retort his now fully functioning mind
had taken milliseconds to formulate. Instead, he tried
to give Black the finger but found his hands were tied.

'Please,' implored Murielle, 'you said ee was not to
be 'armed.'

'Silence!' shouted Lord Black, raising a hand to the
deceitful French beauty.

Pegg similarly gesticulated but, being bound hand and
foot, communicated his feelings with a convulsive jerk
and a wiggle of his eyebrows. Murielle understood what
Pegg had meant by this; the meaning was obvious.

'Don't pretend you care about me, you treacherous
harpy. I trusted you, loved you even, and what do I
get in return for giving myself to someone? Screwed,
that's what. Is it any wonder I'm such a recluse?
There's no going back from this, Murielle, you're nothing
to me now, nothing at all. Any vestige of love I felt
for you drained from my body with my consciousness
after that dart stuck in my neck. You're not Murielle
any more, Murielle, you're just the Scarlet Panther,
and panthers get hunted down and put on display and I
won't be happy until you've been stuffed and mounted
and hung on the wall of my study or maybe the games
room.'

She hung her head in shame.

'May I interest you in something to drink?' Black
offered cordially, gesturing towards the boob cupboard.

Pegg's eyes flicked across to the carriage clock on
the mantelpiece. It was nine o'clock in the morning.
This man was out of his mind. It was insanity to start
drinking at this time of the day unless you were an
alcoholic or a shift worker. Pegg shook his head, the
fire of disapproval flashing in his eyes.

'You don't have to have a 'drink' drink. You could always have a Coke Zero,' said Black with a knowing sneer. Pegg's eyes communicated an unmistakable 'Fuck you, smarty-pants'.

'Suit yourself,' said Black, uncorking a bottle of 800-year-old Famous Grouse and pouring a generous measure into a crystal tumbler. 'I suppose you must be wondering what this is all about,' Black continued, taking a sip and nodding appreciatively.

Pegg looked around the room, assessing the situation, looking for opportunities, weighing up his chances of escape, should he find a way to shed his bonds. The room had four doors, each one guarded by a goon in dark glasses, with an H&K machine gun slung across his chest. Even if Pegg could shake off his shackles, there was no way he'd be able to take on four heavily armed henchmen and Lord Black. The odds were definitely against him and a sense of defeat enveloped him as he slumped back into his chair. Just then, he noticed the inert figure of Canterbury sat in a Parker Knoll armchair to his right. He looked at his cybernetic friend and softened for a split second. Of course, Canterbury hadn't malfunctioned on the jet, he had somehow seen through Muri— the Scarlet Panther's duplicity, picking up on micro-fluctuations in body temperature and behavioural tells, which identified her as an enemy, even before Canterbury's amiable conscious mind had followed suit. Poor Canterbury, he had been loyal to his master on the deepest level and Pegg had repaid him by enforcing program restrictions, sanctioning his directives and being a cunt.

'Terribly sweet really,' sneered Black. 'He carried you in here and sat down, good as gold, without a hint of resistance. I think he was protecting you, you know.

I think he knew I'd kill you if he put up a fight. He picked you up, brought you in here and switched himself off. He hasn't made a peep for hours.'

Pegg looked at his beloved metal compadre, searching his rigid metal endoskeleton for signs of life. If only he could get Canterbury to reactivate, he might stand a chance of putting a plan into action.

Then . . .

He saw it. The glimmer of hope he had been searching for. Blinking at a steady pulse, just beneath his left aural receptor, was Canterbury's earring. The jammy bastard had been awake all along. Pegg's body filled with elation.

'Are you sure I can't get you anything?' persisted Black. 'I'm about to tell you why I set you up and it's going to take a while so you might as well be comfortable.'

Pegg nodded enthusiastically.

'Splendid,' brayed Black. 'Some fresh juice perhaps, or a glass of Volvic?'

Pegg shook his head.

'Evian?' suggested Black.

Pegg shook his head even more fervently and nodded down at his stomach, widening his eyes to ensure Black knew he was indicating to something specific, which is technically illegal in charades.

'Are you hungry?' smiled Black.

Pegg wished he could touch his nose and point at Black to officially confirm he had guessed right, but the enthusiasm of his response to Black's suggestion was enough.

'Ah, breakfast, you would like some breakfast wouldn't you?' declared Black.

Pegg nodded with childish vigour, making his eyes smile as much as he could.

'Some Weetabix perhaps?' Black suggested.

Pegg shook his head, frowning, as if Weetabix tasted like Satan's wang.

'A full English?' Black said triumphantly, convinced that Pegg would relish a plate of sausage, egg, bacon, beans and/or a fried slice.

Pegg was tempted, but rejected the idea with a furious shake of his head.

Black frowned, considering what else he had to offer. Pegg's eyes burrowed into him, willing his arch-enemy to offer the specific item he craved so very much.

'I've got it,' said Black with a triumphant flourish. 'Toast.'

It happened in an instant and was over before Black realised what was happening. Canterbury stood up, his body shell unfolding like an origami swan dropped into a bowl of warm water. His shoulder-mounted rockets flipped out of his epaulettes. The calculations took less than a second, far less time than for the goons to shoulder and aim their automatic weapons. Four rockets deployed with a searing fizz; an instant later, four obliterated bodies slumped against four doors. A thin, blinding laser beam shot from Canterbury's ocular sensors and with breathtaking precision melted the locks on every door, sealing them shut against the shouts of concern erupting without.

With the reflexes of her feline jungle namesake, Murielle dived to the floor as Lord Black pulled a long silver revolver from inside his coat, levelling it at Pegg. With all his strength, Pegg kicked the coffee table across the room, sending it crashing into Black's shins; he squealed in a way that brought a smile to Pegg's face. By the time Black had rallied, Canterbury was upon him, his metal fingers closing around his throat, lifting him three feet off the ground.

Pegg gave a muffled shout. Canterbury's head swivelled like an owl's, looking back at his prone master. Something passed between them. A look of uncertainty from Canterbury and nod of assurance from Pegg, whose eyes said it all: 'You can do it.' With three short bursts of his face laser, Canterbury freed his master of his restraints and gag with staggering pinpoint accuracy.

'Impressive,' smiled Pegg. 'Most impressive.'

'You'll find I'm full of surprises,' replied Canterbury, and in this simple nod to *The Empire Strikes Back*, the second and best of the *Star Wars* films, all was right between them. They were friends again, perhaps stronger than they had ever been. Pegg could have kissed his robotic friend but he wasn't gay or into robots (not since he'd met Murielle at least).

'Now let us finally find out what Lord Black looks like, shall we?' said Pegg, hoping he was all deformed and gross because he needed a laugh.

Murielle had managed to get to her feet. She looked at Pegg half impressed, half bereft. She made to speak but Pegg cut her off.

'I don't want to hear it,' he said angrily with a hint of sadness and regret and resignation and sadness.

Canterbury pulled Black's head round and clasped the corner of the mask in his titanium fingers. He took one look at Pegg, who nodded back at him. The mask came away easily. Pegg staggered back, momentarily thrown.

'You!'

In-betweening

A fter graduating from one of Britain's most august educational establishments with a highly respectable degree, I went to work in Debenhams, Broadmead, as a toy demonstrator, trying to persuade people to purchase those irritating battery-operated dogs that yipped and performed a backwards somersault every 15.7 seconds until the AAs ran out or your soul farted out of your arse.

I wasn't entirely sure what I wanted to do with my life. Towards the end of my academic career, I had become involved in experimental theatre and performed several shows with a company called Bodies in Flight, which included David Icke and Carrier Pigeons alumnus, Barney Power, and Eggy Helen, my now serious girlfriend (whose affections I had finally won on the morning the Gulf War started, although I don't think the incidences were connected).

I continued to work with the company, even as I began to get more gigs as a stand-up comic. A few doors down from my beloved Forever People comic shop, on Park Street in Bristol, a pub called the Mauretania began running a weekly comedy club called the Tongue in Cheek. A compère would introduce two local acts, with an act from the London circuit closing the show. After the second interval, a few minutes would be set aside for an 'open spot', which despite sounding like a suppurating sore was actually an unpaid opportunity for untested acts to prove their worth before a live crowd.

I had already cut my teeth with the Orphans of Jesus at the Dome, when I took a fairly assured five minutes to the Mauretania one Thursday night, having taken the plunge and approached the organisers for the gig. The spot went well and I was invited back to perform a paid ten-minute half spot, subsequently becoming a regular performing full twenty-minute sets, working my way up from opening act to the middle of the show, which was pretty much the best a local performer could hope for.

The Tongue in Cheek's London acts were organised through a chain of South London comedy clubs called the Screaming Blue Murder, booked and run by an entrepreneurial young woman by the name of Dawn Sedgwick. Dawn provided a steady flow of established acts to close the Bristol shows, whilst booking and running London clubs and fulfilling her duties as an agent. The organisers at the Tongue in Cheek, a hugely supportive and amiable young couple (Melanie and David) and an enthusiastic young DJ and comedy fan called Gary Smith, had mentioned to Dawn that I was currently doing very well at the club and suggested that I call her to discuss the possibility of performing a few gigs in London.

And so it was that in May 1992 I travelled to the big city and performed two open spots, one at the Comedy Store in Leicester Square and the other at Dawn's Screaming Blue Murder club in Hampton Wick. I slept on the floor of Andy Thompson's pad in Islington and, he having proved an admirable axeman on 'My Fair Goldfish', I made use of his talents again for the shows. The song had killed at the Dome and there was no reason to doubt its effectiveness in the Big Smoke.

The spots went reasonably well, although at the Comedy Store the other comics were a little dismissive and wore their disdain for newcomers on their sleeves even when they were being nice, and the song felt a little out of place in front of the Thursday-night central London crowd. Nevertheless, booker Don Ward gave me some sage advice and invited me back for another open spot at a later date.

The Screaming Blue Murder was much better. It was more experimental and laid-back than the more meat-and-potatoes Comedy Store, and my quirky, unconventional material played well among the easy-going south London crowd. I met Dawn after the show and on the strength of that performance alone she offered to manage me, if I ever made the move to London. I look back on this moment as an extraordinary leap of faith on Dawn's part, which I appreciated immeasurably. I now had a focus and a goal to get me moving along the path, which felt more and more like the correct one. Bristol had somewhat put me off the notion of becoming a jobbing actor. The course had highlighted the shortcomings of the profession as much as it had equipped me for it and I baulked at the prospect of navigating an ever-struggling arts scene, waiting for the phone to ring. Ironically, after all those years in the education system, I decided to give myself some autonomy and to do the very thing I had done in front of the amassed ranks of the Salvation Army in 1977. Tell jokes.

Living in a one-bedroom flat with Eggy Helen, I continued to perform in Bristol and Bath, saving money from my work on stage and in retail, hoping to earn enough to make the move to London. As my reputation grew, I was booked for larger gigs in the area, opening for Kevin Eldon and Frank Skinner at the Watershed on the Bristol Docks, both of whom I would eventually get to know, particularly Kevin who I have worked with many times and who has become a good friend.

However, the gigs were nowhere near as frequent as they potentially were in London, and selling battery-operated toys hardly generated enough cash to survive, let alone uproot and move to the most expensive city in the country. On one occasion, while moving the furniture round the living room, Eggy Helen and I heard change rattling round inside the plush armchairs and spent several hours retrieving it. By the end of our extensive search, we had recovered thirteen pounds and triumphantly consigned it to a special fund for the hiring of videos and the purchase of wine. The fact that we got so excited about discovering such a small amount of money is a clear indication of our financial status at the time and the utter hopelessness of our desire to move to London.

Helen had aspirations of becoming an actress and there was no doubt that we both stood more chance of realising our dreams in the capital than we did in the sleepy South-West. Life seemed to be uneventfully dripping by and we were both somehow powerless to stop it.

The highlight of our week was generally watching the latest episode of Channel 4's newly imported show *Northern Exposure*,[17] to which we became utterly addicted. Eventually, a sad event provided us with the momentum we needed to escape. Eggy Helen's grandfather passed away, leaving her enough money to make the move, which she did, taking me along with her. Whatever the rules of quantum attraction would throw at us in the next few years, even if it ended in a small amount of blood and broken glass, I would forever be in her and indeed her family's debt.

---

[17] I remained hooked on *Northern Exposure* almost until the show ended for good, drifting away from it after the actor Rob Morrow left to pursue other things. The show became a major influence on my own writing and figured as an example of the magical realism we wanted to convey in *Spaced* when we pitched it to the execs. In 2009, Maureen, then heavily pregnant, Minnie and myself moved into a house in Santa Monica, California, to live while I shot the movie *Paul*. Much to my extreme shock and delight, I discovered my neighbour was none other than Rob Morrow. We became friendly and as a gift to us after the birth of our daughter, Rob and his wife Debbon made us a compilation CD of nursery rhymes, which we still play at bedtime a year later. A trip in the ESTB back to *Northern Exposure* nights in Bristol or to the pitch meeting for *Spaced* with news of this strange coincidence would have surely blown my mind. How the hell did I end up living next door to Dr Fleischman?

Nick

L ondon was an unknown quantity for Eggy Helen and me. We had stayed with friends in Clapham in the south and I had spent those few days in Islington; otherwise neither of us had any real knowledge of the city. I knew where the BBC and the Natural History Museum were, possibly Madame Tussaud's at a push, but in terms of where to live, we didn't have a clue.

Acting on a few recommendations from friends who had already made the leap, we bought a copy of *Loot* and spent an intensive week flat-hunting across the capital. On the fourth day we happened upon an ad for a reasonably priced one-bedroom rental in Cricklewood, north London.

Cricklewood was immediately recognisable to me as the home of seventies comedy threesome, the Goodies, and this tiny sliver of familiarity made the journey up to NW2 feel promising. I had been a huge fan of the Goodies as a kid, totally buying into their zany, junior *Monty Python* vibe. I had even purchased one of their albums and listened to it repeatedly in the front room at my nan's house along with *The Wombles* and *The Story of Star Wars*.

Situated at the quieter end of the bustling high street, the flat was perfect. Clean, modern and totally within our budget, the living room was small but airy, as was the bedroom, and a dark corridor was ingeniously lit by a fortified glass partition window, which allowed light to flow right through the flat to a small but functional kitchen space. The landlord, a roly-poly Irish man, seemed amiable if slightly dodgy and we nodded wide-eyed and hopeful at his request that we present him with five hundred pounds in cash every month without fail or face his jolly Irish wrath.

We took the plunge, signed the contracts and moved in, travelling to London in the back of the removal truck we used to transport our possessions, Rover (still alive at this point) sloshing around on my lap in his bowl. As soon as we arrived, I phoned Dawn and, true to her word, she put me on her books. By this time, Dawn had separated from Screaming Blue Murder and the agency she had worked for and founded an agency of her own, thus Dawn Sedgwick Management was born and as a testament to her tireless work ethic thrives on a much larger scale to this day, with me as her longest standing client. Actors often thank their agents during awards show acceptance speeches and it always sounds somewhat token. I can, however, honestly say that I love Dawn more than the combined ocean of love reserved for my mother, wife, daughter and dog and that is the absolute truth. (*Ben, can you make sure this bit only features in Dawn's personal copy, not the final version? Cheers. S.*)

I began travelling all round London performing open spots in the hope of getting paid bookings and slowly but surely they began to trickle in. For the first time in my life, I was earning a regular if erratic wage from performance.

Without the head start of an agent and the prospect of paid work, Eggy Helen had to find a job outside her vocational flight path in order to help pay the rent, eventually securing a waitressing gig at Chiquito's Mexican restaurant at Staples Corner, a few minutes' drive from our flat.

One evening she returned home from work and informed me that one of the waiters at the restaurant seemed to be quite funny and had a hankering to become a stand-up comic but didn't know how. She had told him that her boyfriend was a pro (which I was but barely) and suggested we meet and have a chat.

A week or so later, I met Nick Frost on the balcony of his flat in Cricklewood. Helen introduced us and for a moment it felt strangely as though I was on a blind date, saying to Nick, 'I've heard a lot about you.' He put on a little demonstration of his funniness to impress me, throwing a few impersonations into the conversation and rebounding around the party with confidence. When I left, I spied him fast asleep in an armchair next to a giant speaker, bolt upright and clutching a can of Red Stripe. I couldn't help smiling. I liked him; really liked him, in fact.

I wrote Nick a list of bookers and clubs to contact (which he still has seventeen years later) and took him to see his first gig, a new-act night at the Cosmic Comedy Club in Fulham.

The compère that night had failed to materialise and the promoter, who had booked me before, asked if I would step in. It was a tough night and I pretty much died on my arse, which didn't instil Nick with a huge amount of confidence in his new mentor. Determined to prove my worth as a comic, I took him out again the following weekend to the Balham Banana, a popular south London club, which ran two shows simultaneously on two levels. This time, the night was a storming success and Nick seemed suitably impressed with my efforts, almost as impressed as he was by the fact he had given comedian Mark Thomas a cigarette in the dressing room.

A few weeks later, Nick took part in the new-act night at the Cosmic and did extremely well, only being pipped at the post by another act who had brought along enough support to win the audience vote at the end. Nick's set was only slightly less well appreciated by a gaggle of Chiquito's staff who had secured the night off to cheer him on. I can clearly recall Nick performing a routine about built-up shoes and parading around demonstrating how someone might walk with an orang-utan sticking out of his arse.

Over the next six months he performed ten gigs in all. Five were great, five were demoralising and nightmarish, and at the end of the tenth set, he decided that it wasn't for him, which frustrated me enormously because in the short time I had known him I realised that he was possibly the funniest person I had met in my entire life.

Despite his reluctance to pursue stand-up, he continued to come to my gigs, and by the time I had parlayed my stand-up career into television, he had seen me perform hundreds of times; he can still recite passages from my set and remembers much of it better than I do. We quickly became inseparable and it all seemed to make more sense to me than any previous friendship, despite our differing backgrounds and experiences. Two years my junior, Nick was like no one I had ever met before. He was blissfully unpretentious and unshackled by the strictures of political correctness. The African chefs at Chiquito's loved him precisely because he could expertly impersonate the variety of sub-Saharan dialects that flew around the kitchen, which he did without a shred of prejudice, making him the subject of much finger-snapping and screaming laughter. If I broadened Nick's horizons culturally, then he broadened mine socially, and crucially taught me how to chill the fuck out.

Over the next few months, I introduced Nick to as much comedy and film as I could, constantly taking him to the cinema or watching videos and going to live performances whenever we could afford it. It seemed odd to me that I worked in comedy and yet the most talented comedian I knew was a waiter at a local restaurant. His natural ability outstripped that of anyone I had encountered on the circuit and I was convinced he had something extraordinary to offer. I resolved to find some way other than stand-up to showcase his talents.

The Logic of Chance

Meeting Nick under such a peculiar set of 'coincidences' threw up a lot of questions for me at the time; predominantly, if there is no fate and our interactions depend on such a complex system of chance encounters, what potentially important connections do we fail to make? What life-changing relationships or passionate and lasting love affairs are lost to chance?

I met my wife on holiday; ten years later we have a daughter. That means that our daughter's very life was determined not just by my and Maureen's decision to go to Thessalonica, Greece, but our decision to go into whatever travel agent we booked the holiday at in the first place at the precise time we did so. Then again, the very fact that we both made that series of decisions suggests that we had something in common in the first place and that synchronicity was slowly drawing us together.

Plainly it isn't an exact science, despite it being a complex interaction of micro-decisions and corresponding thought; perhaps it doesn't always work and we pass by some potential soulmates like the proverbial ships in the night, never quite connecting. Then again, perhaps the system is tenacious and continues to run like a computer program on an infinite loop, so that if at first you don't meet, you are drawn back together for another try.

After Maureen and I met, we realised that, despite the fact that we had never actually met before, we had not only dated friends we had in common but also been in the same place at the same time on several occasions, mainly at gigs where we assembled due to a simple fact that we share a similar taste in music (cultural preferences being one of the more obvious pretexts of quantum attraction).

On another occasion she spotted me in Camden Market, while shopping with her then boyfriend, recognising me from the TV. The boyfriend was a *Spaced* fan and would often eschew Friday nights out on the razz in favour of staying in and watching the show, much to her chagrin. The next time we saw each other was at Gatwick airport, shortly before leaving for Greece. It wasn't until the day we returned to the UK that her decision to sit at the back of the transfer bus resulted in our meeting. Nick and I had made the same decision one stop earlier and so, after a number of near misses, I met the woman who would become my wife and the mother of my child. If Nick and I had not retained that same school-kid desire to seek out those seats, I would have missed her again, but then that tiny, seemingly meaningless decision was another part of the sequence that eventually led not only to us meeting but subsequently discovering we lived just ten minutes from each other in north London.

My dad told me that by the time he met his current wife Kath, they had been in the same room at the same time on four occasions and even been vaguely aware of each other before they finally met and fell in love.

Social venues are a valuable sorting tool in this highly dubious 'science' (that I just made up), since they bring people together en masse and reduce the odds. The Shepherds (there's a whole

(L to R) Edgar Wright, Quentin Tarantino and me at the Arclight Theatre in LA on the opening night of *Shaun of the Dead*. Only one of us is really as cool as he looks.

(L to R) Me, Kathleen Kennedy, Steven Spielberg and Nick Frost on the set of *Tin Tin* in 2009. At no point did we ever lose sight of where we were or who we were working with. It was like *Jim'll Fix It*

I drew this for our producer Nira Park after Nick and I spitballed the idea for *Paul* whilst shooting *Shaun of the Dead*. She stuck it to the pin board in her office where it has remained ever since. The eventual design for Paul is not that far from the original sketch.

The always hilarious Dave Koechner with me and Nick on the set of *Paul*, Madrid, New Mexico in 2009.

M:I:3 2005 (L to R) Maggie Q, Jonathan Rhys Myers, me, Ving Rhames, Michelle Monaghan and Tom Cruise. That's actually a waxwork of me they were all posing with at Madame Tussaud's.

Never did I dream as a seven-year-old boy that I would one day find myself in such a heavenly situation. Me with eleven slave Leias and one Oola on the set of *Paul* in Albuquerque in 2009.

Me, Minnie and the great outdoors. I did not have
a licence for this tractor.

(L to R) Joe Lo Truglio, me, John Carroll Lynch,
Kristen Wiig, Nick Frost and Blythe Danner,
jumping for joy on the set of *Paul*.

Working with the man himself. John Landis with Andy Serkis and me on the set of *Burke and Hare* in February 2010.

I took this picture in my trailer on the set of *Star Trek*. I was worried they would arrest me.

(L to R) Me, Reece Shearsmith, Ray Harryhausen and Andy Serkis at Harry's 90th birthday tribute. Long ago I battled those imaginary skeletons, and now I get to meet the man who planted them so firmly in my brain.

The apples of my eye...

My miniature schnauzer, Minnie.

My California gurl,
Matilda.

My beautiful wife,
Maureen. Classic
Thelma and Louise
shot of us in
Greece where we
met ten years ago.
I thought long and
hard about including
a picture of Mo and
had so many to
choose from but in
the end, I thought
this one really
summed us up.

chapter on this pub later) was definitely an important social nexus, where I nurtured several close friendships. I met complete strangers who went on to become an integral part of my life, all because we were drawn towards the same hub. The charm and appeal of the place was like a beacon, which attracted like-minded people in from all over the country, even all over the planet.

X-Files actress Gillian Anderson joined our team one evening for the pub quiz, having become friends with Chris Martin, who I had become friends with through Maureen, who I met on a bus in Greece. This was an extraordinarily exciting prospect for Nick and me, having been avid fans of the show since our days of living together in relative squalor in north-west London. Now, five years later, we were about to buddy up with our favourite actress for a night of beer and competitive trivia. To fully appreciate the enormity of this coincidence, we need to go back five years to a one-bedroom flat in Ivy Road, Cricklewood.

Nick's girlfriend had recently vacated the flat they shared together after they decided to part ways. On Nick's request, she had taken most of the contents, leaving only a small amount of furniture, a gas heater, an old TV/video combo and a pile of books. Having both recently emerged slightly bruised from serious relationships and being generally unmotivated and directionless to boot, I moved in with Nick and we proceeded to spend much of our time lying around smoking large custom-made joints and watching back-to-back episodes of *The X-Files*; all the while developing a powerful shared crush on Gillian Anderson's Agent Scully. I had purchased box sets of seasons 1, 2 and 3 after my sister Katy had turned me on to the show. (My baby sister has always had impeccable taste in television and to this day has her finger on the pixel, née cathode, pulse.)

Our crush was wilfully boyish, harking back to a time when we kissed pictures and not actual girls. Pictures, after all, didn't sleep with people behind your back and inspire you to unleash hell on interior glazing. Nick taped a cut-out photo of Anderson on to the inside of the mug cupboard so he could look at her every time he made a cup of tea (every fifteen minutes), and when I finally moved into my new flat in Kentish Town, I bought a huge poster of her wearing a blue leather catsuit and mounted it (no pun intended) over my fireplace.

We maintained our love of the show for many years, and when I came to write *Spaced*, I gave Tim my boyish affection for her as a gift. We even shot a scene for the first series in which she appears to Tim as a sort of Obi-Wan Kenobi-ish phantom, bestowing sage advice. Naively, I had written the scene in the vague hope that she might agree to appear. She was performing in *The Vagina Monologues* at the Old Vic while we were shooting and I dropped a note off for her at the stage door, explaining about the show and the scene. She always came across as very cool and interesting in interviews and I couldn't help feeling this might actually appeal to her. Having now received several of these notes myself, I can imagine how she must have felt when reading my request. Flattered but utterly incapable of spreading herself so thin between every entreaty for her attention. The scene was shot with a lookalike but later deleted because it didn't work.

The night she came to the Shepherds, I made sure I had copies of both series of *Spaced* on DVD and passed them to her when I managed to break the ring of rapt male attention that encircled her. I slightly regretted it the next day, since many of the references to her in the show make mention of her as the prime subject of Tim's masturbatory fantasies and I feared she might watch it and get creeped out. I didn't occur to me on the night, however. It seemed crazy to Nick and me that the object of our affections had somehow found her way into our little pub and was sat with us poring over Bernie's quiz sheet, two of the answers on which had been devised specifically for her, after Bernie learned she would be in attendance. Ironically, the questions were about *The X-Files* and, tellingly, Nick and I knew the answers before she did.

Unsurprisingly, the night turned out to be one of the best ever during our time as regulars at the pub. Gillian was charming and funny, and for all the awe that her fantasy royalty inspired, she seemed like the kind of person we'd hang out with whether she was our favourite, fictional FBI agent or not. It was tempting to see her presence in the pub as fateful, even more so being cast alongside her in *How to Lose Friends & Alienate People* in 2007 and becoming proper friends, but it wasn't fate, it was the complex swirls and eddies of quantum attraction, an interaction of millions of tiny choices, preferences and details that magnetised us and drew us all to that particular coterie on that particular quiz night. Although to Nick and me, it was nothing short of an *X-File*.

Something as simple as geographical proximity and a keen interest in manga animation had put Edgar and me in the same auditorium in 1989, but we missed each other that night. It took a more complex butterfly effect to facilitate our actual meeting. That wouldn't happen until seven years later at the Battersea Arts Centre (although Edgar insists it was the Riverside Studios in Hammersmith). We were there to see Matt Lucas perform his psychotic raconteur and rabid thespian, Sir Bernard Chumley, with his then sidekick, David Walliams. Matt invited Edgar to the show having seen his first raw but undoubtedly impressive cinematic offering, *A Fistful of Fingers*, championing him to the Paramount Comedy Channel as a potential director for his and David's first TV sketch show, *Mash and Peas*.

I had met Matt on the comedy circuit and knew David well from university. I had also been working on a show for the Paramount Comedy Channel, called *Dan Doyle: Space Person*, about a British astronaut, stranded in deep space with his dog Shatner and a Hal-style artificially intelligent computer called Alan. I had got the job on the strength of my work as a stand-up comedian, which had also led to appearances on the BBC's *Stand Up Show*, on which I performed a routine about coming from the West Country. Edgar, a fellow West Country boy, had seen the show and approached me in the bar at the BAC/Riverside to say hello.

Eventually, through our connections at Paramount, we found ourselves working on the same show, a strange hybrid sketch/sitcom/stand-up/music show called *Asylum*, the rough tale of a pizza delivery boy trapped in a mental institution along with a group of other hapless 'patients'. The devising process began when Paramount assembled a group of stand-ups to workshop ideas in an attempt to create the show collectively from a sort of comedic think tank. After the first session, a number of the original group dropped out due to moral objections to the show's flippant approach to mental health care (quantum attraction at work). This left us bereft of any female contribution and feelers went out for replacements. I had not long finished filming *Six Pairs of Pants* where I had met Jessica Hynes due to Katy Carmichael (Twist in *Spaced*) bringing her along to the audition for moral support. She had made a huge impression on me during the shoot and I immediately thought of her when it came to suggesting new recruits for *Asylum*. She wasn't a stand-up as such, but in terms of comic chops, she could definitely hold her own among the professionally funny folk, which included comedians Adam Bloom, Norman Lovett, Paul Morocco and Julian Barratt. Jess joined the group and we continued to work, with Edgar and David Walliams taking an executive role in the writing process, building the narrative around characters and improvisations workshopped by the actors.

This was the first time Jess, Edgar and I had worked together as a threesome. The pre-existing chemistry Jess and I had established on *Six Pairs of Pants* meant that we naturally gravitated towards each other in rehearsals, which in turn motivated David and Edgar to write with this in mind. Many of my scenes in *Asylum* involved Jess, who played two characters, the psychotic Scottish Nurse McFadden and a sweet, befuddled patient called Martha, obsessed with Channel 4's *Countdown*. Interestingly, Jess was the only performer in the show not to adopt her own name for her character(s), marking her out as the only real actress among us.

As the series evolved (Edgar and David were still writing as we were shooting), my and Jess's storyline developed into a sweet will-they-won't-they romance which eventually motivates my character (Simon Pegg, the pizza delivery boy) to lead a mass breakout and overthrow Norman Lovett's misguided, experimental psychologist, Dr Lovett.

At the time, I was also shooting a new sketch show for Channel Five, produced by the same people who had created *Six Pairs of Pants*. *We Know Where You Live* was to feature as part of Channel Five's launch package and eventually produced some funny moments from a strong cast which featured Sanjeev Bhaskar, Amanda Holden, Fiona Allen, Ella Kenion and Jeremy Fowlds. I worked on the show for six days a week, and on Sundays, travelled down to a disused children's hospital in Cobham, Surrey, to shoot *Asylum*. It was very hard work and I resented Edgar slightly for his part in dragging me south every week on what should have been my day off. His work method was exhaustive, complicated, and at times his motives were difficult to fathom.

Six days a week I was making point-and-shoot comedy sketches at a breakneck pace, then I'd find myself in Surrey, performing multiple takes on complex set-ups, all the while wondering what the hell was going on. We were, after all, only making a low-budget comedy show for a cable TV channel. Did it really require such studious application of technique and attention to detail?

Despite my exhaustion, which was actually nothing next to that suffered by Edgar who was living and breathing the show, writing, shooting and editing in a perpetual sleepless cycle, I eventually enjoyed the shoot, since it seemed sillier and more edgy than the more conventional fair I was knocking out through the week.

When I finally saw *Asylum* edited together, everything made sense. I was blown away by Edgar's style and technique, and marvelled at his apparent ability to hold the fluid and intricate camera movements of an entire show in his head while creating it in a random order. The whole thing held together like an expensive movie. And justified the time and effort Edgar had devoted to it. Elements of scenes that were shot weeks apart blended together seamlessly, and I experienced the same sense of wonder and admiration for Edgar watching the cut as I had done for the Coen brothers watching *Raising Arizona*.

This particular film has had a huge influence on me as a film-maker, with its frantic directorial style, heightened performances and poetic writing and construction. It was perhaps the first time I realised that comedy could be derived from more than simply the script and the actors. The camera itself became an integral part of building the comedy. The Coen brothers didn't simply point their lenses at the actors and capture the funny; they used their cameras to enhance and augment the comic beats. This device naturally extended into the way the film was edited and scored, creating a beautifully integrated comic masterpiece, which represents a brilliant unifying of the film-making process. I watched the movie twice in a row and decided that if I ever made films or TV shows, they would have to be like this. Of course, I would need to find a director who felt the same way as me, someone who could speak graphically, who could read a script and translate it into a series of visual beats that enhanced the physical action and dialogue, someone with lots of hair and a beard.

Edgar was a director who seemed inextricably plugged into his own vision, who totally understood how the movement of a camera can inform a scene. How it can increase tension or communicate drama, urgency or danger (and he definitely had a beard). Watching just a few moments of *Asylum* in the edit, I knew immediately that if ever I got to make my own TV show, I would want Edgar to direct it. I later discovered that Edgar and I had both attended the opening-night screening of Katsuhiro Otomo's anime masterpiece *Akira* at the Watershed, Bristol, in 1989, and that *Raising Arizona*, *Dawn of the Dead* and *Akira* were Edgar's three favourite films. It's strange to think that sitting in the dark all those years earlier, perhaps just a few seats away from me, was a fifteen-year-old boy who would eventually change my life completely. If the laws of quantum attraction do apply, then it would seem not meeting Edgar would have been harder.

The Wizard of Oz

As Smiley and I sat together in the sweltering heat of an Ozzy beach, a particularly mesmerising ambient house track played on the minibus stereo, building gradually into great swooping loops, promising the return of the pounding backbeat but holding off tantalisingly, as if knowing how much we wanted it. The moment finally arrived when withholding the base drum would have been cruel; we looked at each other and, with goofy whacked-out smiles, said in unison, 'Here we go.'

Life was changing rapidly for me at this point. Eggy Helen and I had broken up just two months before and in the aftermath I had wandered dazed into the Garden Hospital in Hendon with a smashed knuckle on my right hand thanks to the partition window in our flat. Now I was jetting off to Adelaide, Australia, to begin the biggest adventure of my life, with a group of other wide-eyed comics for whom the experience was similarly huge.

It was while on this trip that I forged another of the most significant friendships of my adult life, with a mercurial Northern Irish stand-up, rave bunny and bar-room philosopher called Michael Smiley. I had been aware of Michael for a few years, having first seen him delivering frenetic and oddly absorbing field reports for the magazine show *Naked City*. There was something magnetic about him. Occasionally, you will see someone on television for the very first time, and such is their charisma and presence, you assume they have been around forever and somehow just avoided your attention. This was most certainly the case with Smiley; he had a confidence, an assurance, even a slight air of danger about his persona that gave the impression he had been drafted in from somewhere else, a place where he was king.

A year or so later, I found myself on the same bill as Smiley at the Cosmic Comedy Club in Fulham. I had gone along with Nick Frost in tow, to perform at one of the hellish Christmas party bashes, which sapped the soul but made sense financially. Usually, comedy clubs are filled with people who have paid specifically to see a night of comedy, but at a Christmas party bash the audiences were merely out on a 'works do' and it was a hard job diverting their attention to the stage, particularly when where they really wanted to be was back at the office, drinking red wine out of paper cups and trying to persuade Tina from accounts to photocopy her vagina.

Nick and I both recognised Smiley from *Naked City* and exchanged a few pleasantries in the artists' holding area (an empty upstairs bar). Smiley is not the type of man to suffer fools gladly, and knowing him as well as I do now, I can only imagine what he must have thought of this fresh-faced little smarty-pants student comic and his even younger Essex sidekick.

I saw him again in a bar in Edinburgh the following year and offered a quick hello, which I think he returned with a surly nod. We were both at the festival performing one-man shows. Smiley had become a fixture at the fringe having come second to Dylan Moran in the annual 'So You Think You're Funny' new-act competition (I went out in the heats), whereas this was my first time performing a one-hour show and I felt like a first-year at a big comprehensive. Scouts for a number of Antipodean comedy festivals, including Adelaide and Melbourne in Australia and Wellington and Auckland in New Zealand, were trawling the venues for potential acts to fly over and both Smiley and I eventually made the grade.

The following February my agent informed me that Smiley and I would be on the same flight to Sydney and gave me his mobile phone number to coordinate meeting at the airport. I was very impressed by this – after all, it was 1996 and cellular phones were still something of a luxury. I called the strange, futuristic series of digits and arranged to meet Smiley at Heathrow, along with a number of other acts, including Andrew Maxwell, Simon Munnery and Sean Lock. Thrown into this strange adventure and bonded by the uncertainty we faced, Smiley and I began to warm to each other.

When we arrived in Australia, any cautious circling was abandoned in favour of excitable giggling at this exotic new land. The weather was beautiful, the landscape beguiling, the girls were uniformly gorgeous – and what's more, every household in Adelaide was permitted by law to cultivate nine marijuana plants for personal use. Something about the culture shock and the psychological impact of being geometrically opposed to our lives back home sent us into a spin of hedonistic fervour. Suddenly I found myself relishing my status as a single man and I felt happy and liberated, as though I had been given the chance to start my adult life all over again. I went slightly insane, throwing myself into new experiences. I did a bungee jump, got a tattoo, grew my first beard and had a lot of sex. In the two and a bit months since she'd dumped me, it was the first time I actually felt glad that Eggy Helen had given me the elbow.

We spent most of our days down at Glenelg beach with the increasingly close-knit band of comics and friends we had made along the way. On one occasion, having indulged liberally in the local recreational herb, a sticky and pungent strain of marijuana, I found myself stood silently in the sea with a number of other comics including Smiley and Maxwell, the warm, blue water gently lapping against our hips as we stared into space, every one of us unspeakably happy but somehow struck dumb. After a minute or so of blissful, hazy peace, I lifted my head to my compatriots and uttered a simple devastating truth: 'This is our job.' We remained in a circle for another five minutes before we eventually stopped laughing.

On the surface, Smiley and I in particular were seemingly totally incompatible as friends; our respective credentials read more like a gay version of *Lady Chatterley's Lover*. He was a working-class Northern Irish tough nut, who was married and divorced with two kids and a wealth of life experience that might make a less resilient man feel as though the world owed him a living; whereas I studiously played the fresh-faced, middle-class university graduate who had always had it comparatively easy.

Before our time in Australia had ended, Smiley and I had agreed to share a flat together. Since I was living on Nick's floor in the aftermath of my break-up with Eggy Helen and Smiley found himself similarly transient, kipping on various sofas around west London, we resolved to start house-hunting as soon as we returned. This experience later inspired some of the details of Tim and Daisy's homeless exploits in *Spaced*, a show in which Smiley would eventually play the protean rave-pixie by the name of Tyrone 'Tyres' O'Flaherty.

A few months after we found a flat in Kentish Town, Nick joined us. Having finally given up the ghost on his deserted flat in Ivy Road, he found sanctuary in our spare room, a cell, which soon became affectionately known as 'the crab pit'. By a variety of incidents and accidents, the three of us had been drawn together from wildly disparate backgrounds under one roof to forge an enduring bond that had become nothing short of brotherly.

Michael and Nick were both best men at my wedding to Maureen and are both godfathers to my daughter. It sounds like I'm waxing fatal again, but I'm not; it comes back down to my whole dubious science thing. We might not know we are seeking out the people who best enrich our lives, but somewhere on a deep, subconscious level we absolutely are. Whether that bond is temporary or permanent, whether it succeeds or fails, fate is simply a conflagration of choices that combine with others to shape the relationships that surround us. We cannot choose our family but we can choose our friends, and we do, sometimes before we have even met them.

11

Hanging from the end of Canterbury's outstretched arm was Ben from Century (an imprint of Random House Publishing) a look of terror on his stricken face.

'B-But . . .' Pegg stammered.

'If you put me down, I'll explain it all,' Ben rasped, his face reddening further.

Canterbury lowered the publisher to the ground. He staggered slightly and clutched his bruised neck like a fairy. More of Lord Black/Ben from Century's goons had gathered at the door and were hammering incessantly to get in.

'Stand down,' choked Black. 'Everything's fine.'

'Are you sure, Ben — I mean, Lord Black?' said a voice of muffled concern.

'Yes,' Ben insisted, sinking into a chair and putting his head in his hands.

'Why?' Pegg said simply.

'I did it for you!' muttered Ben.

'For me?' Pegg said incredulously.

'I knew you didn't really want to write a biography,' Ben sighed. 'You seemed so reluctant. I thought perhaps you might require some inspiration and what better inspiration than an adventure? I thought perhaps the book might write itself. So I kidnapped Ms Burdot's dog —'

'Monsieur Pooh?' gasped Pegg.

'Oui,' faltered Murielle, her eyes brimming with desperate tears.

'I threatened to kill him unless Murielle stole the Star of Nefertiti from the Museum of Egyptian Antiquity.'

Pegg's eyes flitted over to the chastened French lovely. She looked at him pleadingly. He knew how much she treasured her Pooh and understood in that moment why she had done what she had done. He caught himself hoping that her deceit had only been partial and that she hadn't faked it, particularly the orgasms which had seemed really real.

'I knew that you knew that I possessed the tablet of Amenhotep IV,' continued Ben, 'and I also knew that you knew the awesome power of the two antiquities combined. It was a simple case of playing off your innate sense of right and wrong and of course your weakness for beauty.'

Murielle and Pegg exchanged a glance and something eased between them.

'And what of Lord Black?' Pegg asked, making sure all the loose ends were tied up neatly.

'Oh, I have always been Lord Black,' smiled Ben. 'Supervillainy is a lucrative sideline. Do you have any idea what I get paid at Century? I mean, it's good but it's not brilliant. It's the authors that earn the big bucks, and what do they do, really?

'Write books?' offered Canterbury.

Ben scoffed, 'You'd be surprised how few of them do. Particularly the money-grubbing celebritwats with their self-indulgent journals of narcissistic twaddle.'

'You've got a Porsche!' Pegg argued.

'It's second-hand,' countered Ben, triumphant at winning

the argument but slightly disappointed that he didn't have a new Porsche.

'So all the dastardly acts of wickedness perpetrated by Lord Black were all down to you?' Pegg enquired helpfully.

'Not all,' said Ben, regaining something of his foreboding malevolence. 'There is one last great wickedness. You see, I decided halfway through this wonderful stratagem that such a story was wasted on an oaf like you. I should do what I've always felt I could do better than any of you philistines — I'd write the book myself and earn enough money to buy a new Porsche.'

'What about *It Looks Like a Cock*?' challenged Pegg, referring to the novelty photobook of naturally occurring and man-made phallic symbols Ben had put together with his simpering sidekick, the notorious hunchback Jack Fogg. 'It sold loads!'

'I'm talking about a real book, you idiot,' snapped Ben. 'A book with a story that has a beginning, middle and end. We've had the first two, all we require now is an end — and what a denouement it will be. I'm going to make millions.'

With the speed of a cobra, Ben grabbed the standard lamp by his side, tore out the cable and jammed it into Canterbury's neck. A surge of electricity coursed through the robot's body, shorting his primary systems, before he had even clattered to the ground. Ben grabbed for the silver revolver and pointed it at Pegg.

'All too easy,' hissed the duplicitous villain/ publishing executive, squeezing the trigger.

Pegg was momentarily confused — he was looking into Murielle's eyes and yet how could this be? She had been on the other side of the room a moment ago and now she was here, her arms clasped tightly around his neck. Her grip loosened slightly and her eyes lost focus. It was then that Pegg realised what she had done and his heart broke in two and then those pieces broke in two so that his heart was in four. Somewhere else in the room he heard Ben fiddling with his pistol, hurriedly loading another bullet into the single-shot chamber. 'How very impractical,' thought Pegg, absent-mindedly plucking one of the throwing blades from his combat suit and propelling it into Ben's forehead. Pegg heard a dull thud and knew his nemesis had croaked.

'Simone.' Murielle's voice sounded distant and strained.

'Try not to speak.' Pegg brushed a strand of hair from her eye.

'I'm sorry,' she whispered. 'I'm sorry I lied. If eet means anything, I only told one lie, everything else was true, I promise.'

'So you weren't faking it then?' Pegg asked tentatively.

'Non,' Murielle whispered.

'The orgasms, I mean,' Pegg pushed.

Murielle smiled and put her hand on the side of Pegg's face and shook her head. Pegg breathed a sigh of relief, secure in the knowledge that he was still great at sex. Murielle shuddered, regaining Pegg's attention. She pulled him close and looked into his eyes.

'I love you,' she whispered.

Pegg immediately thought of Han Solo but decided not to go for the obvious.

'I love you too,' he replied.

Murielle's body went limp, her eyes fluttered into stillness. Pegg knew she was gone but held her closer anyway, burying his face in her hair. A clank from across the room drew his attention and he lifted his head to see Canterbury pulling himself upright. Relief spread through Pegg's body; at least his best friend was still alive, at least everything was not lost. For the first time in his life, since he was a baby, he cried. He cried in a way that was acceptable for a man to cry and had been since the mid-nineties.

'Why do you cry?' asked Canterbury.

'It's an emotional response,' sobbed Pegg. 'Fluid leaks from the tear ducts . . .'

'No, sir,' said Canterbury softly, 'I mean, why are you crying now?'

'Murielle,' said Pegg, his voice cracking, 'she's dead.'

'My scanners would suggest otherwise, sir.' Canterbury gazed at Murielle for a few moments, seemingly searching her inner body. 'Her heartbeat is faint but it's there. It would seem the bullet glanced off a rib and exited through the soft fatty tissue in her abdomen.'

'She's not fat!' said Pegg defensively.

'Sir, she's lost some blood, but if we hurry, we can get her to Hendon Garden Hospital. I'm not a medi-droid but I would wager she'll make a full recovery.'

'Really?' said Pegg, snorting a rope of snot from his upper lip. 'What about Black's goons?' asked Pegg. 'There must be forty of them between us and the jet.'

'Not to worry, sir,' beeped Canterbury. 'If you'd just give the word.'

Pegg lifted Murielle into his arms and smiled at his mechanical confidant. He opened his mouth and whispered a single word.

'Toast.'

Breaking the Telly

Nick and I discovered the spoof news show *The Day Today* by complete accident one Wednesday evening in 1994, and instantly become utterly obsessed with it. The feeling of excitement we got from watching that first episode reminded me of the thrill of finding those few minutes of *Vic Reeves Big Night Out* after *Play It Again, Sam*, or the time when I was finally allowed to watch *The Young Ones*.

And so it was that a short chain of events, kicked off with meeting Graham Linehan and Arthur Mathews after a gig at the Chiswick Comedy Club in west London, would end with me working with the creator of one of my favourite ever comedy shows.

It was 1997 and Linehan and Mathews were the writers of the now classic, then white-hot, Channel 4 sitcom *Father Ted*. The Chiswick gig had gone particularly well and Graham and Arthur came up for a quick chat after my stint was finished.

We hit it off immediately, and a few days later I was invited to take part in a couple of TV pilots they were writing. The first was for a sitcom called *A Bunch of Hippies*, the second was a sketch show called *Big Train*. I loved the sound of both projects and being involved in the pilots was an unmitigated pleasure not least because I felt as though I was finally working with people whose creative motivations were more in line with my own. The *Big Train* pilot was particularly exciting for me as it was to be directed by a huge comedy hero of mine, the brilliant Chris Morris. Chris, along with Armando Iannucci, had been responsible for the aforementioned *The Day Today*.

As if this wasn't enough, I soon after found myself having to sit on the wall outside Talkback's production offices in London's Percy Street waiting for my heart rate to slow down having been given the opportunity to audition for the Steve Coogan vehicle *I'm Alan Partridge*. The first time I was introduced to Steve, I was required to improvise with him in character, wig and all, as Partridge for about fifteen minutes. This was my first experience of performing with a character I had extensive prior knowledge of, and looking into the eyes of Alan Partridge was as intoxicating at the time as looking into the ears of Mr Spock would be twelve years later.

I got the part in *I'm Alan Partridge*, the pilot for *Big Train* was picked up, as was *A Bunch of Hippies* (now just called *Hippies*), although it wouldn't go into production until after *Big Train*. As a result of being introduced to Steve Coogan, with whom I had established an immediate rapport, I was asked to accompany him on tour, along with fellow *Big Trainer* and exceptional comic mind, Julia Davis.

At the same time, after the critical success of *Asylum*, Crispin Laser, a producer at the Paramount Comedy Channel, approached Jessica and me with an idea about creating a vehicle for us to star in together. Naive and confident as we were, we accepted the offer on the proviso that we write it ourselves. We decided to fashion a modern take on the old flat-share sitcom model and create a show that was part *Northern Exposure*, part *X-Files*, a sort of live-action *Simpsons* by way of *The Young Ones*. It started out as *Lunched Out* but soon changed to *Spaced*.

I regarded this new-found autonomy as the perfect opportunity to drag Nick kicking and screaming into the world in which he undoubtedly belonged by writing a character in the show specifically for him. Similarly, Jess saw the show as a chance to return a favour to Katy Carmichael, who had facilitated her inclusion in *Six Pairs of Pants*.

And the final piece of the jigsaw arrived the day that Edgar Wright came round to Jessica's house with a book full of storyboards he had put together for the first episode of *Spaced*. I simply had to marvel at his extraordinary and inventive interpretations of our script and felt so lucky and excited to have him on board. I remember looking up from the book to his face and studying it; trying to see his brain through his ridiculous mop of black hair. I felt as though he had seen into our own heads and somehow extrapolated exactly what was needed to make the show work visually, despite our own inability to describe it. He seemed to be so in tune with the script that it was evident his contribution was the missing part of the creative jigsaw which we hadn't noticed was incomplete.

With Edgar on board as director, we began writing and created the first series piecemeal over the next twelve months, working at each other's houses in between other projects.

It was while writing *Spaced* with Jessica that my love of the zombie was reanimated by Japanese video game company Capcom and the first instalment of their now classic horror survival title, *Resident Evil*.

The game enabled players to experience surviving a zombie outbreak first hand. Set in an old manor house, *Resident Evil* captured the spirit of Romero's mournful, shuffling originals brilliantly, bringing back the same frisson of terror and fascination that inspired my love of these tenacious movie ghouls in the first place.

At the time, the freedom to co-write my own sitcom was

affording me a certain amount of wish fulfilment. Just as I wanted to comically play out the grand tropes of the war movie and deliver a truthful and honest representation of the London rave scene, I realised I had the perfect opportunity to posit myself within one of my most beloved fantasies. The set-up wasn't even particularly tenuous; my character Tim, a shadow version of myself, was, like me, a gamer and as such would doubtless be engrossed in the first sequel to *Resident Evil*, which had soon followed the original game. The show was given to literal metaphors as Tim and Daisy fluctuated between reality and fantasy and it only took a few extra narrative grams of bathtub speed for Tim to find himself living out the game for real.

During the writing process, I discovered that Edgar had been equally beguiled by Romero as a youngster and he jumped at the chance to direct a slice of George-inspired carnage. So it was at nine thirty on a Friday night in October 1999, less than five minutes after Joey, Chandler, Rachel et al. had finished smart-mouthing each other in a fictional Manhattan coffee house, I blew the back of a dead man's head out with a silver, pistol-grip, pump-action shotgun.

We hoped and prayed that there were people out there who hadn't switched channels, as they idly wandered out to make a cup of tea, returning to witness their cosy Friday-night enter-tainment awash with blood. The opening scene of *Spaced*, Episode 3, 'Art', was the first sequence Edgar tackled in the edit after principal photography was complete. He used it as a personal mission statement for demonstrating his intentions for the series; it was the first fully formed moment of *Spaced* ever to exist and it set us out on a journey that would take us much further afield than Tufnell Park, north London. On the morning of the shoot, having completed the scene before lunch, Edgar and I both remarked that it would be fun to do that again sometime.

In the early half of 1998, I disappeared off on tour for six months with Steve Coogan's live show, *The Man Who Thinks He's It*, taking in what must have been every major city in the UK. Together with Julia Davis, we filled in the gaps during Steve's costume changes with characters and material Julia and I wrote with Steve and his long-time collaborators Henry Normal and Peter Baynham. I played a neurotic stage manager attempting an onstage proposal to Pauline Calf's best friend, Michelle, played of course by Julia (Him: 'I've picked your ring.' Her: 'That's no basis for a marriage!'), a hapless actor by the name of Alex D'Arcy (that's D, apostrophe, arsey.) and Paul Calf's new romantic friend, Keith Todd, who together with Julia's militant folk singer, Emma From, had given birth to a mutant child with seven ears (Keith: 'He's an ugly little bastard.' Emma: 'Be quiet, Keith, he'll hear you!' Keith: 'He's back at the hotel.' Emma: 'I KNOW!').

The tour was an amazing experience and Steve was extremely generous in ensuring the cast, dancers and hair and make-up artists all stayed in the very best hotels en route, something he didn't actually have to do. By the time June came round, I was physically and emotionally exhausted, although I barely had time to breathe before starting my next job.

We shot the first full series of *Big Train* that summer and had a thoroughly fun time doing it. There was a real excitement on-set, with both cast and crew aware that something genuinely different and inventive was being hatched. Joining Julia Davis and myself in the cast (Julia and I saw a lot of each other that year) were Kevin Eldon, Mark Heap and Amelia Bullmore, brilliant actors and formidable improvisers all. For the first time in my television career I felt as though I was contributing to a project which represented my own sensibilities completely, as did the rest of the cast. Whether we were protesting a ban on wanking in the office or playing showjumpers desperate to be firemen, we did so with total commitment to the moment, which made the comedy all the more strange and hilarious. Writer

Graham Linehan stepped in to call the shots this time, infusing ingenious comic flourishes, which ensured its unique feel. The show was at once subtle and outrageous, and day-to-day shooting was never short on giggles, particularly from Amelia, Julia and me who couldn't match Kevin and Mark's uncanny ability to keep a straight face. I actually managed to blag Nick Frost a small part in one episode, as a lascivious builder, making eyes at an attractive marionette, marking his first ever appearance on TV.

The show ran on BBC2 later that year and was critically well received, winning an ITV Comedy Award the following year for 'Best Broken Comedy' (whatever the hell that means). A second series followed three years later, which despite being very funny never quite reached the heights of its predecessor. It felt a little belated and, from a purely selfish perspective, I look well fat in it.

After shooting the first series of *Big Train*, it was back to the stage and *The Man Who Thinks He's It*, which transferred to the Lyceum Theatre in London's West End, remaining there for three months. I played out the rest of the year as Steve Coogan's side-kick and was extremely happy to do so. Steve has the kind of mind which is constantly ticking over, and spending time with him is always huge fun. He taught me a hell of a lot . . . about cars.

It was a big year for me, 1998, and in a different book I might have lingered longer on the details, but I feel momentum gathering as the end draws near, and stories about exploits on the road and random anecdotes about the business of filming television shows and even films feel less relevant here, particularly in the light of how this book has evolved during the writing process. What's important is the fact that in the space of twelve months, I found myself working with Bill Bailey, Steve Coogan, Graham Linehan and Arthur Mathews, all of whom had been an inspiration to me as a young comic. Comedy fans are nerds after all, in fact arguably one of the fiercest nerd tribes out there. I felt very lucky, as did Julia, who had sent her home-made comedy showcase video to Steve, never expecting him to even watch it let alone hire her as a result. It was good to have a fellow newbie sharing all the wonder that year; geeking out is always more enjoyable in groups of two or more.

The Single Greatest Pub in the History of Pubs

Most people find a pub they regard as the best pub in the world; the difference with me is that I really did.

The Shepherds, on the corner of Archway Road and Shepherd's Hill, in Highgate, London, became a sort of home from home for Nick Frost and me, when we moved into a nearby house in 1999. From the outside, and indeed from within, it appeared to be a somewhat old-fashioned London boozer, lacking any of the gastro pretensions displayed by so many of the area's watering holes. The carpet was old and sticky, the jukebox a dearth of choice and the clientele an odd mixture of quiet drinkers and rowdy young men.

Behind the bar under the perpetual watch of a grizzled old German shepherd called Bobby was John the landlord, a gruff old Gooner[18] who'd manned the taps in several drinking establishments

[18] A 'Gooner' is a term for a supporter of Arsenal Football Club and is derived from the club's nickname, 'the Gunners', itself derived from the team emblem of a cannon. Presumably the term started off as an insult but was appropriated by the Arsenal fans in much the same way that rappers hijacked the word 'nigger' as a means of disempowering its negative effect. I might be wrong. I don't like football.

over his long career as a publican. His wife Bernie, a mercurial Irish matriarch who would glam up for her weekly excursions to Brent Cross Shopping Centre, worked 'front of house' with an irresistible charm that made her affection something to strive for and be proud of. Together with their daughters, Michelle and Vanessa, they ran the pub as a family affair, with everyone living on-site. This removed the tension from closing time, since the staff only had a staircase to climb to get home.

Nick was the first to go in, immediately loving the pub's simplicity, its lack of frills and transparent attempts to claw at custom. Sitting in the corner he would enjoy a few pints while people-watching, becoming familiar with the regulars, an eclectic mix of people whose drinking patterns were often as regimented as they were prodigious.

I initially resisted the idea of going into the Shepherds, dismissing Nick's persistent patronage as a truculent expression of his tendency to champion the underdog; Panda Pops over Coca-Cola, shop-brand ketchup over Heinz, *The Fifth Element* over *Battleship Potemkin*. Eventually, though, I succumbed and joined him for an evening session.

That first night, we sat together near the door and watched as the various patrons came and went. After a few visits we began to give them nicknames, to amuse ourselves. There was Rugby Jim, a talkative regular who always switched the TV over to his sport of choice; Pollit Bureau, so called because he looked faintly Russian; Peter Stuyvesant, an always sharply dressed septuagenarian with a walking stick who would usually come in five minutes before time was called. There was White Man-Bruised Man, Fat Eye Blind, and a middle-aged woman with long blonde hair who Nick insisted was a retired stripper (his name for her was Fried Gold).

Thursday night was quiz night, which Bernie would host with show-business panache, even if there were only a few people in.

Nick and I joined in one Thursday and did fairly well, probably because there were only three teams. Nevertheless, we decided to make it a weekly engagement, determined to win the first prize of eight free pints or the equivalent in spirits. Not that the prize ever really mattered; it was bragging rights we were after.

Little by little, the Shepherds worked its way into our affections. After about six months we were accepted among the regulars and rarely went anywhere else. We earned the right to call John and Bernie by their first names as well as making friends with the people whose comic monikers became obsolete in the face of their acquaintance.

A few months into our residency, I kicked off my shoes and walked up to the bar in just my socks, a symbolic gesture intended to show Nick just how ensconced we had become. The Shepherds felt like an extension of our own living room, giving a sudden clear definition to the phrase 'public house'.

We brought our friends to the pub and they brought others. Word spread about the quiz and within a year, Thursday nights were packed with teams eager to participate. Our eulogising of the pub may have contributed at first, but it was Bernie's irresistible charm and John's solid management that ensured visitors returned with friends in tow. Closing time was always a sketchy affair and Saturday-night sessions would often extend into the small hours. On several occasions I slept next to Bobby the German shepherd's eventual replacement, Henry, having chatted endlessly to old John, the gentleman formerly known as Peter Stuyvesant. Despite my occasional naps, John's company was always entertaining and represented something magical about the Shepherds, which elevates it above any pub I have ever entered before or since.

It had the distinct feeling of family about it, with John and Bernie at the centre of a rare mix of social types and personalities. We tend to stick to our various groupings on nights out, but the Shepherds seemed to affect its drinkers in such a way that everyone soon became friends. Whether it was a cursory greeting or an entire night's conversation, the connection between regulars was tangible, such was the unifying power of the unique atmosphere. A bit like the Queen Vic in *EastEnders* but without the constant bouts of murder.

Our visits to the Shepherds quickly became habitual, eradicating the need for any other social meeting place. Why go anywhere else, when we had the single greatest drinking establishment sat almost literally on our doorstep? Edgar became increasingly exasperated at my and Nick's reluctance to forgo the succour of our beloved local in favour of the bright lights of Soho or even nearby Islington where he lived at the time. It became something of a sticking point with friends and girlfriends that we never really wanted to travel beyond the tobacco-stained walls of this unassuming pub and the argument always returned to our dogged, one-word defence – why?

Friends who visited the pub usually fell under its spell and joined us even if it meant a cab, bus or Tube ride, particularly on quiz night when the bar would heave with teams from all over London. We made new friends and found ourselves welcomed deeper and deeper into John and Bernie's affections. *Spaced* had started to air on Channel 4 and Bernie was extremely proud that a couple of 'her boys' were on television. As our faces became more recognisable, the pub was a haven from the unnerving sense of visibility that accompanies working in the public eye, since nobody in the pub apart from Bernie seemed to give a shit. This feeling of safety attracted other actors and musicians who loved the sense of normality that pervaded, and the pub soon felt like a small creative hub, bustling with comics, actors and musicians eating toasties, feeding the fruit machine and playing killer up at the dartboard.

In 2001, the then fairly fledging indie outfit Coldplay

performed a small acoustic gig in the corner one evening and raised £300 for the Whittington Hospital baby unit. I had become friends with singer Chris Martin a year or so before through my new girlfriend, Maureen, who worked as a publicist for Sony Music. I had accompanied her to a showcase gig at the Millennium Dome, where she was presiding over press duties for the band Toploader who were headlining the event. Coldplay were on the bill, and after the show, Chris sidled up and expressed an affection for the sketch show *Big Train*, in which I had appeared in 1998. This pleased me enormously since I had already bought his band's first album, *Parachutes*, and seen them perform a set on the indie stage at the V Festival earlier that year.

I liked Chris immediately. He was friendly, funny and infuriatingly self-effacing, something he remains to this day, despite his band's phenomenal success. He invited Maureen and me to the closing gig of their tour at the Shepherd's Bush Empire, which we gladly attended. At the after-show party, I escorted Chris to a nearby cash machine where he admitted he had just wanted to take a breath from all the attention he was getting at the party. It's funny in light of what was about to happen to think of Chris struggling with the notion of success at such an early stage in his career. *Parachutes* had done well both critically and in terms of sales, but the band was only a promising proposition at this point and a somewhat unlikely candidate for global domination.

That night Chris came back to our Highgate home and watched *This Is Spinal Tap* with Maureen and me, cementing what was to become a lasting friendship. Chris began to join us at the pub, which delighted Bernie no end, since the band's rise was meteoric from this point. Their second album, *A Rush of Blood to the Head*, debuted on the Shepherds' jukebox two weeks before it was released into the world, and to this day, Bernie and her family feature regularly on Coldplay guest lists.

By now, Nick and I were helping to mark the Thursday quizzes in the kitchen out back, such was our deep affiliation to John and Bernie. But mostly, life for us at the Shepherds consisted of Nick and me simply sitting and discussing the world while sipping pints or ploughing pound coins into the Simpson fruit machine. Ideas were born and plans were hatched as we luxuriated amid the matchless comfort of our surroundings. On Monday nights, we would sit up at the bar and watch *University Challenge* with John, usually the sole customers. We would throw out answers at the TV, usually falling short of anything Jeremy Paxman would accept as correct. On the odd occasion that we came good on a starter for ten, John would look at us both with an expression of admiration and declare us to be a couple of geniuses.

One of our frequent topics of conversations in the Shepherds was what we would do in the event of a full-scale zombie apocalypse. We would discuss the hypotheses in great detail, tracking our movements from witnessing a stray deadhead in the garden, through running along the rooftops of Archway Road to Pax Guns in order to retrieve a brace of ordnance, then commandeering a vehicle to take us to our choice of hideout. These varied from abandoned castles to Wembley Stadium, the centre of which Nick insisted would afford us a clear view of any stray zombies that breached the perimeter and give us a workable farm space to grow crops for sustenance.

However, this scenario did rely on us being able to get our hands on a vehicle, which we could get into and start without an ignition key. This meant, realistically, the most feasible plan was to remain in the area and the most obvious place to hunker down was the pub. With heavy, bolt-locking doors, thick windows obscured by always drawn curtains which stopped just above head height, to allow light into the bar, survivors could easily move around inside without attracting the attention of the walking dead, stumbling about in the street outside. Aside from an enormous supply of fear-anaesthetising booze, the pub was well stocked with frozen food, and the sandwich toaster alone would provide tasty snacks, as long as the electricity stayed on.

The idea was so inviting, we half hoped the recently dead would start returning to life and attacking the living, if only to give us the justification to remain in the Shepherds all day, every day, without feeling guilty.

Not surprisingly, aspects of our extended fantasy made it into the screenplay for *Shaun of the Dead*, as Edgar and I readily ran with the dead ball, feeding it into the storyline as the solution Shaun proposes in his attempts to save his loved ones. Edgar's own annoyance at our lack of social imagination became the source of Liz's frustration with Shaun, positing the pub at the very heart of the film as the cause of distress and the answer to their problems. Although causing the downfall of the group, the pub does ultimately facilitate their survival and proves a better solution to that of the rival group, who are eventually whittled down to just one.

Shaun of the Dead was written during the height of our love affair with the Shepherds. Its influences on the film are numerous and not just in terms of the plot. The landlord and lady in the film were called John and Bernie, the jukebox had a tendency to self-select if it got bored of underuse and Ed's improvised descriptions of the locals were lifted straight from our early days as strangers in the lounge bar. We might even have kept the pub's name were we not in need of a plot point that provided Shaun's team with a gun. Calling our screen pub the Winchester enabled us to mount an old-fashioned rifle over the bar, which, at a crucial point in the story, reveals itself to be a fully working firearm. By sheer coincidence, the next pub down from the Shepherds on Archway Road is called the Winchester, but it has no relevance or connection to our film, despite what you might have heard.

The Shepherds gave us our central location and character motivation, and served to consolidate the film's singularly British identity, having such an iconic national staple as the local pub at its heart. Parts of the film were conceived and even written within the Shepherds' walls and a tour of the cellar, laid on by a very proud Bernie, enabled us to design a climax that permitted Shaun and Liz to make a credible escape from the burning building above.

In 2002, John and Bernie retired and moved back to Ireland, having decided to leave their pub-running days behind. The last quiz was perhaps the most crowded I have ever seen and chairs were brought down from John and Bernie's living space to accommodate an excess of hopeful teams.

On their last night, the locals old and new gathered to give the couple a rousing send-off. To ensure their memories of the place remained ever-fresh, we commissioned Stuart Free,[19] a talented local artist, to paint a picture of the pub which they could take with them to Ireland. Stuart's paintings centre around buildings and architecture that people see daily and barely glance at. By painting them in sharp detail, he reveals complex and beautiful urban images, finding aesthetic wonder in even the shabbiest shopfront or graffiti-scrawled cafe. His rendering of the Shepherds completely captures the heart of the place in bright angular reds and blacks, set in contrast against the bright green of a nearby tree. Looking carefully, one can notice a number of clever in-jokes. At the doorway, in handsome repose, sits Henry the German shepherd; above the door a sign which read 'Hot and Cold Food' is altered to read 'Hot and Coldplay'; and barely visible through the window a young man in a baseball cap sits at a table with his girlfriend, nursing a pint. The painting was presented to John and Bernie at the end of a wonderful and poignant evening and hangs in the hallway of their home just outside Dublin.

[19] Stuart's work can be purchased from Crouch End and at www.stuartjfree.co.uk.

The pub changed hands and became the Boogaloo, a self-proclaimed juke joint that skews towards a younger, more fashionable clientele and which has honoured the site by becoming a hugely successful and popular hangout with regular quizzes and live music, attracting a whole new raft of punters and artistic types. In fact, the venue seems to be a magnet for artistic significance, far outstripping any of its neighbours in terms of contribution to the cultural history of the area.

Never since have I felt such a connection and affection for a pub as I did with the Shepherds and I miss it even now. I don't ever go into the Boogaloo, not because I object to it in any way – from what I hear, it's brilliant – rather because to drink within those walls again would be like going out on a date with a beloved ex and her brand-new boyfriend or, worse still, making love to an ex and finding it hard to concentrate because of all the new moves she's picked up since you were last together. The building didn't fall down when it stopped being the Shepherds but then it was never the building that stole my heart. It was the unique and alchemical combination of people, atmosphere, simplicity and spirit (as well as wine and beer).

The clientele didn't alter entirely after the change-over. Old John continued to prop up the bar and David Soul, who had come in a number of times before the era ended, reportedly still drank there, perhaps because of the easy-going nature of the other punters that allowed him to be just another guy at the bar rather than Ken Hutchinson, although I couldn't help smiling when he walked in, recalling the big poster of him and Paul Michael Glaser that dominated the wall of my bedroom at Nan's house. Strange that a number of childhood obsessions should converge on the same location, but that's the great thing about pubs: all life is there.

Meeting the Maker

S*haun of the Dead* was released in the UK in April 2004
and premiered in America six months later, after an extensive press tour in the US which required Edgar, Nick Frost
and myself to visit seventeen cities in eighteen days, including
our first visit to the San Diego Comic-Con, where I met Carrie
Fisher and Lou Ferrigno.

Leia and the Hulk weren't the only heroes I was lucky enough
to meet that weekend. Both legendary make-up FX guru Greg
Nicotero and *Dawn of the Dead* actor Ken Foree (whose name
we used for the electrical shop in which Shaun works) were in
attendance and we had heard both had seen the movie. We met
Ken first, an imposing bear of a man, busily signing autographs
for the fans who lined up to meet him. We approached him
fairly gingerly and introduced ourselves. Much to our blushing
delight, he stood up and embraced us with alarming enthusiasm,
which sent us giddy. This man was Peter Washington from *Dawn
of the Dead*, the tough, resourceful SWAT team member who
ultimately rejects suicide in favour of kung fu kicking his way
through a crowd of hungry zombies to join Gaylen Ross's Fran
aboard a helicopter for the film's hugely affecting and open-

ended conclusion. We were beside ourselves with geekish glee as we made a date to meet him at our screening later.

Then we met Greg Nicotero, acolyte of the great Tom Savini in his youth and now a renowned and respected FX technician in his own right, having founded the KNB Effects Group with Howard Berger in 1988 and emerging as one of the most prolific and successful companies of its kind in Hollywood. Greg not only worked on one of my and Edgar's all-time favourite horror comedies, Sam Raimi's *Evil Dead II*, he also worked on and appeared in Romero's *Day of the Dead*, playing one of Captain Rhodes's military goons who, crucially for me as a fan, winds up in Dr Logan's lab as the conscious decapitated head.

Both Greg and Ken were hugely supportive of our film, which meant the world to us. To have the approval of these two men, both of whom had made a big impression on us growing up, was, as another tragic mother killer said, 'consummation devoutly to be wished'.[20] The only greater honour we could have possibly received was bestowed on us a few months prior to Comic-Con, when I picked up the phone to George Romero in the kitchen of my north London flat. His voice sounded distant but familiar as he told me how much he had enjoyed *Shaun of the Dead*, and a huge wave of relief and pride spread through me. He seemed genuinely enthused and flattered that we had written him this cinematic love letter. Amid my ecstatic joy at receiving his approval, I offered him an apology, the response to which I will never forget. It went something like this:

Me: George, I gotta say I'm sorry about the whole speedy reanimation thing. I know in *Dawn* it takes Roger at least thirty minutes before he comes back, but for narrative purposes we

[20] *Hamlet*, Act III, Scene 1. Thought I'd temper the nerdy shit with a classical reference. Shakespeare fans can be nerds too and vice versa.

had to have Philip reanimate almost immediately, so that bit was a little different . . .

George: You know what, Simon, I didn't mind.

A year later, Edgar and I boarded a plane bound for Toronto, heading for the set of *Land of the Dead*, George's fourth instalment in his series, which as I write boasts six chapters, completed by *Diary of the Dead* and *Survival of the Dead* respectively. The situation had arisen entirely through happenstance. Greg Nicotero, who was overseeing the make-up effects for the film, had mentioned in an interview that he thought Edgar and I should make cameo appearances in *Land of the Dead* as zombies. This quickly got back to George, when a journalist asked him if it was true, and George replied in characteristically laid-back fashion, 'Sure, I guess.'

So on a misty night, in an enormous rail depot just outside Toronto, Edgar and I met our hero in the flesh for the first time and were overjoyed to notice he was wearing a *Shaun of the Dead* badge on his jacket.[21]

The next day, we reported to the make-up trailer to have our zombie make-up applied. Both Edgar and I had been head-cast at the KNB workshop in Van Nuys, California, a few months before so that Greg could prepare our latex facial appliances personally. Knowing how much of a fan of *Day of the Dead*'s Bub I was, Greg had found the original moulds for Howard Sherman's make-up and modelled them on to my head cast so that the face he glued over mine was that of my all-time favourite zombie.

If ever there was a moment for making use of the ESTB, it was now. To have stepped from the device into my living room made up as Bub, as I watched *Day of the Dead* at the tender

[21] Our adventure in Toronto was filmed by our long-time friend and collaborator Dan Mudford, and can be found as a short film called *When Shaun Met George* among the extra features on the *Land of the Dead* DVD.

age of sixteen would have been so much fun. Well, at least for the future me. The younger me would have probably fainted or else ruined a perfectly good pair of skin-tight black jeans.

Working with Romero was an extraordinary pleasure and it was hard to not gush every time I sat next to him at the cluster of on-set monitors referred to quaintly as the video village. I wanted to tell him exactly how much his work had meant to me over the years and the effect it had had on me as a person let alone as an artist.

When it came to shooting our scene, the enormity of the moment did not escape me or indeed Edgar. Rather than just be random faces in a shuffling zombie gang, George had given us our own specific moment. In a bustling shanty and allegorical township in the shadow of an exclusive fortified apartment complex called Fiddler's Green, a busy marketplace offered various zombie-based entertainment for anaesthetised survivors looking for a thrill. One such attraction gave the chance to have your picture taken with a zombie. Edgar and I, in full KNB zombie make-up, complete with scleral contact lenses and fake teeth, dangled from chains, gnashing and moaning at grim fun seekers as they posed for photos. Internally, I couldn't help but once again channel Howard Sherman's Bub, even between takes when it felt somehow easier to remain in character. Masks are extremely powerful dramatic tools for actor and audience alike, since they completely alter the wearer both visually and, to whatever degree the actor permits, psychologically. Remaining in character was thus almost inevitable while literally wearing someone else's face, albeit rubber and not an Ed Gein-style trophy.

When George approached us after the first take with notes, I did, however, snap back into human mode, because I wanted to listen carefully as he explained a few beats he required us to hit for the shot and I didn't want to look like a knob.

As he walked back to the video village, I couldn't help turning to Edgar and saying, 'We just got directed by George Romero!' It was a heck of a moment for both of us and its significance sent us into terrifying zombie grins of geekish joy. The same man who had instructed Bill Heinzman (the first and fastest of George's zombie children) to stagger across Evan's City Cemetery in 1968, inspiring Russell Streiner's Johnny to utter the famous line 'They're coming to get you, Barbara', had just instructed us. In geek terms, it doesn't get much cooler than that.

In terms of my childhood zombie love and my eventual participation in a zombie movie of my own, I could not have hoped for better closure on this particular chapter of my life than the world premiere of *Land of the Dead* in Pittsburgh, Pennsylvania, June 2005. The event was attended by a host of luminaries from George's zombie anthology, all of whom I was thrilled to meet.

Before the film began a speech was made in George's honour and a poll was taken among the crowd to determine exactly how many people in the audience had participated in a George Romero film. Edgar and myself rose to our feet, along with the other alumni whose faces we knew so well, to receive a round of applause from the assembled zombie fans who had turned out. Quentin Tarantino, the man responsible for the film that played an important part in my bonding with Nick Frost, playfully insisted we 'sit our punk asses down' since our film was a rip-off of Romero, not a Romero original. After reminding our tormentor that we were in fact in the film we were about to watch, he shut up and we legitimately enjoyed a few moments as bona fide members of the Pittsburgh zombie massive.

The next day, Greg took Edgar, Quentin and myself to the Evan City Cemetery where the opening sequence of *Night of the Living Dead* was filmed and where I enjoyed the bizarre and fun experience of playing zombies with one of my all-time favourite directors.

After the cemetery, we moved on to the Monroeville Mall, the main location for *Dawn of the Dead*. Despite inevitable modernisations, much of the mall remained recognisable from the film, particularly the utility areas and the boiler room, which echoed with the exact same whine of machinery that underscored David Emge's wordless battle with a dead janitor.

On the roof of the building, we stood where Ken Foree had kicked his way to safety and taken off into uncertainty with Gaylen Ross and grinned from ear to ear at being given access to such an auspicious location. It may seem strange to some that two grown men could derive such enormous pleasure from standing on the roof of a shopping centre in suburban Pittsburgh, but Edgar and I, it's fair to say, were standing on top of the world.

Disappointing Interlude

As George Lucas said to his bank manager, 'I'm going to return to *Star Wars* for a while,' and address the dreaded prequels. After defacing the original films as a means of road-testing new effects technology, Lucas produced three ghastly prequels, which all but punched the love out of me. Signs were good at first – the trailer brought tears to my eyes when it premiered on MTV. I sat in front of the television and felt the emotion one feels when reunited with a much loved friend. It had been sixteen years since *Return of the Jedi* and here, unfolding before my eyes, was the confirmation that I would be going back to the universe that had so inspired me as a child.

To add to the excitement, actor and friend Peter Serafinowicz had been cast as the voice of Darth Maul, the new villain, a scary-looking horned fellow with a red-and-black face and demonic contact lenses. A special trailer showcasing the character was released and a group of us piled round to Pete's house to watch it, after it had taken an excruciating twelve hours to download. This was, after all, the era of 56K dial-up modems, nowhere near as speedy as today's broadband fibre optics. Kids these days don't know they're born with their perpetual online status and nanosecond downloads, I remember when it took minutes for a web page to load and iPods were almost an inch thick – an inch! We gathered round Peter's computer and clicked play, barely containing our wonder that one of our own was part of the *Star Wars* universe, that Pete was a Darth. It all seemed like a wonderful dream.

However, it wasn't long before the signs of impending disappointment started to appear, like the dust motes that fall from the rafters seconds before a major earthquake. Thanks to early reactions from critics and fans alike, a nagging doubt had already been poking away at me, but it had largely been kept at bay by my monumental levels of excitement. Of course, there was also the creeping realisation that the special editions were shit and the awful moments of ill-judged slapstick in the trailer didn't help, nor did the slightly flat artificiality of the environments on display.

Before the evidence laid itself out with sickening certainty, the small hints at the fate of my beloved franchise were easy to ignore, even as they became more pronounced. Pete called me after a screening in the States, and with one of the deepest sighs ever to cross the Atlantic, he said, in the rich tones of his lovely, deep, Liverpool accent, 'It's just not very good.' I didn't feel disappointment, I still felt armoured against it; such was my immunity against the failure of my beloved *Star Wars*, I was determined to see it for myself and as quickly as possible. With a small amount of disposable income in my pocket left over from the first series of *Spaced*, I purchased a ticket to New York with the express intention of seeing *The Phantom Menace*.

I arrived in Manhattan one early evening in August of 1999 and checked into the Paramount Hotel on West 46th Street. I dumped my bags and took off into the night to find a cinema that was playing the movie. It wasn't as easy as I expected it to be and I eventually found a small movie theatre on East 34th

Street, bought my popcorn and settled into a front-row seat to watch the film I had waited sixteen years to see.

As the Lucasfilm logo rippled across the screen and the Twentieth Century Fox fanfare blared from the speakers, I bristled with excitement, emitting an involuntary whoop that was echoed by one or two of the other faithfuls in the audience. However, I soon became aware of an uneasy feeling of apprehension in the crowd, which was uncharacteristically quiet for an American audience. The film had been out for several weeks by this point and consequently the majority of the really avid *Star Wars* fans had been and gone and many had not come back. My excitement had already been dampened slightly by the inauspiciousness of the theatre, and this sense of miserable dread was only exacerbated by a problem with the projector that upset the alignment of the image, so that when that moment finally occurred and the *Star Wars* titles appeared on the screen, accompanied by John Williams's iconic score, the bottom half of the lettering was at the top of the screen while the top half protruded from the bottom, fittingly like a row of gravestones. I had a bad feeling about this.

From the opening scene it appeared something was not right. The first line was badly dubbed and, just as Pete had reported, the film simply wasn't very good. In actual fact, Pete's critique had proved somewhat generous. The film was a boring, turgid, confused mess of pretentions and ill-thought-out science-fiction conceits, masquerading as children's entertainment and told with all the dexterity of a four-year-old recounting his summer holiday with a paintbrush.

I left the cinema in a daze and wandered up 34th Street with a couple of fellow Brits who had stumbled out alongside me, obviously experiencing a similar sense of ennui. We hadn't walked more than a block before we found ourselves admitting our disappointment. It was an odd feeling, which came something close to liberation in a strange way; like admitting to an addiction or confessing a terrible crime. I had spent much of my youth championing *Star Wars*, not just in the playground to those who claimed the most recent rip-off was somehow better, but intellectually to cineastes who dismissed it as artistically bankrupt. I would still disagree with the latter charges even now when discussing the first three films, but I always felt an odd defensiveness about my love of the movies, particularly as an adult, which occasionally felt like a burden. Now, I didn't have to endure that burden again. *Star Wars* was undeniably rubbish and there was nothing I could do to change that.

The next morning, I went to see it again, just to make sure. I had awoken as though the previous night had been a bad dream and blamed jet lag, the weight of anticipation and the dodgy projection at the cinema, and resolved to give it another chance. Predictably, it was shit again. Stumbling numbly out of the theatre once more, I realised I was alone in New York and completely bereft. I decided to go and see another film, just to take my mind off *Star Wars*, and noticed that a film called *The Matrix* was playing in the same theatre. Two hours later, I re-emerged into the street full of the excitement and satisfaction that *The Phantom Menace* had failed to inspire. *The Matrix* seemed fresh and cool and visually breathtaking; making wonderful, intelligent use of CGI to augment the on-screen action, striking a perfect balance of the real and the hyperreal. It was possibly the coolest film I had ever seen. Ironically, fraternal directing team the Wachowskis faltered quickly with their sequels, killing their baby in just three years. Credit to George Lucas, it took him twenty-five to murder his.

Return/Revenge

Returning home to begin writing the second series of *Spaced*, I decided to channel my disappointment at *The Phantom Menace* into my character, Tim, and use him to express my feelings on the subject. We were even able to channel some of that dissatisfaction into the first series during the editing process, hastily adding the caption 'Three good *Star Wars* films later' as passage of time after the characters spend an evening watching the original trilogy.

During the filming of the first series, we had approached Lucasfilm's licensing department and asked permission to use various *Star Wars* merchandise for set dressing, as Tim Bisley, like me, was an inveterate fan. They said no to everything, presumably because they were gearing up for a whole new batch of products and didn't want to generate any unnecessary nostalgia for the old stuff. I'm speculating there of course. The truth is, I think they were just being overcautious, in case we took the holy trilogy's name in vain, which at that time seemed like an extremely unlikely event.

By the time the second series went into production, the first series had aired and Lucasfilm's licensing people, seeing that our intentions were honourable and affectionate, were more than happy for us to use anything we wanted. By this time, however, the damage had been done and we didn't really want to. Besides, it would have been hard to justify, since you have to supply context for usage and 'we're going to burn it' doesn't present a convincingly positive proposal. As it was we settled for a number of cardboard boxes pointedly labelled 'Star Wars stuff', as we mounted our scene-for-scene re-enactment of Darth Vader's funeral, substituting *Star Wars* itself as the corpse burning before the grieving son.

Despite everything, I was still first in line for the second prequel, *Attack of the Clones*, even though the title, like its predecessor, sounded like an abdominal complaint. I don't wish the following metaphor to come across as flippant, I must preface it by saying I am fully aware of the horror and hardships caused by domestic abuse in all its forms, but my relationship with *Star Wars* in later years is comparable, symbolically at least, to living with an abusive partner. No matter how let down and violently disappointed by it I felt, I would always return for more, as though nothing had ever happened, making excuses for previous transgressions and dismissing them as anomalous. So it was when I sat down to watch the film at the Odeon Leicester Square at a press screening I had somehow managed to blag tickets for. This film seemed to have the potential to abolish the memory of its predecessor. It promised more action and a more complex character in Anakin Skywalker, thankfully no longer a bowl-haircutted cutie saving the day by accident. There were lots of light sabres and a character that looked a bit liked Boba Fett. It claimed a darker feel, aligning it stylistically with *The Empire Strikes Back*, which could only be a good thing, right?

Sure, as I left the cinema, I had some of that youthful spring in my step and didn't feel that bomb-shocked sense of unease I had experienced in New York. By the time I reached the other side of Soho, however, I realised it had all been an illusion and *Attack of the Clones* had been no better than the first prequel, in fact in some respects it had been worse. Told with the same clodhopping ineptitude, it attempted to win favour by trying to invoke the spirit of the original instalment by making direct references to it, while simultaneously distracting us with lights and flashes to draw focus away from the awful truth.

When *Revenge of the Sith* was released, I was ready to forgive it once more, despite the mountain of evidence to suggest the series was irredeemable. I had been present at the announcement of the title in San Diego on the day I met Carrie Fisher, and noted the slight desperation amid the fans who decided to see the sly reference to the original title of *Return of the Jedi* as a clever circular allusion rather than the desperate attempt to claw back credibility that it probably was.

By this time I had actually become friends with a few people at Lucasfilm, having found my vocal disapproval of the prequels had won unlikely support from people within the organisation. When the original theatrical cuts of the first trilogy were re-released on DVD, free of any of the tampering inflicted upon them in the run-up to the prequels, I received a parcel in the post, containing the discs and an embossed Lucasfilm postcard. The message simply read: '*We thought you might like these.*'

As a result of my new-found connections, I was invited to one of the first screenings of *Revenge of the Sith* at the Twentieth Century Fox building in London's Soho Square. This was undoubtedly the most enjoyable of the three. Still beset by the same problems of style over content and story incoherence, it nevertheless scored points for drawing closer to the original trilogy in both storyline and aesthetics and the promise of seeing the birth of Darth Vader himself.

One scene even involves the action occurring in the corridor of Princess Leia's blockade runner, glimpsed at the beginning of the first film. This moment is doubly powerful in that it is a physical set and not a digital environment, which even enhances the effect of the CGI Yoda, framing him in a realistic setting, making him seem more solid, more present. I actually cried a little bit when Emperor Palpatine initiated Order 66 and wiped out the Jedi, giving kudos to Lucas for his use of cross-cutting, in a sequence reminiscent of the final stages of *The Godfather*. This one was definitely the best of a bad bunch.

Ultimately, though, the film served only to highlight a number of niggling inconsistencies that undermined the continuity of the saga and cast doubt on the credibility of Lucas's grand narrative plan. It's true that a larger, more complex story existed before *Star Wars* and that Lucas had lifted a manageable midsection to create the first film, but it seems hard to believe that the surrounding saga was anything more than a conceptual sketch or a very rough first draft. Oddly, despite the big-budget treatment, the prequels retained the feel of something being made up on the hoof without any regard for consistency and it would seem that nobody had had the scones to point it out.

No one ever said, 'George, if Luke Skywalker is the son of Anakin Skywalker (now Darth Vader) and the forces of good are attempting to conceal him from his father, why didn't they give him a new name or hide him somewhere other than the family home of Darth Vader's stepbrother?'[22] Or, 'Is a bit of bad luck and some mild teenage truculence enough to change a goofy kid into a murderous galactic tyrant?' Or, 'Do you think

---

[22] I actually wrote a little fan fiction about this inconsistency for my MySpace blog, which I dabbled with for a while. I'll stick it in the appendix in case you fancy reading it. The blog was moderated by Harmony Carrigan who founded and continues to preside over Peggster.net, a website about me, which is far better than anything I would hope to produce myself. I made contact with Harmony shortly after I came across the site and we have since become friends. She lives in Memphis, Tennessee, in the US and I'd be lost without her.

the big reveal that Senator Palpatine is in fact the evil Darth Sidious (soon to be Emperor) all that surprising, considering the same actor played a character called Emperor Palpatine in *Return of the Jedi*?' Or even, 'Isn't it a bit unseemly to establish sexual tension between Luke and Leia if they are eventually going to be revealed as brother and sister? Are they from Gloucester?' It seems strange that such a grand and expensive endeavour appears so undercooked at times, almost as though the whole venture was being presided over by one person, refusing to accept any outside input, despite knowing deep down that he had bitten off more than he could chew.

As determined as I was to enjoy *Revenge of the Sith*, having decided that was going to be the case before I saw it, the film ultimately let itself down at key moments, not least the hilarious Darth Vader/Frankenstein debacle, which so undermined one of the most anticipated beats in the story. Anakin Skywalker, having been mutilated and left for dead by the peaceful, monk-like Obi-Wan Kenobi, is rescued by the Emperor and rebuilt as the 'more machine now than man' badass we remember from the original films. When he regains consciousness, he asks how his girlfriend is, in that recognisable voice made oddly whimsical by the vulnerability in his tone, and when informed that she is dead, shouts a big long 'noooooooooooooo' and breaks free of his bindings to stagger clumsily across the Emperor's lab in a wave of snigger-inducing grief. This frustratingly blurs the moment that Anakin Skywalker ceases to be and his evil alter ego takes hold. It seems strange to see the iconic visage of cool, impassive evil attempting to emote. In *Return of the Jedi*, Vader's true humanity is implied in a few moments of stillness, when we can almost see confusion in his static visage, then witnessed fully just before he dies, the majority of his sentiment delivered with the helmet off.

If I had worked for Lucasfilm at the time, I would have strapped explosives to my body, burst into George's boardroom and demanded that he rewrite the scene so that the last vestiges of Anakin's humanity are displayed before the helmet goes on. He lies on the operating table, all but rebuilt, the mask hovering above his face. He wakes, disorientated, looking around, flexing his new cybernetic limbs, scared and confused. He demands to be told what has happened and asks about his wife and even Obi-Wan, clearly not yet fully recalling the events that brought him to this end.

The Emperor then coldly begins to explain, even as the mask begins to lower inexorably towards Anakin's face. Half concentrating on the Emperor's words but distracted, terrified by the claustrophobic fate drawing towards him, he becomes still only at the news that his pregnant lover is dead by his hand. Then the weight of emotion vibrates through and the furious, grief-ridden denial escapes his lips as the mask closes over him, muffling his agony into a protracted silence, then we hear that famous breath as he inhales for the first time and Darth Vader is born. Not that I have thought about it that much.

Despite my irrevocably damaged feelings about *Star Wars* and having already seen *Revenge of the Sith*, I jumped at the chance to go to the premiere in London's Leicester Square, because I had wanted to attend such an event since I was a child and no amount of recent disappointment could eclipse the dreams of the seven-year-old me still filed away in my brain. I wore my Rebel insignia T-shirt and got giddy at the sight of forty imperial storm troopers walking down the red carpet and, in spite of everything, felt a huge surge of affection towards George Lucas when he got up on to the stage and made a short introductory speech.

At the after-show party, I rubbed shoulders with various *Star Wars* alumni, including Peter Mayhew who played Chewbacca (who was in a bad mood – typical Wookiee) and the diminutive

Kenny Baker (who made up for it and proved great company). At one point, a friend from Lucasfilm approached David Walliams and myself and asked if we wanted to meet George. Of course we accepted the invitation and followed our contact through the crowd for an audience with his exultedness.

Lucas was deep in conversation with director Ron Howard who, in his days as an actor, had taken the lead in Lucas's *American Graffiti* before going on to *Happy Days*. Our friend drew Lucas's attention and informed him of our presence, at which point he turned and looked at me with the weary acceptance of a man about to be gushed all over by another thirty-something fan whose life he had changed. He seemed tired and slightly exasperated and in that second I regretted accepting the offer to meet him, but then luckily something cool happened. Ron Howard grinned at me, shook my hand and said, 'Oh man, my kids just love your movie!' I spluttered a thank you, slightly taken aback, and as I chatted to Ron, I noticed George's expression change from bored to slightly more attentive. Suddenly, I didn't feel like just another fan; thanks to Ron, I had been elevated to the status of fellow film-maker and as such found myself welcomed into the conversation. George asked about *Shaun of the Dead* and we chatted about film-making, then he said the most interesting thing, something that shed a surprising light on the artist behind the billionaire businessman. He asked if I minded him giving me a piece of advice. He leaned in towards me and said, 'Just don't suddenly find yourself making the same film you made thirty years ago.' In that instance, everything made some kind of sense to me. Here was a man whose only significant failing was the inability to trust anyone else. He had always been a maverick, since he was a young avant-garde film-maker and sought to operate beyond the grip of any conventional means of production. However, a victim of his own colossal success, he had become the very thing he used to rail against and yet, still possessed of a furious self-reliance, had continued to doggedly guard his own creative output even at the expense of the thing itself.

I fully admit that without Jessica, Edgar or producer Nira Park's significant talent and input, *Spaced* would have been a pale and insubstantial version of what it actually became. As much as you trust yourself in creating a work of artistic entertainment, it is sometimes vital that you find coalition with like-minded people in order to achieve an all-important objectivity, which is impossible to find by yourself. If George had only trusted those around him to nurture and temper his ideas with objective input, he might not only be wealthy but also blissfully content.

Heroes

I t's a hell of a thing to meet your heroes, let alone find your-self working with them. I have been extremely lucky in this respect and, in true ESTB fashion, have found myself working for some of those directors that shaped my tastes as a child. In 2008, while out in LA shooting *Star Trek* for fellow film geek JJ Abrams, I drove down to Giant Studios in Santa Monica to meet Steven Spielberg. It was difficult attempting to summon the concentration required to negotiate the LA freeways while trying to comprehend the hugeness of my impending rendezvous. Steven had recently met with Edgar Wright and Joe Cornish (formerly one half of nineties media teddybearists Adam and Joe), about rewriting the script for his forthcoming film, *Tintin and the Secret of the Unicorn*. Edgar had subsequently suggested Steven talk to me as well.

I parked up at the studios and made my way inside, where I was taken straight to Steven, who was operating the performance-capture camera on a small, elevated stage.[23] He

[23] Performance capture is quite a hard concept to grasp, let alone to explain. Basically, performers wearing special motion-capture suits and headgear act out scenes in a marked-off studio area called the *volume*. The *volume* is defined by

was exactly how I knew him from countless behind-the-scenes documentaries: bearded, baseball-capped and unfailingly charming. We chatted for a while about *Tintin* and other things. I told him about our new film, *Paul*, specifically my and Nick's idea that our alien hero had acted as adviser to Steven over the years, giving him a few key moments and plot details for *E.T.* and *Close Encounters of the Third Kind*. He found this hilarious and pitched in a few ideas of his own, one of which you will see in the finished film, although to divulge that now would be a spoiler.

As our meeting came to an end, Steven casually asked if I wanted to actually be in the film, as he had been thinking about me for the role of one of the Thom(p)son Twins. I spluttered something to the tune of 'That would be great', and when he asked me if I had anyone in mind for the other twin, I immediately suggested Nick Frost, an idea he warmed to straight away.

The beauty of 'performance capture' is that although the computer captures your physicality and facial expressions, the details of both can be manipulated into any shape, a technique exemplified beautifully by the versatility of actor Andy Serkis, who was able to play an emaciated hobbit and a twenty-five-foot

---

the maximum amount of space that can be *captured* and rendered as a three-dimensional environment inside the computers. The scenes are stored as a 3-D event and can then be viewed and manipulated using the performance-capture camera. This means that you only ever need one good take of any scene, which you can then 'shoot' again and again inside the camera from any number of viewpoints. When shooting a live-action scene, the director will usually, at the very least, shoot a master or wide shot, a medium close-up and singles on all the actors, requiring the scene to be performed several times, with complex lighting turnarounds between set-ups. Performance capture eliminates the need for this as once the scene is complete it can be shot from any angle. This means that despite the complexity of the technology, performance-capture filming moves quickly. The average low-budget film will have a principal photography period of about forty days. The principal photography on *Tintin and the Secret of the Unicorn* took about thirty days, although the entire process will take more like three years in the end.

gorilla, wearing essentially the same costume, a skintight body-suit covered in reflective tracking markers.

A year later, Nick Frost and I stepped onto the set of *Tintin* wearing our hugely unflattering bodysuits (which somehow looked cool on Andy Serkis, Daniel Craig and Jamie Bell) to play the almost identical Thompson and Thomson for a man both Nick and myself had long admired. Between takes, Steven was happy to talk about his work and experiences, much to our utter glee. I couldn't help but recall being ten years old and making that crucial choice between *Raiders of the Lost Ark* and the Gloucester Fair or, indeed, sitting alone in the ABC cinema two years later, crying inside my parka while watching *E.T.* I said as much to my mother when I left the studios after my first meeting with Steven in 2008, phoning her breathlessly from the car park at Giant Studios.

As if this wasn't irony enough, I sent a picture of my daughter to Steven shortly after she was born, since he had only seen her grainy sonogram image while we were shooting, and received an email back declaring that he thought she resembled the star child at the end of *2001: A Space Odyssey*. This made me so happy, not only because he had related her to a famous cine-matic baby (as of course he would), but that I found myself in a position where one of my all-time favourite directors was looking at pictures of my baby girl. I can't wait to tell her.

Working on *Tintin* was something of a double whammy profes-sionally speaking, being directed not only by Spielberg but also Peter Jackson, who was co-directing via video link from New Zealand. Peter had been present for much of the run-up to the shoot but then returned home, handing over main duties to Steven. Peter was another director for whom I had had the utmost admiration as albeit a slightly older youngster. His movie *Braindead* (*Dead Alive* as it was known in the States) was a favourite of both mine and Edgar's and was required viewing during our writing of *Shaun of the Dead*, since it was essentially a romzomcom (romantic zombie comedy), despite claims in other corners that ours was the first. I actually reviewed *Braindead* for a cable TV station while working as a stand-up comedian in Bristol on its release in 1992, never knowing I would one day find myself directed by its creator.

After *Shaun of the Dead* was released, we found another ally in Peter, who made very positive noises about the film and gave us a winning quote for our poster. When we came to shoot our ode to the police action film, *Hot Fuzz*, Peter happened to be on a location scout in the UK and agreed to come and perform a cameo as a psychotic Santa Claus who stabs me through the hand in the opening montage of the film.[24]

On the New Zealand leg of our *Hot Fuzz* press tour, Peter not only introduced the film at its Wellington premiere but also played generous host, inviting us to his house for several dinners, giving us an extensive and fascinating tour of Weta, his huge and impressive production facility, and generally showing us some good old Kiwi hospitality. While wandering around his private movie museum, he produced a frame containing one of my shirts from *Shaun of the Dead* and asked me to verify its authenticity. Studios will often make money on the side by selling props and costumes on to collectors and auction houses. A friend had purchased the item for Peter's collection, and while I was there, he grabbed the opportunity to ensure the seller was on the up and up. I checked it over and recognised my own bloody handprints smeared across the front, proudly confirming it to be genuine.

[24] There are actually three Oscar winners in *Hot Fuzz*, two of whom are heavily disguised and seldom recognised. Jim Broadbent is on clear display as Inspector Frank Butterman but tucked away in the cameo drawer is Peter's murderous Santa and Cate Blanchett as Angel's estranged girlfriend Janine, concealed under full CSI protective clothing.

We knelt down either side of it and posed for a picture and I once again experienced that wave of temporal irony joining the spatter of coincidental dots that had brought me to this point and, three years later, would lead to my participation in *Tintin*. I could even trace the irony back to early memories of my father reading me *Lord of the Rings*, as I inspected the models of Isengard and Minas Tirith in the Weta prop stores. What the hell? It's a memoir, it's supposed to be self-indulgent.

A Short History
of the Future

'Hello, Simon, John Landis wants your details.'

In 2009, shortly before I flew to New Mexico to shoot *Paul*, I received an email from Edgar Wright just after I arrived for a four-month residency in the US, telling me that John Landis had asked to see me. I had met John a year before at a screening of *Spaced* at the ArcLight Cinema on Sunset Boulevard in Hollywood. Eight years after it had aired on British TV, the show had finally generated enough interest to warrant a US release and Edgar, Jessica and I embarked on a short press tour to give the occasion a little visibility.

The LA leg consisted of a signing at film-maker Kevin Smith's Jay & Silent Bob's Secret Stash section of the video store Laser Blazer, followed by a screening and Q&A at the ArcLight, moderated by Smith himself. Kevin's support was ironic in itself to Edgar, Jess and myself, since it was his own 1994 movie *Clerks* that had in some ways inspired the three of us to create *Spaced*. It is because of *Clerks'* brilliantly observed moral re-evaluation of the rebel attack on the Death Star in *Return of the Jedi* that

I felt able to channel my love of *Star Wars* into writing the character of Tim Bisley in *Spaced*, since Smith had blazed a trail in culturally specific scriptwriting. Randal, Smith's misanthropic video-shop philosopher asks if it was morally correct to destroy the second Death Star since it was incomplete and would no doubt have carried a population of independent contractors not necessarily politically affiliated to the Empire. After all, as Randall points out, what working-class tradesman is going to pass up a 'juicy government contact with all sorts of benefits'?[25] The whole piece is sharply funny and the argument so beautifully reasoned, it stands out as one of the highlights of the film for me. Unsurprisingly, we eventually made contact with Kevin after *Shaun of the Dead* and were able to tell him how much his work had inspired us. Edgar and I had even attended a screening of *Chasing Amy* in 1998, while Jess and I were writing the first series, and listened to him talk about film-making. Ten years later, we recorded a number of new commentaries for the American release of the show and invited Kevin along to take part, which he did with characteristically laconic profanity.

Kevin was not the only inspiration to feature on the new set of commentaries; along with comedian Patton Oswalt, *South Park*'s Matt Stone and *Saturday Night Live* alumnus and future star of *Paul*, Bill Hader. Also a certain video-shop philosopher turned celebrated movie maverick came along and lent his enthusiastic vocals to the mix.

I had been a fan of Quentin Tarantino since *Reservoir Dogs* and followed his work closely thereafter. The first time Nick Frost and I visited the cinema together was in 1994 to see *Pulp Fiction*, an event that in many respects formed an important part of our bonding process. I took him to see *Pulp Fiction* with Eggy Helen because I thought he would enjoy it. The moment I met

[25] *Clerks*, 1994.

him I noticed he had an acute natural wit and intelligence and the kind of mind that would doubtless respond to Tarantino's playfulness as a director. The following Christmas, Nick bought me a long-sleeved *Pulp Fiction* T-shirt featuring the image of John Travolta and Samuel L. Jackson as Vincent and Jules holding their guns out, demonstrating the awesome power of their partnership. The shirt said a lot about the significance of the film to our friendship. It was an affectionate reminder of our first date. We were partners and we meant business. Ten years later, Quentin Tarantino would refer to Nick as the funniest man in the world.

After *Shaun of the Dead* was released, word got back to us that Quentin had screened the movie in his private cinema for a select group of friends. We subsequently contacted him and secured a quote for our US poster. We were, after all, a foreign film and needed all the endorsement we could get our hands on.

From the very beginning, our own effort was to be resolutely British and the inclusion of any marquee American names would have defeated the object. The very point of *Shaun of the Dead* was that it was happening in a small suburb of north London and not the traditional American context for such events. For this reason, we were already at a slight disadvantage in terms of marketing the film to an American audience, since the only touchstone we had was the genre itself. We felt this was enough, as did our producers, Working Title and Universal, albeit more tentatively. I will always be grateful to Working Title Films for plucking *Shaun of the Dead* from the choppy waters of turnaround. The film had been developed at FilmFour, but when the company downsized, it was (thankfully) cut loose and handed back to us.

The morning Clash frontman Joe Strummer died, Edgar and I sat in an Islington Starbucks with our producers, long-time friend Nira Park with whom we had created *Spaced* and Jim Wilson who we had retained from FilmFour, wondering what was to become of our little film. Fortunately, Eric Fellner, Tim Bevan and Natascha Wharton at Working Title 2 offered to take up the challenge, having expressed some interest before we chose to go with FilmFour. Thus the movie was made by a very British production house, albeit for Universal Pictures in the US, and as such remained resolutely British.

Both Edgar and I believe the decision not to contrive a way of appealing to the American audiences gave the film the precise appeal that secured its eventual success over there. It was a slice of familiar American culture viewed through a glass darkly, recognisable but at the same time fresh. We used the same approach for our next film, *Hot Fuzz*, despite a few early suggestions about visiting FBI agents played by the likes of Jack Black. Our intention was to be true to ourselves and hope that honesty paid off in providing foreign audiences with a different perspective on familiar cinematic ideas.

Shaun wasn't a massive hit theatrically in the States and was considered more of a cult, word-of-mouth sleeper than a smash in the vein of *The Full Monty* or *28 Days Later*. Nevertheless, the support we got from the likes of Quentin Tarantino, Peter Jackson, Robert Rodriguez, Stephen King and of course George Romero gave the film sufficient momentum to become a genuine smash on DVD, to the point where, according to Universal, 40 per cent of American males between seventeen and thirty-nine consider themselves to be fans of the film. How's that for a slice of fried gold?

The relationships we cultivated as a result of *Shaun of the Dead* have persisted, and I firmly believe this is because all those directors recognised themselves in Edgar. A young film-maker with a singular vision, combined with the drive and tenacity to get things done. Edgar and Quentin certainly found themselves kindred spirits, and it wasn't long before Edgar passed on a DVD of *Spaced*, no doubt knowing Quentin would get all the references, not least the ones to his own films.

A few years later, in a recording studio in Santa Monica, Edgar, Jess, Quentin and I sat down to record commentary on episode one, series two of *Spaced*, which featured a shot-by-shot recreation of a scene from *Pulp Fiction*, in which Bruce Willis returns home to find a machine gun discarded on the kitchen worktop and John Travolta using the toilet. In *Spaced* it is Daisy who finds the gun, while its owner Mike Watt is in the bog. The moment was intensely personal for me, since the scene featured Nick as the careless Uzi owner, recreating a scene from a film which had united us as friends, for the viewing pleasure of the very filmmaker that created the original. I only wish Nick had been there, if only because we were knocking back the margaritas, and if there's one thing Frost loves, it's a salted Mexican booze bowl.

At the *Spaced* screening in Hollywood's much loved ArcLight Cinema, guests including our new raft of commentators were milling around in the bar before the show. To my barely disguisable delight, Edgar introduced me to John Landis and pretty much made my night. The circularity at work here was fairly dizzying, not only because it was Landis's movies that had so informed my tastes long ago in those darkened front rooms, but also because we had paid specific tribute to him in *Spaced*. At the end of episode five of the first series, an evil vivisectionist is stalked on Hampstead Heath by a feral dog and unwittingly quotes one of the victims in *American Werewolf* just before he is attacked. It never occurred to us as we made our very low-budget comedy for Channel 4 that we would one day be able to show it to the very people that inspired us.

The second time we met, John took me to see *Terminator Salvation* at the Directors' Guild and then for dinner at the Kate Mantilini

Restaurant on Wilshire Boulevard, the location of Robert De Niro and Al Pacino's famous face-to-face in Michael Mann's *Heat*. There he told me about his plans to direct a film called *Burke and Hare* in the UK. He said the story revolved around two notorious 1820s Edinburgh killers who, between them, bumped off seventeen people and sold their cadavers to medical science.

Less than a year later we began shooting in London with myself and Andy Serkis as the titular 'heroes' in a film that boasted, among its players, three of the original cast members of *American Werewolf in London*: David Schofield, John Woodvine and Jenny Agutter. Even more interestingly (for me), *Burke and Hare* also contained four members of the cast of *Spaced*: Jessica Hynes, Michael Smiley, Bill Bailey and me. And with that pleasing flourish of circularities, I think it's time to bring proceedings to a close.

Wait a minute! I hear you cry. What about [insert thing you wanted to know about here]?

Well, I probably have enough anecdotes about my professional life to fill a whole other book, but to be honest I'm not sure how interesting that would be for any of us. Unless you are blithely indiscreet or just mercenary, you have to be a little bit more guarded and careful when talking about other people in the public eye. I'm not harbouring any devastating secrets or vendettas, but the truth would have to be modified to protect others and no amount of Meredith Catsanus or Eggy Helen-style pseudonyms would fully insulate against clever people working things out or, perhaps worse, misconceiving. My professional life has been eventful and emotional and I have met a wide variety of people. It hasn't all been plain sailing; there have been struggles and conflicts and not everyone I have met has been a delight, but I'm just not that interested in dishing the dirt, and besides, I don't really have that much dirt to dish. The journey has been fun and exciting, but there are few things less beguiling than 'hilarious' celeb stories, which culminate in the crushing sensation that you really had to be there and a vague feeling of resentment that you weren't. And anyway, as Johnny Morris used to say at the end of *Tales of the Riverbank*, that's another story.

In the end, this memoir has turned out to be far more personal than I ever intended. My first inclination when faced with the task of writing a book about myself was to keep it strictly professional, for fear of constantly defaulting into tales of dogs and hosiery, but the truth is, the most interesting stuff to write about, and hopefully to read, took place as a prelude to the whole showbiz malarkey. Ultimately, we are all products of the experiences we have and the decisions we make as children, and it remains a peculiar detail of the human condition that something as precious as a future is entrusted to us when we possess so little foresight. Perhaps that's what makes hindsight so intriguing. When you're young the future is a blank canvas, but looking back you are always able to see the big picture.

Epilogue

The jet lifted off from the roof of Hendon Garden Hospital, a sleek black exercise in vertical grace. Nobody noticed as the silent bird drifted into the sky, apart from a tramp but his description of events would have seemed dubious on account of him being drunk and mental.

Simon Pegg sat in the cockpit next to Canterbury, his friend and faithful robotic butler. Very little had passed between them since they delivered Murielle Burdot, aka the Scarlet Panther, to the A&E department with a gunshot wound to her back.

The doctors had whisked her away to the ICU and an hour or so later reported her condition to be stable. Pegg felt a honey warmth spread through his body at the news and fought back his tears of joy, not wanting to look like a whoopsie in front of the cops who had been called as a matter of course.

Pegg had participated in a short interview, which the rozzers kept brief because they fancied him so much. Besides, this wasn't the first time Pegg had rocked up to an NHS hospital carrying a woman with a bullet in her back and it certainly wouldn't be the last.

Pegg looked over at his treasured friend, watching him for a moment as the android cycled through various flight procedures with obvious efficiency. A smile stretched across Pegg's face and he found himself filled with a wave of devotional love. Was it possible to love a robot? Pegg mused to himself as he considered his friend. There had been that incident with the BJ5000 at the Birmingham NEC in 2005, but that was hardly love, more like gratitude.

'Is everything all right, sir?' chirped Canterbury, breaking Pegg from his reverie.

'Yes,' said Pegg, 'I was just thinking how much it sucks.'

'What sucks, sir?' enquired Canterbury.

'Murielle's going to be in hospital for at least six weeks,' Pegg sighed. 'What am I going to do?'

'You could always write your book, sir,' suggested the intuitive automaton, a hint of amusement in his smooth synthetic tones.

'Is that an attempt at humour?' asked Pegg, fighting to conceal his smile.

'Not at all, sir,' replied Canterbury. 'I was just thinking, with the benefit of a moment's solace, you might finally find the motivation to put finger to iPad.'

'What shall I write about, though?' asked Pegg honestly, reminding his mechanical companion of the young man who put him together from a shop-bought robo-kit so many years before, ingeniously adding a number of specialised modifications without invalidating the warranty. In fact, with the exception of the flashing earring and the spray-on tits, Pegg's additions to Canterbury's hardware and programming had created a unique individual, whose experience and ability to learn at a geometric rate had made him all but human.

Canterbury looked at his master for a moment and felt a fizz of data sparkle across his silicon synapses. If he didn't know better, he would have concluded it to be love, little knowing how much it was reciprocated.

'Write what you know, sir,' said Canterbury. 'Write what you know.'

Pegg laughed, an explosive chuckle that surprised even him.

'Perhaps Ben from Century wasn't as mad as we thought,' mused Pegg. 'I suppose, in the end, he helped me more than he knew. It's funny, but I wish he was here so I could thank him.'

'Perhaps you should have thanked him when you pulled the knife out of his brain,' suggested Canterbury helpfully.

'It slipped my mind,' admitted the handsome adventurer and sex expert.

'Much like that blade slipped his,' quipped Canterbury.

Pegg roared with laughter for six minutes. When the laughter subsided, Pegg and Canterbury looked at each other for a moment, Canterbury's ocular illuminations pulsing in the moisture across the surface of Pegg's crystal-clear eyes.

'I'm sorry I doubted you,' Pegg said suddenly.

Canterbury said nothing for a few seconds, his fixed face unreadable. Then he spoke.

'I forgive you, sir.'

Pegg smiled, a look of relief melting through his expression of concern.

'When we get back, I'm going to give you a full overhaul,' Pegg enthused. 'I'm going to paint over those tits, and get rid of that earring, I don't care what those wankers at Comet say, they can go fuck themselves.'

'I'd appreciate a lick of fresh paint, sir, but you can leave the earring. I've grown to like it.'

'Whatever you say,' said Pegg, grinning broadly at his best friend.

They sat in comfortable silence for a minute or two.

'I was thinking . . .' Pegg began hopefully. 'When Murielle is fully recovered, I might ask her to come and stay with us for a while.'

Canterbury couldn't be sure but it seemed as though Pegg was almost asking his permission.

'That sounds like a capital idea, sir,' said Canterbury, as if Pegg hadn't been thinking about it since he discovered Murielle was still alive. 'Shall I make up the guest bedroom in the east wing?'

'That won't be necessary,' said Pegg.

Canterbury wasn't looking at his master but he could hear the slight smile on his face.

'Perhaps you could start thinking about some recipes,' suggested Pegg. 'I'd like to put on a nice dinner for her on her first night at the manor.'

'How about quail tagine with prunes and almonds?' Canterbury offered.

'Perfect,' said Pegg.

Pegg stretched and looked out of the viewscreen into the darkness of the night. The future seemed full of potential, full of warmth and even fun, not just the grim promise of danger that usually haunted the time before him.

'Where shall we go now?' Pegg asked absent-mindedly.

'Zihuatanejo,' said Canterbury.

'Zihuatanejo?' replied Pegg.

'Mexico,' continued Canterbury. 'Little place right on the Pacific. You know what the Mexicans say about the Pacific?'

'You keep asking me that,' said Pegg, a note of frustration in his voice.

'Might I suggest we just go home, sir?' Canterbury said happily. 'I think you earned yourself a rest.'

And with that, the sleek black jet cut into the velvet blackness and slid away through the night, towards Pegg's top-secret hideout in Gloucester, between Brockworth and Upton St Leonards, near the ICI factory but with nice views of the Cotswolds and a huge swimming pool.

Appendix

I wrote this shortly after playing through *Star Wars: The Force Unleashed* on the PS3. It features the characters of Rahm Kota, Kazdan Paratus and Shaak Ti, the last remaining Jedi Knights after the execution of Order 66. Shaak Ti is glimpsed in *Revenge of the Sith*; the other two exist within the expanded universe of the game which charts the rise of the rebellion between Episodes III and IV. The other characters should be familiar to anyone who has watched the original *Star Wars* saga more than three times. If that criteria fits you, read on; if not, I'd give it a swerve.

The Plan

Massassi Temple, Yavin 4. Mon Mothma and Bail Organa are seated around a large stone table discussing the aftermath of Order 66 with the last remaining Jedi: Shaak Ti, Kazdan Paratus, Rahm Kota, Obi-Wan Kenobi and a holo-transmission of Yoda. Captain Madine enters looking worried.

MADINE

Our spies bring disturbing news from the Imperial Sector. Anakin Skywalker is alive.

KOTA

What?

MON MOTHMA

How can this be?

KENOBI

But I stood on the lava banks of Mustafar and watched him die.

SHAAK TI

I still don't understand why you didn't help him. He was your padawan.

OBI-WAN KENOBI *shrugs*.

YODA

Master Kenobi?

KENOBI

I was tired.

YODA

Grave news, this is.

KENOBI

I wouldn't worry. He was in a terrible state when I left him. Both his legs were off and he was on fire.

KOTA

That's another thing. Why did you just leave him there?

KENOBI

I dunno.

PARATUS

If what Obi-Wan says is true, can Skywalker really be much of a threat?

MADINE

The Emperor has rebuilt him. Apparently he's more machine now than man.

KENOBI

Creepy.

MADINE

What is more, intelligence reports suggest that he has been reborn as the Sith Lord, Darth Vader.

KENOBI

Cool name.

YODA

Feared this, I did. A terrible ally the dark side has found

MON MOTHMA

What about the babies? Surely he will seek them out.

YODA

Hidden, they must be.

KOTA

Hidden and separated.

KENOBI

Awwww.

YODA

Right, General Kota is. Strong is their bond, easy to sense.

ORGANA

I will take Leia. My wife and I have long yearned for a daughter. We will raise her as our own. Concealed by the bright light of royalty.

KENOBI

Nice.

MON MOTHMA

What about the boy?

PARATUS

He needs to be hidden as far away as possible.

KENOBI

How about Tatooine? I have a friend there who has always said, if there's a bright centre to the universe, Tatooine is the planet that it's farthest from.

MON MOTHMA

Who is this friend?

KENOBI

His name is Owen Lars.

SHAAK TI

Can he be trusted?

KENOBI

Oh yes.

PARATUS

How did you make his acquaintance?

KENOBI

He's Darth Vader's stepbrother.

EVERYONE

What?

KENOBI

It'll be fine, seriously. He won't think to look there.

ORGANA

Are you sure?

KENOBI

Positive.

KOTA

Master Yoda?

YODA

Out of ideas, I am.

PARATUS

Very well. Leia Organa and Luke Lars –

KENOBI

Skywalker.

EVERYONE

WHAT?!

KENOBI

He should be called Luke Skywalker. Come on, it sounds cooler.

MON MOTHMA

What is it with you and names?

KENOBI

I think it's important. Why do you think I changed my name to Obi-Wan? Nobody's going to be frightened of a Jedi called Benjamin.

> YODA

Fear leads to aggression . . .

> KENOBI

Yeah, yeah. If I had a credit for every time you wheeled that one out –

> YODA

Up shut!

> MON MOTHMA

Really, this bickering is pointless.

> YODA/KENOBI

Sorry.

> KOTA

Doesn't keeping his name defeat the object of hiding him?

> MON MOTHMA

Yes, what if Vader vanity surfs?

> ORGANA

Mon Mothma is right. He may have a Galactanet alert attached to his name. What if he checks to see what people are saying about him and happens upon an article about Luke winning a spelling competition or a pod race or something?

> KENOBI

Never gonna happen.

> KOTA

Very well, if you're sure.

> KENOBI

Hey, have I ever let you down?

> YODA

Anakin Skywalker, did you train?

> KENOBI

Oh, throw that in my face, why don't you!

> KOTA

Silence. General Kenobi, we will abide by your wisdom . . .

KENOBI *makes a nah-nah face at the holographic* YODA.

KOTA

But you have to go and live on Tatooine.

KENOBI

WHAT?

KOTA

You have to go and live in a little house on Tatooine and keep an eye on him.

KENOBI

Oh man! It's boring on Tatooine. And what about all the sand-people? You have to make that funny noise to scare them off and I can't do it because I've got a deviated septum.

PARATUS

You'll have time to learn.

KENOBI *looks sulky*.

KOTA

It's either that or we change his name and hide him somewhere less obvious.

KENOBI

All right then, I'll go.

ORGANA

Good.

KOTA

Then it is settled.

PARATUS

Very well.

SHAAK TI

Let us ready a shuttle.

YODA *fizzles out*.

MON MOTHMA

I have a bad feeling about this.

Index